Trinitarian Interpretation in Light of the Identity of YHWH as the Triune God

Trinitarian Interpretation in Light of the Identity of YHWH as the Triune God

A Biblical, Historical, and Theological Approach

Alias K. Eldhose

Foreword by Glenn R. Kreider

WIPF & STOCK · Eugene, Oregon

TRINITARIAN INTERPRETATION IN LIGHT OF THE IDENTITY OF
YHWH AS THE TRIUNE GOD
A Biblical, Historical, and Theological Approach

Copyright © 2024 Alias K. Eldhose. All rights reserved. Except for brief quotations in critical publications or reviews, no part of this book may be reproduced in any manner without prior written permission from the publisher. Write: Permissions, Wipf and Stock Publishers, 199 W. 8th Ave., Suite 3, Eugene, OR 97401.

Wipf & Stock
An Imprint of Wipf and Stock Publishers
199 W. 8th Ave., Suite 3
Eugene, OR 97401

www.wipfandstock.com

PAPERBACK ISBN: 978-1-6667-8320-9
HARDCOVER ISBN: 978-1-6667-8321-6
EBOOK ISBN: 978-1-6667-8322-3

VERSION NUMBER 01/05/24

Scripture quotations taken from the (NASB®) New American Standard Bible®, Copyright © 1960, 1971, 1977, 1995, 2020 by The Lockman Foundation. Used by permission. All rights reserved. lockman.org.

The Scriptures quoted are from the NET Bible® https://netbible.com copyright ©1996, 2019 used with permission from Biblical Studies Press, L.L.C. All rights reserved.

Scripture quotations are from the New Revised Standard Version Bible, copyright © 1989 National Council of the Churches of Christ in the United States of America. Used by permission. All rights reserved worldwide.

Scripture quotations are from the ESV® Bible (The Holy Bible, English Standard Version®), © 2001 by Crossway, a publishing ministry of Good News Publishers. Used by permission. All rights reserved. The ESV text may not be quoted in any publication made available to the public by a Creative Commons license. The ESV may not be translated in whole or in part into any other language.

The Hebrew text used is from the Biblia Hebraica Stuttgartensia (BHS). Copyright © 1967, 1977, 1983 Deutsche Bibelgesellschaft. Used by permission.

Greek Scripture quotations marked (NA^{28}) are taken from Novum Testamentum Greece, 28th revised edition, edited by Barbara Aland and others, © 2012 Deutsche Bibelgesellschaft, Stuttgart.

Unless otherwise noted, quotations from the Septuagint are taken from Rahlfs's Septuaginta. LXX Septuaginta edited by Alfred Rahlfs. Copyright © 1935 Württembergische Bibelanstalt/Deutsche Bibelgesellschaft (German Bible Society), Stuttgart.

To Terry and Laurie Ledbetter in whom
I see Christ's love personified.

Contents

Foreword by Glenn R. Kreider | ix
Preface | xiii
Acknowledgments | xv
List of Abbreviations | xvii

1. Introduction | 1
2. Trinitarian Correlates in Theological Interpretation | 36
3. YHWH *Is* Trinity | 79
4. Bridging the Gap | 132
5. Conclusion | 151

Bibliography | 163

Foreword

How should the references to "God" in the Hebrew Scriptures be understood? Is the God of Abraham the same God as revealed in Jesus of Nazareth? Is he an undifferentiated or undefined God or is he the Trinity? Does the term YHWH refer to God the Father, as is often assumed? Or is YHWH the Trinity?

In this work, the author identifies a problem in theological interpretation of Scripture, what he calls the "isolationist tendency." Rather than understanding YHWH as the Trinity, many of these interpreters interpret YHWH in the Old Testament as a reference to the Father. Then, the New Testament is read christologically and pneumatologically. Rather, this author defends the thesis that the theological interpretation of both the Old and New Testaments must be founded on the identification of YHWH as the triune God. Thus, rather than seeing the Old Testament as the revelation of God the Father, he argues that YHWH is a reference to the Trinity. This does not mean the Trinity was revealed in the Hebrew Scriptures; the Trinity is revealed in Jesus. What it does mean is that the differentiation of persons of the one God, Trinity, is clearly revealed in Christ and the coming of the Spirit and the God who is revealed prior to the coming of the Son is essentially Trinitarian.

Although the Christian tradition has always rejected the Marcionite view that the Old and New Testaments reveal two different gods, there has been a tendency to differentiate between YHWH in the Old and YHWH in the New. In the same way that "God" is used to refer to each person of the Trinity, "YHWH" too refers to the essence the three persons share. One God, in three persons, and YHWH is his name. The Father is YHWH, the Son is YHWH, and the Spirit is YHWH.

Among the implications of his work, the author argues that when the Hebrew Scriptures refer to God as Father of Israel, that designation lacks the closeness and intimacy of Jesus' references to his heavenly Father, and to ours, as he taught his disciples to pray (Matt 6:9). The inter-Trinitarian relationship of intimacy is the foundation and source of the intimacy we experience with the triune God. And this intimacy within YHWH is the significance of that name in the Hebrew Scriptures.

The book begins with an excellent overview of the history of theological interpretation of the Bible and the various understandings of Trinitarianism within practitioners of the Theological Interpretation of Scripture. The author argues that YHWH has always been Trinity, even though the Trinity was revealed explicitly in the incarnation of God the Son and the sending of the Holy Spirit, and thus the Hebrew Scriptures reveal the God who is Trinity.

The author then illustrates the significance of his claim in two biblical texts, one in the Old Testament and the other in the New. In the judgment on the rebels in the garden, YHWH declares that he does not want the man and woman to eat from the tree and live forever (Gen 3:22). In John 6:51 and 58, Jesus declares that those who eat his flesh and drink his blood will live forever. Also, in John 7:37–39 (cf. John 4), Jesus declares himself to be the source of living water. YHWH does intend his followers to have eternal life, but not through the tree of life in the garden due to the fallenness of the creation as a consequence of human sin, but through the provision that YHWH will deliver through himself, in Jesus. The redemptive language in the gospel of John deliberately echoes that of the judgment oracle in Genesis 3, thus indicating that Jesus is YHWH.

A second illustration is in 1 Corinthians 10, where Paul asserts, "The Rock that followed them was Christ" (1 Cor 10:4). Since YHWH is the Trinity, when Israel resisted God in the wilderness (Num 21:5–9) they were resisting Christ, the Rock that followed them. The author argues that the God who was revealed in the Hebrew Scriptures, the Trinity, is the God who is revealed in Jesus of Nazareth. There are not two gods. YHWH is the Trinity and Jesus is YHWH. Thus, reading the revelation of the Trinitarian God in the Old Testament is not the revelation of one person in the Godhead but the revelation of the one God who is Trinity. In the same way that the Israelites offended YHWH who was with them, the Corinthians are in danger of offending the same Lord. Unless the Corinthians change their ways, they will face a similar consequence of the rebellious Israelites, because YHWH is with them too.

These two illustrations are sufficient to demonstrate the claim the author has made. Many other illustrations of this Trinitarian reading could be cited. Biblical scholars should be encouraged to discover them.

This is an important work and makes a significant contribution to the discipline of hermeneutics. The author has read widely and interacted deeply with the literature of Theological Interpretation of Scripture. He is appropriately both affirming and critical of those voices. He elevates the Trinitarian God of the Old and New Testament Scriptures and he shows how reading the Scripture through this lens points forward to the coming of the Messiah and how reading the Old Testament through the revelation of the Trinity in Jesus helps the reader of Scripture to recognize how those texts are not just christological and pneumatological but Trinitarian. This book advances the conversation and deserves a place in the libraries of biblical scholars.

Glenn R. Kreider, PhD
Professor of Theological Studies
Dallas Theological Seminary

Preface

THE IDEA OF A *Trinitarian interpretation* of Scripture first occurred to me in a seminar on theological method under Dr. Glenn Kreider. Soon, I discovered that the many works on theological interpretation of Scripture (TIS) lacked clarity, although they claimed to be *Trinitarian* in nature. Often, Trinitarian interpretation in such proposals appeared to be a placeholder for christological, pneumatological, ecclesial, or figural interpretation. The lack of clarity in those proposals stemmed from an *isolationist tendency* among scholars who identify YHWH as the first person (God the Father) of the Trinity. Additionally, the proposals for a Trinitarian interpretation did not seem to make any material differences in the way one read the Scripture.

The subsequent research convinced me that a solution to this isolationist tendency required a careful consideration of several factors: (1) a thorough exegetical study on the identity of YHWH in the Old Testament, (2) a reevaluation of the great *Shema* and the ensuant understanding of *monotheism*, (3) a contextual evaluation of the many references to God as Father in the Old Testament, (4) a proper appraisal of the *differences* in Jesus's appellation for God as his *Father*, and (5) a comparative study of select Hebrew Old Testament texts, the LXX translation of YHWH in those texts, and the New Testament's ascription of those texts to Jesus where YHWH was the referent in the Old Testament.

The thesis of this book is that Trinitarian interpretation must be founded upon the proper identification of YHWH as the triune God. Reconsidering the identity of YHWH in light of the relevant Old Testament and New Testament passages along with the early church's understanding of the appellation "Father" for God leads to the conclusion that YHWH is multiple persons, in other words, the triune God. Therefore, Father is YHWH, the Son is YHWH, and the Spirit is YHWH just as the Father is God, the Son is God, and the Spirit is God. If the identity of YHWH is triune, then it will help explain the New Testament's use of the Old Testament and will facilitate a robust practice of Trinitarian interpretation that overcomes the isolationist tendency. Case studies on Gen 3:22 and 1 Cor 10:4 will demonstrate how a proper Trinitarian interpretation can be undertaken once YHWH is understood as multiple persons.

Acknowledgments

ALTHOUGH THIS BOOK BEARS my name and I take full responsibility for its content, I could not have done it without the help of many who came alongside me in the writing of my dissertation of which this book is a revision. I am grateful and indebted to the readers of my dissertation, Dr. Glenn R. Kreider, Dr. Nathan D. Holsteen, and Dr. Abraham Kuruvilla, whose valid critiques and insightful suggestions brought clarity to my thinking and strengthened my arguments. Dr. Richard A. Taylor who was the director of PhD Studies at DTS provided valid comments with regard to Hebrew Grammar and exegesis and formatting issues. Besides my dissertation committee, my friends Dr. Abraham Joseph, Jonathan Platter, and Nancy Kerstetter read various drafts of my dissertation. Finny Varghese and Joseph Lee, my fellow doctoral students, were constant sparring partners. A special thanks to all of them.

I am thankful to the Lord and grateful to Terry and Laurie Ledbetter, to whom this book is dedicated, for their love, kindness, and constant support since the time we met them, especially during my studies at DTS. Their home became our home away from home. Thankful for the many Thanksgiving and Christmas meals that we had at their home. I am also thankful for the constant encouragement and friendship of Dr. Stephen George, the president of Asian Christian Academy of India, to convert my dissertation into a book.

This journey could not have been possible without the unconditional love, prayer, and support of my covenant partner Mercy Eldhose, who held the fort together when my head was buried in books. Babe, though I will never understand the true depth of your sacrifice, I am forever grateful to you. My twin boys Jonathan and Nathaniel constantly nudged me toward the finish line by asking rather some curious questions such as "when will you become a doctor?" Or "being a nurse, can mom work with you?" (They thought I was getting a degree in medicine!) My parents Mr. and Mrs. K. M. Alias and my parents-in-law Mr. and Mrs. K. V. Mathews were constant sources of encouragement. I am grateful for the help and support I received from the staff of Wipf and Stock Publishers. Special thanks to managing editor Matthew Wimer, assistant managing editor Emily Callihan, and the editorial administrative assistant George Callihan for their tireless support from my initial contact to the publication of this book. Special mention and thanks to my copy editor Christopher Klimkowski, whose copy editing skills made the final product a much enjoyable one.

Many friends, church families, and family members came alongside me during my studies at Dallas Theological Seminary. I fondly remember each of their love and support.

List of Abbreviations

AB	Anchor Bible
Abr.	Philo, *On the Life of Abraham*
ACCS	Ancient Christian Commentary on Scripture
1 Apol.	Justin, *First Apology*
Autol.	Theophilus, *To Autolycus*
BECNT	Baker Exegetical Commentary on the New Testament
BDAG	Bauer, Walter, et al. *Greek-English Lexicon of the New Testament and Other Early Christian Literature.*
BDF	Blass, Friedrich, et al. *A Greek Grammar of the New Testament and Other Early Christian Literature.*
BBR	*Bulletin for Biblical Research*
BETL	Bibliotheca Ephemeridum Theologicarum Lovaniensium
BTCB	Brazos Theological Commentary on the Bible
C. Ar.	Athanasius, *Orations against the Arians*
CBQ	*Catholic Biblical Quarterly*
CCL	Corpus Christianorum Latinorum
CCSL	*Corpus Christianorum: Series Latina*
CD	Church Dogmatics
ConcC	Concordia Commentary
CurBR	*Currents in Biblical Research*

DDD	Toorn, Karel van der, et al., eds. *Dictionary of Deities and Demons in the Bible*.
Decr.	Athanasius, *Defense of the Nicene Definition*
Dial.	Justin, *Dialogue with Trypho*
DJD	Discoveries in the Judaean Desert
DTIB	Vanhoozer, Kevin J., et al., eds. *Dictionary for Theological Interpretation of the Bible*.
EvT	*Evangelische Theologie*
FAT	Forschungen zum Alten Testament
Haer.	Irenaeus, *Adversus haereses*
IJPR	*International Journal for Philosophy of Religion*
IJST	*International Journal of Systematic Theology*
ISBL	Indiana Studies in Biblical Literature
JBL	*Journal of Biblical Literature*
JECS	*Journal of Early Christian Studies*
JSNT	*Journal for the Study of the New Testament*
JSNTSup	Journal for the Study of the New Testament Supplement Series
JSOTSup	Journal for the Study of the Old Testament Supplement Series
JSJ	*Journal for the Study of Judaism in the Persian, Hellenistic, and Roman Periods*
JTI	*Journal for Theological Interpretation*
JTISup	Journal for Theological Interpretation, Supplements
JTS	*Journal of Theological Studies*
LCL	Loeb Classical Library
Leg.	Athenagoras, *The Plea for Christians*
LNTS	Library of New Testament Studies
LSJ	Liddell, Henry George, et al. *A Greek-English Lexicon*.
Mos.	Philo, *On the Life of Moses*

NA²⁷	Nestle, Eberhard, et al., eds. *Novum Testamentum Graece.* 27th rev. ed.
NA²⁸	Nestle, Eberhard, et al., eds. *Novum Testamentum Graece.* 28th rev. ed.
NAC	New American Commentary
NCBC	New Century Bible Commentary
NICNT	New International Commentary on the New Testament
NICOT	New International Commentary on the Old Testament
NIDOTTE	VanGemeren, Willem A., ed. *New International Dictionary of Old Testament Theology and Exegesis.*
NIGTC	New International Greek Testament Commentary
NPNF²	Nicene and Post-Nicene Fathers, Series 2
NT	New Testament
NTL	New Testament Library
OBT	Overtures to Biblical Theology
OECS	Oxford Early Christian Studies
OECT	Oxford Early Christian Texts
Or. Bas.	Gregory of Nazianzus, *Oratio in laudem Basilii*
OSHT	Oxford Studies in Historical Theology
OT	Old Testament
OTL	Old Testament Library
PNTC	Pillar New Testament Commentary
ProEccl	*Pro Ecclesia*
4Q372	4QApocrypha of Joseph
4Q460	4QNarrative Work and Prayer
SBL	Society of Biblical Literature
SBT	Studies in Biblical Theology
SC	Sources chrétiennes. Paris: Cerf, 1943–
SJT	*Scottish Journal of Theology*
STI	Studies in Theological Interpretation

StOr	Studia Orientalia
SubBi	Subsidia Biblica
Syn.	Athanasius, *On the Councils of Ariminum and Seleucia*
TBN	Themes in Biblical Narrative
TDNT	Kittel, Gerhard, et al., eds. *Theological Dictionary of the New Testament.*
TGST	Tesi Gregoriana, Serie Teologia
ThTo	*Theology Today*
Tim.	Plato, *Timaeus*
TIS	Theological Interpretation of Scripture
TJ	*Trinity Journal*
Trin.	Augustine, *The Trinity*
TS	Theological Studies
TWOT	Harris, R. Laird, et al., eds. *Theological Wordbook of the Old Testament.*
VCSup	Supplements to *Vigiliae christianae*
VT	*Vetus Testamentum*
WBC	Word Biblical Commentary
WUNT	Wissenschaftliche Untersuchungen zum Neuen Testament

1

Introduction

Need and Purpose For Study

RECENT DECADES HAVE SEEN a surge of interest in *Trinitarian interpretation* of Scripture. This interest is most prominently evident in the nascent field of theological interpretation of Scripture (hereafter, TIS). Although the literature on TIS invariably employs Trinitarian interpretation, the usage itself has been ambiguous at best.[1] Most practitioners of theological interpretation contend that their interpretation is "Trinitarian," but a survey of their works reveals that, often, Trinitarian interpretation is a placeholder for christological, pneumatological, ecclesial, or figural interpretation.[2] The incongruity within these proposals for Trinitarian interpretation is further complicated by a tendency that can be labeled *isolationist*.[3] *Isolationist tendency* refers to the practice of assigning the Old Testament (hereafter, OT) primarily to God the Father (P1) and the New Testament (hereafter, NT) to the Son (P2) and to the Spirit (P3) because of the identification of YHWH in the OT as the first person of

---

1. Cummins, "Theological Interpretation," 193.

2. Watson, *Text, Church and World*, 152–53, 255–57; Watson, *Text and Truth*, 16, 182, 248; Billings, *Word of God*, xiii, 36–37, 104–48. Watson emphasizes a christological interpretation and Billings emphasizes a pneumatological interpretation.

3. A good example of what I mean by *isolationist tendency* can be found in Bartholomew, *Introducing Biblical Hermeneutics*, 10–11. See also Bartholomew, "Listening for God's Address," 4; Schultz, "Hearing the Major Prophets," 335–36.

the Trinity, leading to the separation of the works of the Father, Son, and Spirit from each other.[4] Isolationist tendency raises questions concerning the NT's use of the OT, especially Jesus' own claim that the OT bears witness to him (Luke 24:25–27, 44–45; John 5:39–47). Whether intentional or not, isolating the works of the Father, Son, and Spirit from one another has become a common misstep in such proposals.[5] Implicit in such proposals is an inherent misinterpretation of YHWH in the OT as P1.

Christine Helmer, for example, suggests that Christian theological interpretation generally identifies YHWH as P1: "Theological differences between the two witnesses have never been considered grounds for divorce; in fact, Christian theological interpretations of the unity of the two testaments, with the exception of these two theologians [Marcion and Schleiermacher], identify the God of Israel with God as Father of Jesus Christ."[6] Identifying YHWH as P1 raises questions concerning the way in which the OT quotations and allusions are used in the NT. The solutions to this dilemma range from prophecy/fulfillment structure to atomistic interpretation.[7]

Such proposals for Trinitarian interpretation face similar questions such as "how can one legitimately read the OT texts christologically or pneumatologically if they are not primarily christological or pneumatological in content and intent?" Or "how could God be one (Deut 6:4b) if the NT presents Jesus Christ and the Holy Spirit as equally God?" To answer such questions, christological and pneumatological interpretations often project Christ or the Spirit back onto the OT texts where P1 had already been assumed as the original referent. This leads to objections from those who define interpretation of the text as the one that emerges from a historical, grammatical, and contextual reading. If the identity of the divine agent (YHWH) in the OT texts makes room for the presence

---

4. The *sigla* P1, P2, and P3 indicate the first person of the Trinity (God the Father), the second person (Jesus Christ the Son) of the Trinity, and the third person of the Trinity (God the Holy Spirit) respectively. "T" stands for the Trinity. They will be used throughout to clarify the referent.

5. Thomas, "Telos," 213. Thomas calls the isolationist tendency a danger. "Dangers appear when interpretation isolates any one of the three members of the Triune God to the neglect of others." Cf. Greidanus, *Preaching Christ*; Spawn and Wright, *Spirit and Scripture*.

6. Helmer, "Trust and the Spirit," 64.

7. For example, see Beale, *Handbook*; Kaiser, et al., *Three Views*; Porter and Stovell, *Biblical Hermeneutics*; Porter, *Hearing the Old Testament*; Moyise, *Old Testament in the New*.

of multiple persons (YHWH is identified as more than one person), then the NT attribution of the OT texts to Christ or the Spirit makes sense. Questions such as these emerge because of the constant identification of YHWH as P1 in these proposals. Those questions can be better answered if YHWH is identified as the triune God. It will not only answer the direct question of the identity of YHWH in the OT, but also the ancillary question, "what to make of the NT uses of the OT?" Thus, the identification of YHWH as P1 remains one of the major reasons for the isolationist tendency in Trinitarian interpretation.[8]

The isolationist tendency that exists in current proposals also adds credence to the objections of those who oppose a Trinitarian interpretation. John Goldingay acknowledges the multivalence in current proposals for Trinitarian interpretation. He objects to the nomenclature Trinitarian interpretation in such proposals and dismisses it as having any real purchase on OT exegesis.[9] Among his several objections to a Trinitarian interpretation, Goldingay observes that these works misidentify the God of Israel as the Father of Jesus Christ.[10] The God who is called "Father" in the OT is not simply the first person of the Trinity; instead, "Yahweh is God—period; therefore Yahweh is Father, Son and Spirit."[11] According to Goldingay, Christian theological interpretation can become Trinitarian interpretation only if it recognizes YHWH, the God of Israel, as the triune God.[12] Thus, Trinitarian interpretation of Scripture requires meticulous analysis to determine its biblical appropriateness as an interpretive lens and make it palatable for TIS (and for that matter biblical interpretation in general).

The thesis of this book is that Trinitarian interpretation must be founded upon the proper identification of YHWH as the triune God.[13]

---

8. Goheen and Wright, "Mission and Theological Interpretation," 175. Goheen and Wright suggest that it was God the Father who was at work in the OT. Chapters 2 and 3 explain how identifying YHWH as God the Father leads to isolationism and how that affects Trinitarian interpretation.

9. Goldingay, *Need the New Testament?*, 157–76. Regarding the multivalent approaches within TIS—whether TIS can be a robust method for its stated purpose or not—see Porter, "What Exactly Is Theological Interpretation," 234–67. Porter is sympathetic to many of the concerns that TIS raises, but he is not convinced that TIS, in its present state of competing theories and proposals, can achieve that end. See also Rae, et al., "Christ in/and the Old Testament," 7–11.

10. Goldingay, *Need the New Testament?*, 166–68.

11. Goldingay, *Need the New Testament?*, 167.

12. Goldingay, *Need the New Testament?*, 169.

13. Identifying YHWH as the triune God impacts the OT and NT texts. It will allow

4   Trinitarian Interpretation in Light of the Identity of YHWH as the Triune God

Reconsidering the identity of YHWH in light of the relevant OT and NT passages along with the early church's understanding of the appellation "Father" for God leads to the conclusion that YHWH is the triune God. YHWH is Father, Son, and Spirit just as the Father is God, the Son is God, and the Spirit is God.[14] The Nicene-Constantinopolitan creed makes it amply clear that this one God is the Father, Son, and Spirit.[15] God's personal name יהוה in the Hebrew Bible is often translated κύριος in the LXX, which in the NT is used interchangeably for God (general term), God the Father, and Jesus Christ.[16] Further, the NT argues that Jesus came to reveal YHWH (the one true God of the OT) and he reveals him as the Father, Son, and Spirit (John 1:18; 10:30; 14:7–11; 17:21; 1 Cor 8:6; Eph 4:4–6; Phil 2:9–11; cf. Isa 45:18–25; Exod 3:2–15; 6:3; Judg 6:11–24; 13:24–25; 14:6, 19; 15:14; 16:20).[17]

There is a difference between the references to God as "Father" in the OT (Deut 32:6; Isa 9:6; 63:16; 64:8; Jer 3:4, 19; Mal 1:6; 2:10) and Jesus' reference to God as his Father (John 5:17–18; 10:30). In the former case, YHWH is called "Father" not in the intra-Trinitarian sense, but as the Father of the nation Israel (cf. Isa 9:6—Christian tradition takes Jesus as the referent of the phrase "everlasting Father").[18] In the latter case, Jesus calls God his "Father" in the intra-Trinitarian sense (John 5:17–19;

OT to be read in a new perspective. Additionally, it has the potential to offer a different approach for understanding the NT's use of the OT, which will significantly impact the NT reading itself. Case studies on Gen 3:22 and 1 Cor 10:4 in chapter 4 will amplify this point.

14. Chapter 3 will present detailed arguments for YHWH = Trinity.

15. "We believe in one God, the Father. . . . And in one Lord Jesus Christ, the only-begotten Son of God, begotten from the Father before all time. . . . And in the Holy Spirit, the Lord and life-giver, Who proceeds from the Father, Who is worshipped and glorified together with the Father and Son. . ." In Leith, *Creeds of the Churches*, 33. The emphasis is on "We believe in one God" and the rest is an explication of who that one God is.

16. For a thorough analysis of יהוה as κύριος ὁ θεὸς or κύριος see the word study on יהוה and πατήρ in chapter 3.

17. The juxtaposition of the OT passages here will make better sense once they are explained in chapter 3. See also Saner, "*Too Much to Grasp*"; McDonough, *YHWH at Patmos*.

18. Goldingay, *Need the New Testament?*, 167. If calling God "Father" in the OT meant that it was a clear reference to P1 in the Trinitarian sense from the vantage point of the OT itself, one would have to assume that the Jews understood it to be so, which seems to be not the case (cf. John 5:18).

10:30; 17:5—here Father is the Father of the Son). Calling God "Father" does not mean that P1 is inferred in all such cases.[19]

Paul, alluding to the Shema, writes that there is only one God and he identifies this one God with Father, Son, and Spirit (1 Cor 8:6; Eph 4:4–6; cf. Eph 3:14–19). The New Testament and the early church understood God to be one; yet they directed their worship of this one true God in the figure of Jesus by addressing prayer, thanksgiving, and worship to him, always assuming that in their worship of Jesus they were worshiping YHWH (Isa 45:22–24; cf. Phil 2:9–11).[20]

A theological interpretation based on the identity of YHWH as the triune God is more comprehensive and biblically accurate. It has the potential to mitigate the overwhelming tendency for isolationism prevalent in the current proposals for Trinitarian interpretation. It will also help answer detractors' objections regarding the legitimacy of Trinitarian interpretation in the first place. As indicated earlier, the main reason for their objections stems from the fact that the current models on Trinitarian interpretation misidentify YHWH as P1. If the identity of YHWH as the triune God can be established on sound biblical reasoning, then it will help make better sense of Jesus' claims that the OT bears witness to him (John 5:38–57; Luke 24:44), just as the new way of understanding the same Scripture was ushered in once Jesus explained the OT Scriptures to the disciples (Luke 24:25–27, 44–47). Identifying YHWH as the triune God is necessary for biblical interpretation to overcome Marcion's straitjacket.[21] Although the church has rejected his proposal of the OT God being different from the God in the NT, history of interpretation

---

19. It is significant to note that, according to John 5:18, the Jewish people wanted to kill Jesus because he called God his "Father" along with breaking the Sabbath by healing a man who was disabled for thirty-eight years. It can be inferred from their conspiracy to kill Jesus that they understood Jesus' claim of God being his "Father" was somehow different from YHWH being called Father in OT. Otherwise, it would not make sense. This distinction between God being called "Father" in the OT and Jesus calling God his Father needs to be maintained in order to correct the misidentification of YHWH in the OT as "God the Father" (P1) in the Trinitarian sense.

20. Yeago, "New Testament," 154–58.

21. Harnack, *Marcion*, 65–92. What is meant by "Marcion's straitjacket" is his view of God in the OT as quite different from the God who is revealed in Jesus Christ. It is acknowledged that calling any interpretation Marcionistic is strong language, but it is used to call attention to how serious the identity of YHWH to Christian interpretation is. Even if current interpretations do not appropriate Marcion's language, and even condemn it, the hermeneutical construals themselves reveal a certain degree of difficulty with the identity of God in the OT in that he stands in an antithetical position to the benevolent God who is revealed in the NT.

reveals that the church has not always overcome the tendency to differentiate between God in the OT and in the NT.

Not only is there an isolationist tendency in Trinitarian interpretation, but also a chasm between proposals and practice. To bridge that chasm, this book will present a distinctly Christian and thoroughly Trinitarian reading of Gen 3:22 and 1 Cor 10:4, which will also demonstrate the impact of the identification of YHWH as the triune God for TIS.

Limitation of the Study

While the determination of the identity of YHWH as the triune God has ramifications for OT and NT theology and biblical interpretation in general, this book will mainly focus on its impact on TIS. As a result, this book primarily addresses the works of those who contribute to the field of theological interpretation. This book assumes the creedal confessions of the early church as uncontested and will not attempt to prove the doctrine of the Trinity.

Organization

A survey of the field of theological interpretation today tells a remarkable story of biblical interpretation (in modern times) finally coming of age to recognize and become comfortable with the influence of prior judgments (faith commitments) on one's interpretive practice. But this progress is not without its own struggles. TIS, as a movement, is a melting pot of ecumenical genealogies (Karl Barth [Protestant] and Hans Urs von Balthasar [Roman Catholic]), converging disciplines (biblical studies and systematic theology), and diverging philosophical frameworks (modernity and postmodernity). A careful look at these new and changing conditions are important to understand why literature on TIS often focuses on questions such as the locus of meaning in biblical texts (behind the text, in the text, in front of the text), what has "priority" in interpretation (author/text vs. reader/ecclesial community), and the nature of the text (human vs. divine). Thus, mapping the field of theological interpretation today provides a sketch of the ecumenical nature of the field and the impetus for theological interpretation, while shedding some light on the reasons for apparent incompatibility among the many proposals.

The brief historical sketch presented in chapter 1 is an attempt to provide some answers to the question "why is theological interpretation viewed as a new idea since the church has always practiced theological interpretation?" The historical sketch also gives rationale for a lack of progress in Trinitarian interpretation that goes beyond the standard practice of identifying YHWH as P1. It becomes evident that the history of biblical interpretation has experienced radical changes since the time of Renaissance to the extent that since the nineteenth century the focus has been on the very texts of Scripture (focus was on literary, philological, and historical matters) without much regard for its theological shape and intent.[22] These changes affected the view of history in modern biblical interpretation. History came to be viewed independently of any relation to revelation, which represents a radical shift. Thus, the biblical guild followed the practice of the natural sciences in search of what came to be known as objective interpretation. The idea was that if biblical interpretation could be undertaken without any recourse to prior confessional commitments, such interpretation would be free of any influences from outside the text. This view took strong hold in the academy. To regain credibility for theological interpretation meant that there needed to be a break from many of the assumptions of modern hermeneutics. This required the rehabilitation of church traditions and the history of interpretation in the first place and then incorporating that into biblical exegesis. What we witness from the time of Barth are the efforts of scholars from various disciplines and backgrounds coming together to do and promote theological interpretation by recognizing history as part of the history of revelation.[23]

Chapter 2 takes a closer look at the various Trinitarian proposals offered in TIS to understand the rationale behind them and to highlight the ambivalence and deficiency in such proposals in embracing

---

22. Childs, *Biblical Theology*, 13–17. The reason Childs provides for the beginning of the biblical theology movement (BTM) in the United States is very much applicable to TIS as well. TIS is indebted to BTM for making a case for the theological dimension in the Bible—a "strange new world" in Barth's view (Childs, *Biblical Theology*, 33). Childs later suggested that there is a certain coercion in the texts of Scripture that requires multilevel interpretation. Childs, "Recovering Theological Exegesis," 17, 21.

23. Porter, "What Exactly Is Theological Interpretation," 247, 258. Porter misses this point in his analysis of the field. He seems to view method as monolithic and not multivalent, but TIS is forthright about the ecumenical nature of its endeavor. The conclusion of his analysis that there are competing theories and inconsistent application of salient features within TIS should not be surprising to those familiar with TIS because by nature and design, it is ecumenical in all aspects.

the Trinitarian identity of YHWH—something that is indispensable for a comprehensive approach to Trinitarian interpretation. The adjectival phrase Trinitarian interpretation is often a misnomer for christological, pneumatological, ecclesial, or figural reading in these proposals. Not only do these proposals fall short of articulating Trinitarian interpretation, but also exhibit a chasm between theory and practice.[24]

Ascertaining the identity of YHWH requires an analysis of the meaning of יהוה in the OT, what the Shema reveals about YHWH (monotheism versus monolatry) in its immediate background, what the multiplicity of persons identified as YHWH reveals about who he is, and how and why the NT ascribes to Jesus what was once said exclusively of YHWH. The attempt to understand the Christian view of the identity of the one true God also requires an understanding of how πατήρ was used as an appellation for God in the OT, how Jesus used πατήρ for the first person of the Trinity, and how the early Church understood the "Fatherhood" of God in defense of the Christian doctrine of God. What emerges from this study is that the identity of YHWH never excluded the possibility of having multiple persons in that identity and as a result YHWH can, without inconsistency, be identified as the Father, Son, and Spirit.[25] The claim that YHWH is Trinity is to be understood similar to that of the creedal statement in which all three persons of the Godhead are called God, but not three Gods. Just as "God" refers to the essence of the Godhead that all three persons share, YHWH is the name of that essence that they share.[26] Therefore, it is incumbent upon students of Scripture to pay careful attention to the identity of YHWH as the triune God to overcome the isolationist tendency so prevalent in much of the theological interpretation today. Chapter 3 concludes that YHWH has always been the Father, Son, and Spirit.

Chapter 4 provides a distinctly Christian reading of Gen 3:22 and 1 Cor 10:4 based on the identity of YHWH as the triune God. Genesis 3:22 mentions that יְהוָה אֱלֹהִים did not want Adam and Eve to eat from

---

24. Childs, "Recovering Theological Exegesis," 18. Childs observes that there were attempts in the past to recover theological interpretation but they failed mainly because there was a chasm between what they set out to achieve in theory and what they did in practice.

25. Sommer, *Bodies of God*, 38–57, 59.

26. Soulen, *Divine Name(s)*, 127–257. Soulen argues that YHWH is mentioned several dozen times in the NT using periphrasis and synecdoche. The common occurrence of YHWH is by the first century Jewish appellation, "the NAME." Soulen's proposal will be discussed in chapter 3.

the tree of life and to live forever. LXX translates the Hebrew phrase וְאָכַל וָחַי לְעֹלָם ("eating and living forever") as καὶ φάγῃ καὶ ζήσεται εἰς τὸν αἰῶνα. This phrase is repeated only twice more in the entire Scripture; it is found in John 6:51 and 58. Since the identity of YHWH has been established as triune, Jesus' statement about eating his flesh and drinking his blood so that the one who eats his flesh and drinks his blood could live forever makes perfect sense. YHWH wanted humans to live with him forever, but sin became a barrier. Instead of letting humans live in their sin forever by eating from the tree of life, YHWH banished them from the garden so that YHWH could make the provision for them to live forever through the very act of eating—a partaking of God in an intimate, life-giving relationship with God. This way of looking at Gen 3:22 in light of John 6:51, 58 enriches the reading of both passages.[27]

In 1 Cor 10:4, Paul writes, "And the rock that followed them was Christ."[28] This phrase and the passage in which it appears are sometimes labeled Pauline *midrash* because it is assumed that what Paul was doing here was simply following the midrashic tradition.[29] A closer look at this passage in light of the other NT passages such as 1 Cor 10:9, Jude 5, and Jesus' own statement about the bread of life (John 6:32–58) and the "living water" (John 7:37–39; cf. 4:13–14), leads to the conclusion that the identity of YHWH as triune provides a better lens to understand Pauline theology and Paul's reading of the OT narratives. As chapter 3 argues, he identified Jesus with YHWH and that is why he could say in v. 9 that the people of Israel tested Christ in the wilderness (cf. Num 21:5–9). If the identity of YHWH for Paul is triune (Rom 10:9–13; 1 Cor 8:4–6), then he sees no inconsistency in Christ being the one the Israelites tested in the wilderness. This conclusion not only makes sense in light of Pauline theology, but also in light of the overall NT approach of quoting, referencing, and alluding to the OT. Paul and the early church were convinced that they did not find another God in Jesus, but a new way of understanding the God who was revealed to the fathers in the OT.

---

27. This interpretation is different from figural interpretation in one significant way: figural interpretation sees YHWH as the first person of the Trinity. Any reference to Christ is only in the figural sense, but as I argue in chapter 3 the identity of Jesus is inseparably tied to the identity of YHWH in that Jesus is YHWH just as the Father is YHWH and the Spirit is YHWH. See chapter 3 for the rationale for my position.

28. Unless otherwise specified, all translations are my own.

29. Enns, "The 'Moveable Well,'" 23–38.

Chapter 5 summarizes the arguments for the identity of YHWH as triune, which is consequential to theological interpretation and Trinitarian interpretation in particular. The argument for the identity of YHWH as triune is biblically sustainable as already shown; if appropriated carefully and consistently, it has the potential to mitigate the isolationist tendency prevalent in current proposals. It will help answer the detractors' objections, leading to a more robust Trinitarian interpretation.

Mapping Theological Interpretation Today

Theological interpretation of Scripture can be described as a distinctly Christian approach to reading Scripture informed by theological convictions about the identity of God and the Bible's theological character and its intent to hear God speak so that the church can live faithfully before the Lord.[30] The modern rise of theological interpretation has to be understood in its proper context. Throughout church history, many theologians and biblical scholars have established the fact that the church always believed in theological interpretation.[31] Due to the rise of Enlightenment epistemology, many have abandoned the idea of theological interpretation and embraced the idea of historical criticism that dismissed the legitimacy of theological interpretation as was practiced by the church and confessional theologians.[32]

While theological interpretation is not a new concept, its place in modern scholarship is relatively new because many in the academy abandoned that practice long ago, although the church has always practiced some form theological interpretation.[33] Today there is recognition within some quarters of the academy that theological aspects are part of the biblical texts (the intratextual pressure) themselves and not an import onto the texts (the extratextual pressure); as a result, biblical interpretation

---

30. Scholars differ in defining TIS. For example, see Moberly, "Theological Interpretation," 163; Martin, *Pedagogy of the Bible,* 21; Vanhoozer, "What Is Theological Interpretation?," 24; Green, "(Re-)Turn to Theology," 1; Fowl, *Engaging Scripture*, 22.

31. For example, see Warfield, *Right of Systematic Theology*, 38. Warfield argues in this essay that dogmas or doctrines are rooted in facts and they enter into the essence of Christianity (44–92).

32. Bowald, *Rendering the Word*. In the first chapter, Bowald especially focuses on how the Enlightenment epistemology impacted biblical interpretation.

33. For a rationale against theological interpretation, see Jowett, "On the Interpretation of Scripture"; Räisänen, *Beyond New Testament Theology*.

must attend to the theological aspects of the biblical text. There is also a concerted effort to articulate that fact in various forums and formats.

It is this story of the renewed interest in theological interpretation that is being told here. Thus, to understand its modern genesis and the apparent incoherence of methods and proposals, one has to pay attention to its two genealogies (Protestant through Barth and Roman Catholic through Balthasar), the convergence of various disciplines (biblical studies and systematic theology), and the diverse philosophical backgrounds (modern and postmodern) of the advocates.[34]

Two objectives guide the following survey. The first is to present a brief historical and genealogical background (to show why TIS is viewed as something new) by paying special attention to its ecumenical nature in which Protestants and Roman Catholics, as well as scholars from other biblical and theological backgrounds, collaborate. The second objective is a by-product of the first—to shed some light on the reasons (apart from identifying YHWH as P1) for the prevailing isolationist tendency in Trinitarian interpretation.

Two Genealogies: Karl Barth and Hans Urs von Balthasar

Theological interpretation of Scripture as a movement has been fraught with questions such as the locus of meaning in scriptural interpretation,[35] the role of authorial intention,[36] the role of tradition (and whose tradition),[37] and the role of the reading community.[38] These questions have a long history and some of that history is important to explain why theological interpretation was not always the preferred method of

---

34. For an excellent historical introduction to TIS, see Treier, *Introducing Theological Interpretation*. For the major emphases in TIS and some of its major contributors, see Fowl, *Theological Interpretation*. For what TIS is and its defining features, see Hays, "Reading the Bible," 5–21; Vanhoozer, "What Is Theological Interpretation?" For a manifesto that looks at the past, present, and the future course of TIS, see Bartholomew and Thomas, *A Manifesto*.

35. Spinks, *Crisis of Meaning*. Spinks provides a good summary and thorough analysis of the ongoing debates about the locus of meaning in TIS. He presents the paradoxes that still exist in TIS due to differing views of the meaning of the text by analyzing the works of Kevin Vanhoozer and Stephen Fowl.

36. Vanhoozer, *Is There a Meaning*; Vanhoozer, "Imprisoned or Free?, 51–93.

37. Lane, "Tradition," 809–12.

38. Holt and Spears, "Ecclesia as Primary Context," 72–93; Fowl, *Engaging Scripture*, 62–96; Treier, "What Is Theological Interpretation?," 144–61; Fowl, "Multivoiced Literal Sense," 35–50; Fowl, *Theological Interpretation of Scripture: Classic*, 127.

interpretation in academic circles. The history presented here is eclectic, but this history tells the particular story that led to TIS as a movement and how that complicated history continues to present challenges for identifying YHWH in the OT as the triune God.[39]

From Scripture to Bible[40]

Seventeenth and eighteenth century intellectual and social changes in the West presented orthodox Protestantism with enormous challenges to be overcome.[41] The developments in natural sciences, philosophy, and social and political life affected biblical interpretation, directly in many cases.[42] These changes affected the OT and the NT scholarship more than theology.

In the eighteenth century, John David Michaelis proposed a new direction in OT scholarship starting with the demotion of modern Jewish scholarship.[43] He contended that the Hebrew language had been a dead language from before the time of the Christian era; therefore, any Jewish contribution to the study of the Hebrew language and Bible from the time of the Second Temple period was insufficient.[44] He advocated a separation of Hebrew language from its afterlife in the religious life of the Jewish people because religious experience could be a corrupting influence.[45] A familiarity with the ancient Near Eastern (hereafter, ANE) languages and cultures was necessary to understand biblical Hebrew. The Renaissance cry of *ad fontes* ("to the sources") had already been well received by Michaelis's time. So his insistence on the study of the Hebrew language in its ANE background was nothing new. What was new was his emphasis on disconnecting such a study from the history of biblical interpretation,

---

39. Spinks, *Crisis of Meaning*, 32. Spinks describes the current debates in TIS as a "crisis of meaning."

40. Legaspi, *Death of Scripture*, 5. The use of "Scripture" seems to have a religious tone whereas the use of "Bible" emphasizes its quality as a classic text.

41. Livingston, *Modern Christian Thought*, 2.

42. Methuen, "On the Threshold," 665–90. Some of the scientific discoveries contradicted then-prevalent biblical interpretations. This resulted in questioning the veracity of the Scripture itself and not just its interpretation.

43. Methuen, "On the Threshold," 680–84; Legaspi, *Death of Scripture*, 86–87.

44. Michaelis, *Beurtheilung der Mittel*, 1:1–2. He called Rabbinic Hebrew "Euro-Hebrew" because it was full of Aramaic and Arabic loan words. Legaspi, *Death of Scripture*, 87.

45. Legaspi, *Death of Scripture*, 104.

especially from the Jewish perspective because such a study would allow exploring the OT independently of any prior commitments to the concept of divine revelation.

During the same time, Siegmund Jakob Baumgarten (1706–1757) sought a separation of the natural and supernatural understanding of Scripture.[46] His pupil Johann Salomo Semler dropped the supernatural understanding and argued for biblical interpretation free of dogmatic influence.[47] He separated the "outward" and the "inward" religion.[48] All religions including Judaism are historically conditioned (therefore, the OT can be treated more as a historical artifact) and they fell into the category of "outward" religion. On the contrary, "inward" religion for Semler was moral and personal.[49] In the process, he distinguished between Scripture and the word of God. Scripture belonged to the historical past; it does not speak to the present situation. On the other hand, the word of God refers to those biblical texts that have propositional values (often understood to be of moral or virtuous nature) and applicable for all times.[50] Semler was Michaelis's contemporary and collaborator; together they promoted a form of critical scholarship that has become the academic model for biblical studies.[51]

By the nineteenth century, dogma was considered an incursion on the plain teachings of the Bible because dogma was viewed as "a work of the Greek spirit on the soil of the Gospel."[52] Biblical theology replaced dogmatic theology in the academy.[53] J. P. Gabler made a clear demarcation between religion and theology.[54] By contrasting religion (biblical

---

46. Baumgarten, *Evangelische Glaubenslehre*, 81, 426. Baumgarten wrote that there is a natural understanding of the Bible aided by philology and historical-critical study and a supernatural understanding of the Bible arising from the viewpoint of Scripture as divine communication. Law, *Historical-Critical Method*, 43. Law's work presents a brief, but good portrait of the development of historical criticism with special attention on major players and their contribution. I follow Law's historical sketch here.

47. Law, *Historical-Critical Method*, 43.

48. Semler, *Historische Einleitung*, 35–40.

49. Law, *Historical-Critical Method*, 44.

50. Semler, *Abhandlung*, 60.

51. Law, *Historical-Critical Method*, 43–44.

52. Harnack, *History of Dogma*, 17.

53. Biblical theology also reached a crisis point at a later time because many who practiced biblical theology were interested in literary, philological, and historical matters. Childs, "Recovering Theological Exegesis," 15.

54. Gabler, "Oration on the Proper Distinction," 494–95.

theology) with theology (dogmatic theology), he maintained that "religion is passed on by the doctrine in the Scriptures, teaching what each Christian ought to know and believe and do in order to secure happiness in this life and in the life to come. Religion then, is every-day, transparently clear knowledge, but theology is subtle, learned knowledge, surrounded by a retinue of many disciplines, and by the same token derived not only from the sacred Scripture but also from elsewhere, especially from the domain of philosophy and history."[55] William Wrede makes a similar observation in the field of NT studies. "New Testament is not concerned merely with theology, but is in fact far more concerned with religion."[56] Biblical theology, according to Wrede, is an intellectual exercise done objectively, correctly, and sharply as possible like any other science without being adulterated by systematic theology.[57] If the meaning of a text is bound up purely in its immediate context and nothing more, then the systematization of doctrines have no place; at the same time, no particular doctrine, not even the doctrine of God, could influence the reading of a text.

Benjamin Jowett, an Oxford scholar in classical Greek and theology, posits that if the study of Plato and Sophocles simply follows the conventions of classics because meaning is understood to be the plain, literal sense, then biblical interpretation should also be similar in that it should simply attempt to arrive at the original meaning of the text when it was first uttered by the prophet or the evangelist by applying the same rules that are applied to the classics.[58] Arguments such as this undermine the fact that Christians take only the Bible and no other books (religious or otherwise) as inspired, inerrant, and sacred. They already accord special status to the biblical text so the Christian treatment of Bible as a special book should afford it certain interpretive privileges that are not accorded to other books.

Historical critical scholars maintain that biblical studies and theology are different because theology is influenced by philosophical, dogmatic, and cultural elements.[59] Ernst Troeltsch epitomized this kind of

55. Gabler, "Oration on the Proper Distinction," 495.
56. Wrede, "Task and Methods," 116.
57. Wrede, "Task and Methods," 69.
58. Jowett, "On the Interpretation of Scripture," 378.
59. Law, *Historical-Critical Method*, 25–80; Collins, *Bible after Babel*, 4–11. For an alternative view of historical criticism and its incongruity, see Barr, *History and Ideology*, 32–58.

historical critical scholarship when he argued for the autonomy of the historian from all forms of authority or superstructure because such authorities were corrupting influences in bringing out the meaning of the texts themselves.[60]

Stephen Chapman argues that biblical scholarship in modernity changed the way history was viewed, especially biblical history. According to him, history came to be viewed without any "recourse or relation to revelation at all, which begs the question anew and even more urgently; if the biblical canon is fully contingent, a mere accident of history, what unity can it possibly have and what convincing rationale can be given for its limits? In purely historical terms, how can one restrict one's inquiry to only these books, and how can one perceive anything in them other than irreducible diversity?"[61] In much of modern biblical scholarship, biblical interpretation became a matter of attending to the literary, philological, polemical, and cultural features of the text.[62] Consequently, Christian convictions and Christian reading of Scripture found little to no place in the academic study of the Bible.

The Struggle to Read the Bible as Scripture

Historical critical scholarship affected both Protestant and Roman Catholic interpretation alike. It is against this background that we see the emergence of two important figures—Karl Barth and Hans Urs von Balthasar[63]—who mustered the courage to emphasize the role of dogmatic (doctrinal) presuppositions in biblical interpretation.[64] Together, they

---

60. Troeltsch, "Historische und Dogmatische," 729–53. Van Harvey, according to Collins, lucidly summarized the three major pillars of historical-critical scholarship found in Troeltsch, which are: (1) autonomy of the historian, (2) the principle of analogy, and (3) the principle of criticism. Collins, *Bible after Babel*, 5. See also Harvey, *Historian and the Believer*. Seth Heringer adds correlation as another point that Troeltsch argued. Heringer, "Problem of 'History,'" 28–29.

61. Chapman, "Modernity's Canonical Crisis," 658–59.

62. Legaspi, *Death of Scripture*, 3–4.

63. Barth and Balthasar are natural choices here because of their long-standing correspondence and mutual admiration. More than Henri de Lubac, it was Balthasar who pushed Roman Catholic theology to interact with Protestant theology, especially with Barth even when many had reservations about Barth.

64. Dahlke, *Karl Barth*; Palakeel, *Use of Analogy*.

represent the Protestant and the Roman Catholic branch of theological interpretation.[65]

Barth's focus on theological interpretation has one unique and noticeable feature—a pastoral heart. In his sermon entitled "The New World in the Bible," delivered on February 6, 1917, Barth challenged the then prevailing attitude toward the Bible as a book of only historical import.[66] He argued that biblical history and events are not static but are dynamic in the sense that the same God is still speaking when one reads these texts. God is present in the text, Christ is present in the text, and the Spirit is present in the text. As a result, the response to the Bible should be more than a mere fascination with history, it should reflect a genuine desire to know this God.[67]

In *Der Römerbrief*, Barth reveals a contrasting approach to biblical interpretation to that of historical critical interpretation, which he calls "inner dialectic."[68] In the preface to the second edition, he argues that historical critical exegesis is not an end in itself but only the first step. Barth writes, "I have nothing whatever to say against historical criticism. I recognize it, and once more state quite definitely that it is both necessary and justified. My complaint is that recent commentators confine themselves to an interpretation of the text which seems to me to be no commentary at all, but merely the first step towards a commentary."[69] He further argues that the interpretation of the text requires more than disjointed notes on words and phrases. It requires attention to the identity of God who is revealed in it. Unlike those who restrict the identity of Jesus

---

65. The mutual appreciation and willing cooperation of Protestant and Roman Catholic scholars make TIS not only a strong ecumenical movement, but also a forum where Protestants and Roman Catholics share common concerns and strong agreements since the Reformation had set them on a collision course. This brief overview of the historical background is important because some of the major arguments of historical criticism such as the plain, literal sense, authorial intention, reading Scripture like other classics, emphasis on the human aspect of the text, the disjunction between "what was meant" versus "what it means," and so forth continue unabated in many works on TIS.

66. There is a minor dispute on the actual date of the delivery of this lecture. For example, compare Barth and Thurneysen, "Briefwechsel," with Barth, *Das Wort Gottes*.

67. Barth, *Word of God*, 16–29. Barth is said to have gone through three stages of evolution in his own theological thought (liberal, dialectical, and analogical) which his works, according to some scholars, reveal with certain clarity. Palakeel, *Use of Analogy*, 14. This evolution in Barth's thoughts presents an example of the struggle to read the Bible as Christian Scripture after the academy had relegated Scripture to the status of a mere academic Bible.

68. Barth, *Der Römerbrief*.

69. Barth, *Romans*, 6.

to a mere historical figure, Paul claims that this Jesus is the Son of God and reveals God. Not making this connection misses Paul's own view of Jesus.[70] By arguing this way, Barth keeps the language and content of Scripture together.[71] He also states there is no disjunction between what was written then and what is understood now because through the words of Scripture God speaks to us today, just as he did a long time ago when the Scripture was first communicated.[72] For Barth, God's ability to speak to the readers of Scripture at any time, not just to the original audience, is integral to biblical interpretation. Past history is not detached from present history because the same God is actively speaking today just as he did with the original audience. Barth makes the case that the word of God is active because God is active. For him, the identity of God is important for interpretation.

The study of Anselm's *fides quaerens intellectum* became a decisive turning point in Barth's theology.[73] Joseph Palakeel writes, "Barth deciphered a new theological epistemology in the Anselmian principle *fides quaerens intellectum*, where faith (*fides*) is defined as 'knowledge and affirmation of the word of Christ,' or of the church's creed and the task of understanding (*intellectum*) is 'reflecting on what has been said and affirmed beforehand by creed.'"[74] Theology is concerned with "faith-knowledge, namely the knowledge that springs from faith in God's revelation in Jesus Christ."[75] Barth expounds the importance of this decisive revelation of God in Jesus Christ who is the *Logos*.[76] For Barth, all temporality in the time and eternity dualism needed "radical reinterpretation according to christological and Trinitarian modes of thought."[77] The Christian view of history has to have faith as its starting point. God's action in Christ becomes the key to interpreting Scripture.

---

70. Barth, *Romans*, 11–12.

71. Treier, *Introducing Theological Interpretation*, 16.

72. Barth makes this point from his practical experience as a pastor who struggled to preach to his congregation from the works of the so-called commentators because the words of Scripture had only historically annotated values. Barth, *Romans*, 9.

73. Barth, *How I Changed My Mind*, 43; Hartwell, *Theology of Karl Barth*, 42–47; Busch, *Karl Barth*, 205–9.

74. Palakeel, *Use of Analogy*, 18.

75. Palakeel, *Use of Analogy*, 18.

76. Barth, *CD* 2.1, 97.

77. Hunsinger, *How to Read Karl Barth*, 14.

Although Barth did not abandon the skills he acquired through his training in historical-critical study as a theological student, his theology continued to develop. He relegated historical criticism to its proper role—as the first step in biblical interpretation and not its *telos*. The word of God became the only criterion of the *Dogmatics*. Barth in the second draft of his *CD* tries to exclude anything "that might appear to find for theology a foundation, support, or justification in philosophical existentialism."[78] What prompted Barth in his conviction concerning the word of God was the attitude of scholars who concurred with the arguments of natural sciences and historical criticism to the degree that they argued for the ability of human beings to know God apart from divine grace. Barth insisted on a christological center (though his view was much more nuanced than the way he has been appropriated). Apart from Christ and the grace that is received through him we cannot understand the Scripture. His emphasis on a christological center continues to shape TIS as many have picked up an interest in christological interpretation of Scripture.[79]

Barth influenced Roman Catholic theology in equal measure as Protestant theology with his willingness to shift the foundation of his theological exegesis from a primarily historical critical foundation to that of dogmatic elements, while generating excitement and controversy with his view on *analogia entis* ("analogy of being").[80] *Analogia entis*, in Barth's view, is the "invention of the Antichrist."[81] Roman Catholic theologian Erich Przywara wrote on *analogia entis* in 1932 and his entire system revolved around this concept.[82] Based on Thomas Aquinas's view of the identity of God's essence and existence, Przywara stated that since humans have their being from God's being, they can know God from the

---

78. Barth, *CD 1.1*, xiii.

79. Chapter 2 will make this point more evident.

80. Here Bible becomes Scripture again.

81. Barth, *CD 1.1*, xiii. Balthasar argues that Barth has provided sufficient evidence in *CD 2.1* that *analogia entis* should be completely palatable to Barth's theological program under his own concept of *analogia fidei*. Balthasar, *Theology of Karl Barth*, 164–67, 257. cf. Barth, *CD 2.1*, 82–84.

82. Dahlke, *Karl Barth*, 63. See also Przywara, *Analogia Entis: Metaphysics*. Barth and Przywara corresponded on this issue in 1929 and 1931 before Przywara published his book in 1932. He wanted Barth to review his forthcoming book on *Analogia Entis* and Barth did not oblige to review the work citing his lack of interest in such matters. Dahlke, *Katholische Rezeption Karl Barths*, 81–86. Przywara himself writes about his correspondence with Barth in the preface to the first volume. Pryzwara, *Analogia Entis: Metaphysics*, xxi.

point of their creatureliness because their existence proves the existence of God.[83] Thus, philosophical reflection on "being" is capable of leading one to the knowledge of God similar to the knowledge of God revealed in the Roman Catholic Church because they stand in continuity with one another. The imperfect knowledge of God available through philosophy can be perfected in and through the church.[84]

According to Keith Johnson, Przywara was invited as the guest lecturer for Barth's seminar on Aquinas at the University of Münster (February 5–6, 1929). During that meeting, Barth disagreed with Przywara's view of *analogia entis* because Barth was convinced that God's revelation was manifest in Jesus Christ. Apart from that revelation in Jesus, one cannot understand the identity of this God or have any relations with him.[85] Barth may have had Przywara in mind when he was writing about *analogia entis* in *CD*, although he does not mention him by name, because none of the works he mentions regarding Roman Catholic theology uses *analogia entis*.[86] Barth wanted to rid Protestant theology of liberal Protestantism. In his view, Roman Catholic theology adopted similar positions as the liberal Protestants who postulated that God was merely a human construct or that God can be known apart from revelation in Jesus.[87]

Barth's solution was *analogia relationis* ("analogy of relation"). The Father and the Son are revealed in the man Jesus—the *imago Dei*—and it is in him that we find our relation to God (John 17:20–21).[88] Our knowledge of God is not based on human capacity to postulate the existence of an ultimate being based on the concept of "being" itself, as Przywara argues. Sin came into the world and brought a barrier between God and man. As a result, man is not able to know God on his own. Man can know God only based on his relationship to God made possible by Jesus. Because of Jesus, God loves humans with the same love with which the Father loves the Son and the Son loves the Father. Human knowledge of

---

83. Pryzwara, *Analogia Entis: Metaphysik*, 192–316.

84. Johnson, "Reconsidering Barth's Rejection," 637–38.

85. Johnson, "Reconsidering Barth's Rejection," 634–42.

86. Dahlke, *Karl Barth*, 63.

87. Dahlke, *Karl Barth*, 65–66. Dahlke posits that Roman Catholic theology had real internal concerns and fears due to the rise of theoretical and practical atheism and agnosticism in the eighteenth and nineteenth centuries.

88. Barth, *CD* 3.2, 219.

God must consist of this intimate relationship with him and not through human ability external to this relationship.[89]

The fact that man cannot know God by his own capability due to sin is important for Barth because this makes him depend on God for understanding his word. God is in heaven and man is on earth, but there is a relationship between God and man. The relationship between such a God and such a man is the theme of the Bible, argues Barth.[90] Barth brought biblical interpretation closer to theological interpretation that was once viewed as naïveté.

Despite the many criticisms against Barth in Roman Catholic quarters, he gained admiration and a following (some silently), as in Protestant circles.[91] In the years leading up to, during, and soon after Vatican II, Roman Catholic theology was faced with the role and place of historical critical scholarship. Jean Daniélou and Henri de Lubac led the charge against the philosophical foundations of historical criticism as they contended that Catholic theology should retrieve its traditional and historical interpretation.[92] The continued resistance toward modernity within Roman Catholic circles led to the reconsideration of the contribution and influence of medieval theology, which gave birth to neo-Thomism

---

89. Barth, *CD* 3.2, 220–22.

90. Barth, *Romans*, 10.

91. Some were more critical of Barth's work than others. For example, see Balthasar, *Theology of Karl Barth*; Betz, "Beyond the Sublime," 1–50, 367–411; Johnson, "Reconsidering Barth's Rejection"; Johnson, "Karl Barth," 219–21; Hart, *Beauty of the Infinite*, 241; Fehr, *Offenbarungsproblem*.

92. Williamson, "Catholic Biblical Interpretation," 103–4. See also Daniélou, *God and the Ways*; Lubac, *Exégèse médiéval*. Regarding the important role *Nouvelle Théologie* (Daniélou and Lubac being chief among the *ressourcement* theologians) played in the resurgence of Roman Catholic theology that is critical of historical-critical theology, see Boersma, *Nouvelle Théologie*. In the preface, Boersma cites the important contribution *nouvelle théolgie* made to the Catholic-Protestant dialogue and collaboration. Boersma, *Nouvelle Théologie*, vii–ix. For the contribution of Lubac to TIS, see Storer, *Reading Scripture to Hear God*.

(neo-scholasticism).[93] The nature and ability of man is elevated where the need for grace becomes more of a natural extension.[94]

Balthasar became quite disturbed by the direction of Catholic theology. This is particularly evident in his letter to Barth:

> Certainly the outrageous element of truth which has become Christian through Protestantism has not been truly and fully assimilated in Catholic theology; the Counter-Reformation was too strongly a *Counter*-Reformation; the burden of medieval theology is enormous; for this theology was relatively justifiable in the situation at that time, but it remains with impunity. I hope that your great work will help to foster this self-reflection in Catholic theology too; and that it likewise achieves the same

---

93. Brezik, *One Hundred Years of Thomism*, 7–22; Brown, "Sacramentality," 627.

Against post-Cartesian philosophy that privileged epistemology over metaphysics (cognition or thought versus being), neo-Thomism posited "being" as primary and that mankind can have a degree of certainty in his knowledge of God starting with his own being because human being is a representation modeled after God, the Supreme Being. Pope Leo XIII had issued the encyclical *Aeterni Patris* in 1879 and *Providentissimus Deus* in 1893, which encouraged Catholic scholars to study biblical languages and new scientific criticism to argue against it and made neo-Thomism the official philosophical position of the Roman Catholic Church. However, the Catholic attitude toward historical-critical scholarship has not always been negative. Pope Pius XII issued the encyclical *Divino afflante Spiritu* on September 30, 1943, encouraging critical engagement with historical critical studies. Bechard, *Scripture Documents*, 115–39.

The 1965 Vatican II document *Dei Verbum* under the Pontificate of Pope Paul VI was more in line with the historical-critical scholarship than traditional scholarship and divided Catholic theologians into two camps: those who argued for *Dei Verbum* to be fully endorsing historical criticism (Brown, *Critical Meaning of the Bible*; Fitzmyer, *Biblical Commission's Document*; Fitzmyer, *Interpretation of Scripture*) and those who were skeptical of such an interpretation (Dulles, "Vatican II," (2006) 17–26).

Under the direction of Pope John Paul II, the Pontifical Biblical Commission published *The Interpretation of the Bible in the Church*, which encouraged the church to appropriate critical exegesis while also engaging with other methods of interpretation. Pontifical Biblical Commission, *Interpretation of the Bible*. In his encyclical *Fider et Ratio* in 1998, Pope John Paul II struck a balance between faith and reason. John Paul II, *Fides et Ratio*.

It is in this historical milieu that the quest for theological interpretation in Roman Catholic circles began in earnest. It is instructive to keep this history in mind to make sense of the continuing struggles within TIS, given its ecumenical character. Therefore, some are open toward an ecclesially driven interpretation (more in line with Balthasar and the Catholic interpretation), while others resort to and insist on the concept of *sola scriptura* (more in line with Barth and Protestantism). See, for example, Vanhoozer, *Drama of Doctrine*, 7–12; Lindbeck, *Nature of Doctrine*; Fowl, *Engaging Scripture*; Fowl and Jones, *Reading in Communion*; Watson, *Text, Church and World*; Reno, *Genesis*, 9–14.

94. Dahlke, *Karl Barth*, 130.

courageous distance from its stages of development as you yourself have taken from the whole history of theology.[95]

Balthasar was convinced that Catholic theology was in need of course correction for it to embrace a theological, not a philosophical, foundation as its starting point.

Neo-Thomism became a point of tension for Balthasar. Contrary to the neo-Thomistic contention of general grace (available in creation because God had imbued it with his grace) and special grace (available in Jesus Christ) as one and the same because of its origin in God, Balthasar, through his many interactions with Barth and his works, sensed the acute need for Christ to be the starting point of Catholic theology; for the grace provided in Jesus Christ is unique because he is God himself.[96] By attacking Neo-Thomism's anthropological foundation, Balthasar wrote, "the theologically relevant concept of nature is finally not to be had from philosophical analysis. If this is ever to be reached, we will have to look elsewhere, that is, from the perspective of faith, which alone can tell us what grace and revelation are in themselves and how *they themselves* are defined against the background of what we—now theologically—can term 'nature.'"[97] Balthasar challenged the then dominant practices within Catholic scholarship.

Many of the architects of Vatican II were neo-Thomists—the ones who were emboldened, after *Divino afflante Spiritu*, to engage with critical Protestant scholarship and were influenced to varying degrees by that engagement.[98] As a result, post-Vatican II Catholic theology shows signs

---

95. As quoted in Dahlke's work. Dahlke, *Karl Barth*, 98–99. This letter was dated May 4, 1940, more than two decades before Vatican II. It highlights the growing tension in some Catholic quarters with the direction of Catholic theology, especially with regard to its philosophical and biblical underpinnings.

96. For Barth's influence on Balthasar, see Balthasar, *Glory of the Lord*, 52–56; Frei, *Doctrine of Revelation*; Torrance, *Karl Barth*, 216–17; Hütter, "Barth between McCormack," 105–9; Wigley, "Balthasar Thesis" 345–59; Wigley, *Karl Barth*; Dahlke, *Karl Barth*, 21–55. For a critical view of Balthasar's characterization of Barth, see McCormack, *Barth's Critically Realistic Dialectical Theology*; Dorrien, *Barthian Revolt*.

97. Balthasar, *Theology of Karl Barth*, 276. Balthasar did not find the use of philosophy in theology itself problematic, but he did when philosophy served as the foundation.

98. Fiorenza, "Systematic Theology," 36–37. According to Fiorenza, Roman Catholic theology became open to modernity post-Vatican II. Catholic theology splintered mainly along the lines of those who favored modernity and historical criticism and those who favored classical models and premodern interpretation. Fiorenza, "Systematic Theology," 64–66.

of divergence within Catholic thought between those in favor of critical scholarship and those who wanted to follow Balthasar's lead to read Bible as Scripture.[99]

Barth made a lasting impression on Protestant biblical interpretation. David Steinmetz stated that precritical exegesis was in fact superior to historical critical exegesis and that the most primitive meaning of the text is the only meaning of the text.[100] David Yeago's influential essay challenged the scholarly biblical guild through his explication of Nicene dogma as biblically and theologically sound.[101] He wrote that the Nicene *homoousion* was "neither imposed *on* the New Testament texts, nor distantly deduced *from* the texts, but rather describes a pattern of judgements present *in* the texts, in the texture of scriptural discourse concerning Jesus and the God of Israel."[102] Brevard Childs, a pupil and exponent of Barth's theological hermeneutics,[103] wrote a programmatic essay on the need for theological exegesis as part of interpreting Scripture.[104] In it, Childs says one cannot help but read Isa 53 as pointing to Christ.[105] The rise of theological interpretation in the last few decades owes much to the work of these men, especially to Barth and Balthasar.

---

99. For examples of ardent defenders of historical-critical exegesis among Catholic scholars, see Brown, *Critical Meaning of Bible*, 23–44; Fitzmyer, *Biblical Commission's Document*, 26–44.

For examples of Catholic scholars who are critical of overreliance on historical-critical exegesis, see Ratzinger, "Biblical Interpretation in Conflict," 29; Potterie, "Biblical Exegesis," 33; Dulles, "Revelation, Scripture, and Tradition," 35–58; Dulles, "Vatican II," 17–19; Carey, *Avery Cardinal Dulles, SJ*, 306–488; Gadenz, "Hiatus between Exegesis and Theology," 63–84.

100. Steinmetz, "Superiority of Pre-Critical Exegesis," 27–38. For more supporting arguments on the merits of pre-critical exegesis, see Jenson, *Ezekiel*, 22–26.

101. Yeago, "New Testament."

102. Yeago, "New Testament," 153. Yeago also emphasized the role of tradition, especially the truly catholic form of that tradition as embraced by Luther in interpreting Scripture—an important element in TIS. cf. Yeago, "Catholic Luther," 13–34.

103. For Barth's influence on Childs, his student, see MacDonald, "Theological Interpretation," 85–101; Scalise, "Canonical Hermeneutics," 68–72; Xun, *Theological Exegesis*, 226; Gignilliat, *Karl Barth*, 1–25.

104. Childs, "Recovering Theological Exegesis," 16–26. He expresses his indebtedness to Yeago at the beginning of the essay.

105. Childs, "Recovering Theological Exegesis," 24. "How can one claim to read Isaiah as the voice of Israel in the Hebrew Scriptures and at the same time speak of its witness to Jesus Christ? It is not only possible, but actually mandatory for any serious Christian theological reflection. Because Scripture performs different functions according to distinct contexts, a multi-level reading is required even to begin to grapple with the full range of Scripture's role as the intentional medium of continuing divine revelation."

As in Protestant circles, Catholic theologians also paid attention to the need and validity of theological interpretation, not just as a part of the repertoire of options, but as an indispensable and primary task of interpreting Scripture.[106] A constant refrain in Catholic debates after Vatican II was whether or not to treat historical criticism as complementary or as the only legitimate way in Catholic theology and interpretation. According to Hans Boersma and Matthew Levering, there are at least three important stages of development in post-Vatican II Catholic interpretation that address the vexing question of the complementary nature of historical criticism to theology.[107]

The first stage of this development is credited to Francis Martin who, following Gregory of Nyssa, thought of history in terms of temporality and stated that the biblical history of salvation is unique in that the realities presented in it continue to be present today unlike other time-bound realities in history.[108]

Joseph Ratzinger, who represents the second stage, contends that the modern understanding of history as "pure facticity, which is composed of chance and necessity" needs to be recalibrated in light of the participatory nature of time in God's eternity.[109] He argues that an exegete does not occupy a neutral position above and outside the church's history of interpretation, but he has to first view the Bible as one book, as does the church, and that it presents a coherent history; and the locus of interpretive authority therefore must lie in this view of the church's history and the Bible's life in the community of believers.[110] For him, Jesus Christ is the linchpin of biblical interpretation.[111]

The third stage in this development is the contribution of Denis Farkasfalvy who emphasized the eucharistic or liturgical nature of the development of early Christian doctrines.[112] Challenging the conclusions of form criticism and redaction criticism, Farkasfalvy proposed that the

---

106. A few examples of Protestant theologians who are interested in theological interpretation are Fowl, *Engaging Scripture*; Vanhoozer, "Imprisoned or Free?"; Treier, *Introducing Theological Interpretation*; Watson, *Text and Truth*; Seitz, *Word without End*; Green, *Practicing Theological Interpretation*; and Billings, *Word of God*.

107. Boersma and Levering, *Heaven on Earth?*, 4–6.

108. Martin, *Sacred Scripture*, 239; Boersma and Levering, *Heaven on Earth?*, 4.

109. Potterie, "Biblical Exegesis," 23.

110. Potterie, "Biblical Exegesis," 29; Ratzinger, *Jesus of Nazareth*, xvi–xxi.

111. Ratzinger, *Jesus of Nazareth*, xix.

112. Farkasfalvy, *Inspiration and Interpretation*, 63–87.

synoptic gospel narratives must be viewed from the point of "coming and being encountered"—an oft-repeated phrase in those gospels—and this is something that is repeated in the Eucharistic theology of the early church. In such a context of the early church's Eucharistic theology, Jesus was presented not merely from the objective past, "but as the one who, at the beginning of an episode, 'arrives' and becomes approachable once again, as the one who encounters the human needs and religious problems of living individuals . . . a solution unavailable from merely human resources."[113] Thus, Farkasfalvy concluded that historical reality does not exhaust the truth, but is absorbed into the eucharistic and liturgical tradition of the church.

Roman Catholic theology has gone through stages of reconciling the role of historical criticism in reading Scripture. Those who are theologically oriented see an indispensable yet diminished and complementary role for historical-criticism in reading Scripture.[114] Today, several scholars of international acclaim embrace the need for theological interpretation of Scripture and are hard at work in producing commentaries, monographs, journal articles, and essays.[115] The works of Barth and Balthasar set the stage for TIS, and their collaboration and mutual admiration for each other have given a strong ecumenical shape to it.[116] The

---

113. Farkasfalvy, *Inspiration and Interpretation*, 73.

114. Ayres, "'There's Fire in That Rain,'" 33–51; Daley, "'In Many and Various Ways,'" 13–31; Levering, *Participatory Biblical Exegesis*; Johnson and Kurz, *Catholic Biblical Scholarship*; Murphy, "Profiling Christ," 173–87; Reno, *Genesis*; O'Keefe and Reno, *Sanctified Vision*. This list is not exhaustive by any means.

115. Brazos Theological Commentary on the Bible by Baker, The Church's Bible by Eerdmans, Ancient Christian Commentary on Scripture by InterVarsity, and The Two Horizons Old Testament and New Testament Commentary by Eerdmans are a few examples of commentary series devoted to theological interpretation. JTI is exclusively dedicated to the promotion of theological interpretation. Similarly, JTISup series publishes monographs on theological interpretation. Examples of edited works are Green and Meadowcroft, *Ears That Hear*; Boersma and Levering, *Heaven on Earth?*; Bartholomew and Thomas, *Manifesto*. This short list attests to the exponential growth TIS had in the last two decades or so, an encouraging sign.

116. For a different point of view on the genealogy, see Treier, "What Is Theological Interpretation?," 149–53. According to him, Barth and postmodern concerns (where the role of ecclesial or reading community takes priority) shaped TIS. His focus is on the tension between the two *loci* of interpretive authority, namely, *sola scriptura* and churchly reading. His article is helpful in understanding some of the important elements that influenced particular theologians and shaped their works, but his analysis eludes the prior ecumenical consensus that evolved out of Barth-Balthasar engagement which is of historical import that shaped both Protestant and Catholic scholars who came after them. However, his view of the church's dogmatic heritage as a treasure

struggle with the appropriate role of historical criticism still continues even within TIS, which has much in common with the struggles of Barth and Balthasar—the struggle is against not just a hermeneutical system, but more importantly against the academy that for centuries have argued in favor of historical critical interpretation.

Converging Disciplines

The convergence of biblical studies and systematic theology offers much hope for TIS.[117] However, the very fact that scholars from biblical studies and systematic theology collaborate creates tension that is both healthy and at times contentious.[118] Trinitarian interpretation does not get much attention in the present exchange of ideas. This may be in part due to the felt need among scholars to forge a common ground before they can consider ideas that challenge both disciplines because there are still lingering questions concerning several aspects of these converging of disciplines. One of such concerns is the extent to which historical criticism, a defining feature of biblical studies for a long time, can be appropriated.[119]

---

worth pursuing is commendable for its aim. In *Introducing Theological Interpretation of Scripture,* he mentions Barthean and Catholic background, but differs in one significant way—he does not trace the important role Balthasar played in the emergence of Catholic theological interpretation as is done here. I believe that the particular genealogy traced in this book sheds an important light in this respect—in the relation between Barthean and Catholic theology that paved the way for TIS. This could also help explain some of the continuing tension between Protestant and Catholic proponents of TIS.

117. It must be pointed out that the line of demarcation with regard to the attitude toward and appropriation of a certain ideology or hermeneutical position between scholars of different discipline is not straightforward. However, as a general rule of thumb, this distinction holds true of the advocates of TIS. This is not an attempt to assign strict categories to the scholars but point out their preferences and how that shapes their theories and practices.

118. Treier, "What Is Theological Interpretation?" Treier provides a short but helpful list of scholars who are engaged in TIS who fall into biblical and theological disciplines. Watson exhorts discarding the ideological divide between biblical studies and systematic theology to fully embrace a theologically driven interpretation of Scripture. Watson, *Text and Truth,* 2–9. Watson also acknowledges the challenges that emerge when biblical studies and systematic theology begin to converse and attempt to converge. Watson, *Text, Church and World,* 11–14.

119. Burnett, "Historical Criticism," 290–93; Green, *Practicing Theological Interpretation,* 43–70; Fowl, *Theological Interpretation of Scripture: Classic,* 15–24; Rae, *History and Hermeneutics*; Heringer, "Problem of 'History'"; Rae, "Theological Interpretation," 94–109.

Some argue for a measured and tamed appropriation of historical criticism, while others appear extremely cautious and see less value in it.[120] The real question concerns what controls the narrative—historical-critical elements or confessional elements. Theologian Webster advocates a moderate appropriation of historical criticism. The dogmatic critique of historical criticism is its denial of the role of Scripture's "natural history" in the "communicative divine economy" that is part of its ontology, says Webster.[121] On the other hand, biblical scholars like Childs and Watson are more comfortable with the appropriation of historical criticism.[122] Despite the consensus on several issues among the practitioners of TIS, some important disagreements linger.[123] There are competing views on the extent to which one should appropriate historical criticism in theological interpretation. If historical criticism does not have the same sway in TIS as it had in much of modern scholarship, then the foundational question concerning the identity of God in the Bible can become the starting point in theological interpretation.

Another vexing question that emerged as a result of this convergence is regarding the *locus* of meaning in biblical texts.[124] The question on the locus of interpretive authority emerged as a corollary to the question of the locus of meaning, but soon became equally or more important of a question than the locus of meaning itself. The question on the locus of meaning in the text is centered on whether the author (authorial intention) or the reading community (the church in the case of TIS) has priority in determining the meaning of a certain text. Answering to the locus of meaning can reveal to some extent what theory and method of theological interpretation one advocates.

Kevin Vanhoozer and Stephen Fowl represent those who prioritize "authorial intention" and those who prioritize "reading community" respectively. Vanhoozer, for example, argues in his earlier work that the author has priority in determining the meaning.[125] His immediate

---

120. See, for example, Burnett and Fowl above. Burnett sees historical-criticism as unavoidable, but, contrastingly, Fowl sees little value in it.

121. Webster, *Holy Scripture*, 19.

122. Childs, "Recovering Theological Exegesis," 22–23; Watson, *Text, Church and World*, 1–2, 12–14, 171.

123. Porter, "What Exactly Is Theological Interpretation," 243–47. Porter evaluates the works of some of the prominent exponents of TIS and showcases the inconsistencies within the field based on his reading of the field and his evaluation of its merits.

124. Spinks, *Crisis of Meaning*.

125. Vanhoozer, *Is There a Meaning*, 43–74, 250–55.

concern at this time was the erosion of biblical authority, especially in radical hermeneutics proposed by Jacques Derrida (deconstruction) and Stanley Fish (reader-response criticism), when texts seem to assume a life of their own without a substantial role for biblical authors.[126] Not only did Vanhoozer argue for "authorial intention" to be the *locus* of meaning, he also argued for *sola scriptura* to be the *locus* of interpretive authority.[127] By insisting on *sola scriptura*, Vanhoozer wanted to draw a line between what he considered to be a slippery slope in determining the meaning of the biblical text by its use in the believing community and his view of meaning from the vantage of "status" in Christ.[128] Though he modified his position on "authorial interpretation" in his later work "Imprisoned or Free?," he has not abandoned his preference for it and he presents it in a more nuanced way in which the master/slave relationship becomes a metaphor for the mutual dependence of the author and the reader to determine the meaning of the text.[129] In this mutual dependence, the hierarchy goes from the master to the slave.[130] Webster, similarly, cautions against the "ecclesially" vested and oriented meaning and interpretive authority.[131] Watson emphasizes the critical role of authorial intention in determining the meaning of the text, which he calls the "literal sense," to

---

126. Derrida, *Writing and Difference*; Fish, *Is There a Text*. See also Foucault, *Madness and Civilization*.

127. Vanhoozer, *Drama of Doctrine*, 11–12. Vanhoozer appropriates the speech-act theory of J. L. Austin via Nicholas Wolterstorff to argue that the meaning of the biblical text needs to be located within "divine authorial discourse." His arguments are set up against the cultural-linguistic model of postliberal theology of Hans Frei, George Lindbeck, and David Kelsey who placed substantial weight on the role of the reading community. Cf. Austin, *How to Do Things*; Wolterstorff, *Divine Discourse*; Frei, *Eclipse of Biblical Narrative*; Lindbeck, *Nature of Doctrine*; Kelsey, *Uses of Scripture*.

128. Vanhoozer, "Imprisoned or Free?," 54–58.

129. Vanhoozer, "Imprisoned or Free?," 59n21.

130. Vanhoozer, "Imprisoned or Free?," 71. What the divine author is doing with the text of the human author can be seen mostly at the canonical level. The emphasis even in his modified version of authorial intention is on what the human author is doing with what he has written—the illocutionary force of the text. Ricoeur and Wolterstorff influence this particular nuance in his work. For a critical view of the appropriation of speech-act theory to overcome the human/divine author dichotomy, see Seitz, *Character of Christian Scripture*, 80–82.

131. Webster, *Holy Scripture*, 44–57. He argues that the chronological priority of Scripture over the church (there was Scripture before the church was born) necessitates priority in interpretive authority. The church is corrected, encouraged, and guided by the word and not vice versa because the church exists in a space created by the word.

counter the argument that meaning is determined by readers rather than the authors.¹³²

Fowl, on the other hand, argues that the ecclesial community has priority in determining meaning of the biblical text.¹³³ After discussing the merits of determinate (emphasizes the stable character of the meaning of the biblical text),¹³⁴ anti-determinate (emphasizes the "otherness" in the text that stands over and against the dominant reading—contra determinate interpretation),¹³⁵ and underdeterminate types of interpretations (focuses on interpretive aims, interests, and practices instead of focusing on textual meaning alone—this is his preferred choice),¹³⁶ Fowl turns to Jeffrey Stout's theory of meaning¹³⁷ and asserts that instead of using the term "meaning" we should use a form of explication that captures the essence of what is being said because there is ambiguity in the term "meaning" itself. Thus, he concludes: "I argue that theological convictions, ecclesial practices, and communal and social concerns should *shape and be shaped by* biblical interpretation."¹³⁸

Not only is Fowl concerned about the ineffectiveness of a determinate model for theological interpretation, he is equally concerned about the possibility of drowning out the multivoiced meaning of the text and the ecclesial context of its reception and interpretation unless a more nuanced understanding of "meaning" is conceived.¹³⁹ Vanhoozer, on the other hand, is concerned about the possibility of interpretive anarchism

---

132. Watson, *Text and Truth*, 11, 95–126. Watson does not abrogate the unique role of the reading community, but like Vanhoozer, he prioritizes the author's role in determining meaning and sees a chronological priority for the author in the author-reader collaboration in determining meaning.

133. Fowl, *Engaging Scripture*, 56–61.

134. Fowl, *Engaging Scripture*, 33–34.

135. Fowl, *Engaging Scripture*, 42–44. See also Critchley, *Ethics of Deconstruction*, 26.

136. Fowl, *Engaging Scripture*, 56.

137. Stout, "What Is the Meaning," 2–3. Stout prefers explication (explication as elimination) as proposed by W. V. Quine and aided by Dennis Stampe's assertion that grammatical context determines a particular interpretation. He concludes that theoretical terms should serve interests and purposes (5). See also Quine, *Word and Object*, 258–59; Stampe, "Toward a Grammar of Meaning," 267–302.

138. Fowl, *Engaging Scripture*, 60.

139. Fowl, "Multivoiced Literal Sense," 35–50; Fowl, *Engaging Scripture*, 59–60; Fowl, "Further Thoughts," 125–30. Accommodating the criticism from several quarters of his dismissal of authorial intention, Fowl has consented to a chastened view of authorial intentions in text without necessarily changing his view of meaning. Fowl, "Role of Authorial Intention."

running rampant without a proper defining framework and the loss of *sola scriptura* as the locus of interpretive authority.[140] These two concerns can be generalized as representing the field based on one's preference for either author-centered, author-driven interpretation or ecclesially located meaning. The quest for the best approach to determining meaning in theological interpretation has been equally impacted by another feature of TIS, the diverging philosophical underpinnings of the advocates. The question on the locus of meaning brings us back to the issue of what dictates theological interpretation—whether a theory of meaning that prioritizes historical contingencies in the text or the Christian view of Bible as sacred text.

Diverging Philosophical Foundations

Literature on TIS demonstrates the influence of either modern or postmodern philosophical hermeneutics on its advocates.[141] Though they may not explicitly mention their philosophical commitments, their works bear the hallmarks of a particular philosophical preference. Stanley J. Grenz declared that evangelicals have utilized the tools of modernity (the scientific method, empirical approach to reality, and common sense realism) in their quest to demonstrate the credibility of the Christian faith.[142] Many within TIS similarly utilize different aspects of modernity in varying degrees.

If confidence in human reason and the ensuing autonomy that guarantees objectively verifiable knowledge can be identified as the defining

---

140. Vanhoozer, *Drama of Doctrine*, 11–12. See also Treier and Vanhoozer, *Theology and the Mirror*, 85; Ramm, *Pattern of Religious Authority*, 21. For Ramm, the locus of interpretive authority lies with the triune God in his self-revelation.

141. Although no one fits neatly into any one category, all of them exhibit some dominant way of thinking in their interpretive approaches. There are more ways than one to describe "modernity" and "postmodernity"; however, modernity, as Stanley Grenz puts it, can be described based on the epistemological assumptions such as the certainty of knowledge apart from any external authority, objectivity, and human freedom, especially individual freedom. Grenz, *Primer on Postmodernism*, 4. Postmodernity is a reaction against confidence in the certainty of objective knowledge and individual freedom in determining truth or reality. Ermarth, "Postmodernism," 587–88. The major disagreement is about whether words are "referential" (correspondence to reality) or "reflexive" ("self-referential"—words refer to other words and not to realities in the world) in nature. See Alston, "Truth: Concept and Property," 11–26.

142. Grenz, *Primer on Postmodernism*, 161.

feature of modernity,[143] then postmodernity has poked a hole in the autonomy of human reason and confidence in the certainty of objective knowledge that comes with it.[144] The emphasis on the "individual" has been replaced by emphasis on "community."[145] The rise of postmodernity questioned the existing paradigms of biblical interpretation (the dominant paradigm being historical criticism that is said to have been fashioned after scientific investigation) and the elements such as presuppositions and subjectivity, which were once considered anathema, now have been rehabilitated and become integral to theological interpretation.[146]

Appropriation of tradition has also been rehabilitated through the works of philosophers such as Hans-Georg Gadamer, eventually aiding TIS in significant ways. Acceptance of tradition allowed precritical exegesis to be viewed favorably and positively.[147] Some in the evangelical camp, such as Grenz, Fowl, and others, found postmodernism and especially the concept of community in postmodernism particularly appealing to

---

143. Gadamer, *Truth and Method*, 279.

144. Lyotard, *Postmodern Condition*, xxiv, 81; Taylor and Winquist, *Postmodernism*, xv; McGowan, *Postmodernism*, 4–5. Postmodernity is a reaction against modernity. This reaction affects all aspects of language, art, culture, society, and religion. Nonfoundationalism recasts truth against a background that has done away with Enlightenment epistemology. Deleuze, "Image of Thought," 63–103.

145. Fish, *Is There a Text*, 13–15, 97, 147–80. Community driven grammar and meaning do not eliminate objectivity, but objectivity, as understood in modernity, has been redefined. See also Treier, *Introducing Theological Interpretation*, 51–55, 146–47. Treier highlights how postcritical interpretations have contributed to a renewal in biblical interpretation that assesses and views precritical interpretation favorably and its usefulness to TIS along with the ongoing tensions and wavering between the modern and postmodern camps within TIS in chapters 1–4 of this book. These chapters are particularly instructive in that they demonstrate the fact that TIS is not monolithic given its diverse philosophical, hermeneutical, and disciplinary homes.

146. Grenz, *Primer on Postmodernism*, 161–74. Grenz characterizes twentieth century evangelical theology as blindly drinking from the fountain of modernity. While cautioning against some of the issues in postmodernity that are detrimental to Christian belief, Grenz encourages an adoption of modified postmodernism against evangelical appropriation of modernity. The need to go beyond foundationalism is clarified and explained further in Grenz and Franke, *Beyond Foundationalism*, 28–54. This postmodern turn to the community is best exemplified in Grenz, *Theology for the Community*.

147. Gadamer, *Truth and Method*, 278–84. Gadamer challenged the long-held belief of objective interpretation by questioning the modern tendency to dismiss presuppositions and interpretive traditions. At the same time, he challenged deconstruction and the complete annihilation of verifiable and dominant truth (contra otherness or *différance*). See also Michelfelder and Palmer, *Dialogue and Deconstruction*, 1–5.

theological interpretation.[148] A few examples are in order to illustrate this point.[149]

Vanhoozer, in the conclusion of his programmatic chapter on postmodernity, asks two questions that are telling of his view toward postmodernity: "Is postmodernity a 'culture' into which the Gospel may be translated, or is it a condition from which the Gospel must be liberated?"[150] This way of framing the matter is rooted in the conviction that there is no consistent core (truth is relative) for postmodernity, and modernity can offer that certainty because Christian faith articulates definitive truth claims.[151]

Critiquing George Lindbeck's cultural-linguistic model, Vanhoozer cautions that just as Friedrich Schleiermacher's turn to human experience paved the way for Ludwig Feuerbach's concept of God as man's projection of his own ideal self, Lindbeck's turn to corporate experience would lead theology to be mere cultural anthropology.[152] Therefore, Vanhoozer sets out to rescue biblical interpretation by wresting the interpretive authority from its ecclesial location and depositing it back to *sola scriptura*.[153] Vanhoozer represents the modernist camp in TIS. Webster agrees with Vanhoozer and strongly opposes placing the locus of interpretive authority in the ecclesial community.[154] Watson, similarly, juxtaposes Lindbeck's proposal with what Paul calls the "people who suppress the truth" (Rom 1:18) because religion is man's response to primal divine revelation.[155]

---

148. Grenz's *Theology for the Community* is developed around the concept of community starting with the Trinitarian community of the Father, Son, and Spirit.

149. For a modernist approach, see Watson, *Text, Church and World*; Watson, *Text and Truth*; Vanhoozer, *Is There a Meaning*; Vanhoozer, *Drama of Doctrine*; and Jeanrond, *Text and Interpretation*.

For a postcritical/postliberal approach, see Fowl, *Engaging Scripture*; Kelsey, *Scripture in Recent Theology*; Lindbeck, *Nature of Doctrine*. For an overview of these differences in worldviews see Bartholomew, "Uncharted Waters," 1–35; Treier, *Introducing Theological Interpretation*, 33–35. For an increasing appeal to premodern interpretation see Steinmetz, "Superiority of Pre-Critical Exegesis"; Yeago, "New Testament"; Bokedal, "Rule of Faith," 233–55; O'Keefe and Reno, *Sanctified Vision*; Young, *Exegesis and Theology*.

150. Vanhoozer, *Cambridge Companion*, 22.

151. Vanhoozer, *Cambridge Companion*, 23–25.

152. Vanhoozer, *Drama of Doctrine*, 175.

153. Vanhoozer, *Drama of Doctrine*, 11–12.

154. Webster, *Holy Scripture*, 42–52. Webster, like Vanhoozer, singles out Lindbeck and the emphasis on ecclesial community. Since Scripture precedes church, the argument for ecclesially driven hermeneutics is faulty.

155. Watson, *Text and Truth*, 274n41.

On the other side of the spectrum stands Fowl who is representative of the camp within TIS that puts strong emphasis on an ecclesially driven and controlled interpretation.[156] Fowl, following Lindbeck's emphasis on the church's grammar and intratextual reality, argues that ecclesial community holds the key for ascertaining the meaning of biblical texts.[157] Lindbeck stated that the scriptural world created by the intratextual reality is able to absorb the universe, thus providing interpretive framework within which the believers seek to live and perform.[158] Lindbeck was concerned about the influence of extratextual reality that interrupts church's faithful practice because such a reality is extraneous to the texts themselves.[159]

In his critique of Lindbeck, Watson finds this aspect troubling.[160] Fowl sees Watson's criticism as a misreading of Lindbeck and defends Lindbeck. He was contrasting a theological account that uses language and concepts that are derived from Scripture with "non-theological accounts of 'human experience.'"[161] The modernist–postmodernist tension

---

156. Fowl, *Engaging Scripture*, 56–127.
157. Fowl, *Engaging Scripture*, 23–24.
158. Lindbeck, *Nature of Doctrine*, 116–18.
159. Fowl, *Engaging Scripture*, 22–24.
160. Watson, *Text, Church and World*, 124–25, 133–36, 151–52.

161. Fowl, *Engaging Scripture*, 24. Fowl complains that Watson's problem is a lack of constructive interactions with interpretive pluralism, kinds that do not necessarily make claims that Watson find objectionable. See also Brett, "Four or Five Things," 357–78; Fowl, "Ethics of Interpretation," 379–98.

Brett, having discussed the differences in "emic" and "etic" aspects in diachronic approach, concludes that if Sausser's synchronic method is given careful consideration, those who argue for a diachronic approach can sense that authorial intention and historical contexts—the extrinsic factors—do not come ready-made, but need to be reconstructed. If that is the case, interests in texts should have priority over extrinsic factors. He calls for abandoning the quest for an all-inclusive method; instead, one needs to appreciate the pluralities of interests and interpretive methods as positive. Brett, "Four or Five Things," 371–77. Fowl rejects E. D. Hirsch's arguments for a determinate sense of meaning with the example of the use of μορφῇ θεοῦ (Phil 2:6) in J. B. Lightfoot's commentary on Philippians. He argues that Lightfoot's diachronic view of μορφῇ θεοῦ as attributes of the Godhead based on its use in Plato and Aristotle needs correction in light of a synchronic approach that takes the use of μορφῇ θεοῦ (visible appearance of God) in the NT, in LXX, and in the Sibylline Oracles. Fowl contends that this synchronic approach is actually better than the nineteenth-century philological and reconstructionist methods because synchronic approach is actually closer to the presumed meaning of the text (Fowl dislikes the term "meaning") than the diachronic method. He argues that the plurality of methods, especially the rise of postmodern theological methods, are better suited for biblical interpretation because they embody the intratextual reality that is self-evident. Fowl, "Ethics of Interpretation," 387–98. For

in TIS continues along the fault lines. Consolidation of these ideological differences into a more inclusive reading strategy can potentially result in much more congruent construals of interpretive aims, methods, and practices. It is incumbent upon the practitioners to find a common ground where what excites and drives the interpretive practice is to personally hear God speak by pulling the curtain on the labyrinth of historical and other factors that impede such a practice.

Conclusion

This brief history of TIS as a movement shows what launched such a movement and the different stages of its growth. It is an ecumenical movement; diversity is expected among proposals (sometimes diametrically opposed ones). Since the time of Renaissance humanism, biblical interpretation began to focus its attention on the literary, philological, and historical aspects in biblical interpretation. Eventually, theological elements were excluded from the interpretive norms. By the time Barth challenged such norms in biblical interpretation, the academy had already been accustomed to not having any confessional elements as part of biblical interpretation. So Barth sought to reform Protestant biblical interpretation by "challenging the location of revelation in history rather than in the biblical witness."[162] His works influenced Protestants and Romans Catholics alike. Balthasar was chief among the Roman Catholics who were influenced by Barth's works. While Barth sought to reform the Protestant interpretation, Balthasar sought to reform the Roman Catholic interpretation. Their efforts paved the way for theological elements to be considered as part of interpretation.

In spite of the differences within TIS, theological convictions that were once deemed unsuitable for biblical interpretation are now given further consideration and many of those convictions have been restored. For example, the role of tradition (especially *regula fidei*), the importance of listening to the voices from the past (history of interpretation), and the role of the ecclesial (faith) community that were part of the pre-critical interpretations are now admitted as relevant for biblical interpretation. Even then, there are differences among the practitioners

---

a detailed discussion on Phil 2:6 and the advantage of a synchronic method, see Fowl, *Story of Christ*.

162. Chapman, "Modernity's Canonical Crisis," 658.

of TIS as to what matters are of utmost importance and how to go about doing theological interpretation because of different interpretive and ecclesial traditions the participants represent. As a result, much of the works on TIS are devoted to discussions of meaning, interpretive authority, method, and the role of tradition and community in interpretation. Often times, the adjectival phrase *Trinitarian interpretation* appears within these discussions. In the process of these discussions, Trinitarian interpretation itself gets a passing mention, as the next chapter makes clear. When it gets mentioned, its function is that of a placeholder only to be later replaced by other emphases.

2

Trinitarian Correlates in Theological Interpretation

TRINITARIAN INTERPRETATION GETS FREQUENT mention in the works devoted to theological interpretation. However, the idea of a Trinitarian interpretation itself is often left underdeveloped in such proposals. What we find instead are arguments for christological, pneumatological, ecclesial, or figural interpretation, or theories concerning the need for a Trinitarian interpretation without explaining how any one of these emphases can be fully Trinitarian. The works of the Father, Son, and Spirit are separated from each other in these proposals. YHWH is identified as P1 *alone*.

The revelation in Christ as the starting point for Trinitarian interpretation is not a problem in itself. In fact, a Christian interpretation of both the Testaments assumes that Christ in the NT makes the identity of YHWH in the OT explicit. But Christ as the starting point becomes a problem if YHWH is identified solely as P1, especially when there is a need to justify the NT references and allusions to the OT texts that have P2 as the referent from the NT's perspective. As a result of identifying YHWH as P1, these works tend to project Christ back onto the OT texts because Christ, in them, becomes part of the OT only in a typological sense. But, if YHWH can be identified as T, then it will allow the NT attribution of OT texts to Christ to be viewed differently and such attributions would not appear to violate the original intent. Moreover, this will allow one to overcome the isolationist tendency and embrace a robust understanding of Trinitarian interpretation.

This chapter will summarize the various proposals for a Trinitarian interpretation and their supporting arguments. In the course of this chapter, it will become evident that Trinitarian interpretation remains a placeholder in such proposals because of their tendency to isolate the persons of the Godhead. This chapter is a diagnosis of the problem and chapter 3 will offer a solution to overcome the isolationist tendency by making the case for the identity of YHWH as the triune God.

Christological Interpretation

Christological interpretation is one of the prominent ways of arguing for a Trinitarian interpretation. The crux of the arguments includes the centrality of the gospel message for Christian faith and theology, the need to understand the OT in light of the person and work of Christ, and the finality of revelation in Christ that leads to deductive reasoning in which the new revelation in Christ somehow appears to be superior to the old. Speech-act theory also plays an important role (perhaps a historical accident) in these proposals. The ensuing interaction with various works reveals that in making a case for christological interpretation, these proposals identify YHWH as P1.

Francis Watson

Francis Watson provides a christological model for TIS. Watson, unlike some other biblical theologians, presents a case for theologically driven biblical interpretation.[1] *Text, Church, and World* and *Text and Truth* complement each other in that the thoughts of the first volume are corrected (where necessary) and expanded in the subsequent volume.[2] The first

---

1. Watson, *Text, Church and World*, vii, 12–14. For a lengthy discussion on Watson's theological position and how he is perceived from the vantage point of a triangle typology devoted to the priority of human or divine agency in interpretation, see Bowald, *Rendering the Word*, 73–82. Bowald's triangle typology, however arbitrary it may be, offers a glimpse into Watson's emphases in his works and also some of the self-contradictory views as he moves from one work to another.

2. For an example of Watson changing his earlier conviction, see his shift in thinking on the intra-Trinitarian relation and its extension in God's creation of humans as

follows his taxonomy of text, church, and world by paying attention to narrative and canonical theology, postmodern radical hermeneutics and postliberal theologies, and ideological criticism (especially feminist). The second volume is divided into two parts: the first part attends to the fault line that exists between biblical scholarship and systematic theology, and the second part focuses on the issues that compartmentalize OT and NT interpretations and proposes a solution to overcome the impasse.[3]

Watson conceives the relationship between the OT and the NT as mediated in and through Jesus Christ. Gospel narratives about Jesus are programmatic for his arguments, but they are not taken in isolation, but within the contours of the canonical Scripture.[4] For Watson, "literal meaning" is comprised of verbal meaning, illocutionary and perlocutionary force, and the relation to the center.[5] Theological interpretation hinges on its "relation to the centre," which is a christological one.[6] He writes,

> The real question is whether or not it is granted that the Christian canon exists, that it has a centre, that this centre is the self-disclosure in Jesus of the triune God who is creator, reconciler and redeemer, and that an exegesis of a particular text cannot be regarded as *theologically* normative if it conflicts with what must be said at this centre.[7]

Not to confuse his statement of a christological center with the kind of interpretation that finds Christ in every OT passage or allegorical interpretation, Watson writes that though the OT texts in any of their parts are not about Christ alone, all of the OT is to be understood in relation to Christ for whom the OT Scriptures are retrospectively seen to prepare the way.[8]

In critiquing the arguments for the interpretation of the Old Testament "in their own right," Watson contends that "from the standpoint of Christian faith, it must be said that *the Old Testament comes to us with*

---

male and female. Watson, *Text and Truth*, 304n26. cf. Watson, *Text, Church and World*, 149–51.

3. Watson, *Text and Truth*, 9.
4. This argument sounds like a canon within the canon.
5. Watson, *Text and Truth*, 1,123.
6. Watson, *Text and Truth*, 16.
7. Watson, *Text and Truth*, 248.
8. Watson, *Text and Truth*, 184. He has not explained how this proposal is different from figural reading.

Jesus and from Jesus, and can never be understood in abstraction from him."[9] Christian Scripture requires a *Christocentric* (not *Christomonistic*) reading because in Jesus the God of Israel is disclosed in the triune name of the Father, Son, and the Spirit.[10]

Under this interpretative schema, Jesus, the center of Christian Scripture, holds the key to unlocking the meaning of the OT texts. To demonstrate his view, Watson enters into a discussion of the creation account in Genesis 1. He sets up his argument in interaction with and against Jürgen Moltmann. Moltmann perceived creation as a dynamic and not static reality.[11] For him, it has a past, a present, and a future, and creation will have its eschatological telos in God himself when he completes his creative activity. For Moltmann, the primary relationship Israel has with God begins with the idea of God as the covenant maker and not creator.[12] Challenging this view, Watson argues that the nation of Israel knew YHWH primarily as the creator and then as the covenant maker and redeemer (Exo 4:11; Jer 31:35–36; Amos 4:13).[13] Since YHWH is both the creator and the redeemer, creation constitutes the foundation on which covenant and redemption are built.[14] The faithfulness of the creator to his creation, says Watson, was a necessary presupposition for the people of Israel to be certain that the covenant God of Israel would be faithful to his covenant.[15]

Extrapolating the idea of creation further, Watson finds a clear correlation between the seven days of creation narrative in Gen 1 and the Gospel narrative of the life and ministry of Jesus.[16] This allows him to postulate, contra Moltmann, that creation remains the foundation on which the covenant history is built.[17] Sensing the dangerous tendency in modern natural theology, Watson writes, "Yet there is another way in which biblical understanding of creation can be misstated. God's creation

---

9. Watson, *Text and Truth*, 182.

10. Watson, *Text and Truth*, 185.

11. Watson, *Text and Truth*, 227. See also Moltmann, *God in Creation*, 4–5, 119–21, 198.

12. Moltmann, *God in Creation*, 54–66; Watson, *Text and Truth*, 227.

13. Watson, *Text and Truth*, 232–34.

14. Watson, *Text and Truth*, 234. "The creator as the future redeemer and the redeemer as the creator."

15. Watson, *Text and Truth*, 231.

16. Watson, *Text and Truth*, 237–41. The emphasis is on the creatureliness or humanity of Jesus.

17. Watson, *Text and Truth*, 239.

of the world can be removed from its proper context as the beginning of the divine-human history attested by the biblical narrative, and re-established as an independent idea isolated and abstracted from the history of the covenant."[18] He states that the business-as-usual way of doing biblical theology needs to be reconsidered to make the exercise more theologically and scripturally compatible and acceptable so that it can be moored to a christological center.

Similarly, he develops a theological anthropology by examining the relation between the image of God in Gen 1 and Jesus Christ, the image of the invisible God (2 Cor 4:4; Col 1:15; 3:10–11). If Jesus Christ is the image of God according to the NT and Christ "occupies the same semantic space as its counter part in Genesis," then a Christian account of the image of God cannot be complete without properly accounting for its relation to Christ. The Genesis text in itself is insufficient for Christian theological anthropology.[19] The natural extension of this thought is that if Jesus Christ is indeed the image of God, then our identity as human can only be fully comprehended in the person of Christ. Christ is the center for Christian theology. Watson suggests that it becomes obvious from a mere observation of the fact that the Christian canon divides Scripture into "old" and "new" based on the person of Christ.[20] He emphasizes this point in *Text, Church and World*.[21]

Although Watson emphasizes a christological center for biblical interpretation, he has not abandoned the language of a Trinitarian interpretation. God as creator is triune, declares Watson.[22] Every act of creation involves God's mouth, his hands, and his breath—a reference to the trinity.[23] The rationale for his Trinitarian interpretation emerges from his understanding that it is the triune God who called the world into being.[24] By arguing this way, he could assert that those who attempt to separate Jesus from his life in the trinity do so by ignoring the high Christology of the Pauline Epistles and early Christian confessions. From within the framework of a Trinitarian hermeneutic it can be argued that the exegesis

18. Watson, *Text and Truth*, 242.
19. Watson, *Text and Truth*, 282.
20. Watson, *Text and Truth*, 286–87.
21. Watson, *Text, Church and World*, 138.
22. Watson, *Text, Church and World*, 144.
23. Watson, *Text, Church and World*, 145.
24. Watson, *Text, Church and World*, 152–53. See also Cummins's comments on Watson's Trinitarian framework. Cummins, "Theological Interpretation," 186.

Trinitarian Correlates in Theological Interpretation 41

of texts will simultaneously be an exegesis of reality as presented in the Scripture.[25] But the fact that Jesus has always been part of the triune life of God has not been received favorably by many because of the concept of an evolutionary Christology (Christ was not always God, but the church eventually made him to be so).[26] Watson sees a christological reading of the OT and NT texts as legitimate and it affords theological clarity to biblical interpretation. It is this kind of christological interpretation that he views as Trinitarian interpretation.

In his response to Christopher Seitz's criticism of his work, Watson notes that his view of Christian Scripture having a christological center is contingent on a phenomenological description of the structure of the Christian canon in which both parts (OT and NT) can only be heard through their interdependence.[27] The impetus for this conclusion is found in the Lucan post-resurrection narrative of Jesus' interpretation of the OT Scriptures—a rereading of the same text, but with one noticeable and irreducible difference, which is the reality of the resurrected Lord who retrospectively activates the same texts in the new context.[28] Here Watson follows Gerhard von Rad, who points out the existence of the concept of rereading in the OT itself. He compares God's promise to Abraham, Isaac, and Jacob of a land (the land of Canaan) with Joshua's entrance into the promised land (Canaan) after the exodus from Egypt. God's promise to the ancestors is now seen as a temporal one in light of a permanent life in the promised land under Joshua. The earlier promise is reread in light of the new reality—a reactualization of the old event in new context.[29] God's promise now finds multiple fulfillments. Watson finds support in von Rad for his argument for rereading the OT from a christological center because the OT itself warrants the possibility of a rereading.

To answer Seitz's charges that his proposal makes it less of a Trinitarian interpretation, Watson responds by saying that no Christology is independent of a Trinitarian concept.[30] Seitz, on the other hand, challenges Watson's christological interpretation of the OT.[31] He finds a lack

---

25. Watson, *Text, Church and World*, 255–64.
26. Watson, *Text, Church and World*, 257.
27. Watson, "Old Testament as Christian Scripture," 227.
28. Watson, "Old Testament as Christian Scripture," 229–30.
29. Rad, *Old Testament Theology*, 1:322.
30. Watson, "Old Testament as Christian Scripture," 231.
31. Seitz, "Christological Interpretation of Texts," 209–26.

of Trinitarian application in this interpretive schema.[32] Working from within *regula fidei*, contends Seitz, would have allowed Watson to present a truly Trinitarian interpretation. In the current form, Watson's rejection of a discrete voice of the OT to be heard in exegesis (contra Brevard Childs) pits the God of Israel against Jesus because it is assumed that when the discrete voice of the OT is ascertained, one is reading of a God who is different from Jesus Christ. If his program were to be truly Trinitarian, argues Seitz, then it would not have pitted Jesus against the God of Israel whose voice is somehow different from the voice of Jesus.[33]

In Seitz's assessment, Watson has made a claim that is nowhere attested in the NT. According to Paul in Eph 2, the gentiles were without God and were brought to that God in Jesus. So how does Watson's separation of the God of Israel from Jesus comport with the NT teaching?[34] Seitz's criticism of Watson is important in another sense. Watson himself implies that the God of the OT is P1.[35] In his critique of James Dunn's view of Pauline theology, Watson argues that Paul's view of God was not a mere extension of the Jewish monotheism. Instead, it was always Trinitarian.[36] The identity of God for Paul is embedded in his actions. God is called the one who raised Jesus from the dead.[37] God is also identified in his relationship to the Son: "If Jesus is the Son of God, then God is the Father of our Lord Jesus Christ."[38] Watson implies that God in the OT is P1 and he can only be understood in relation to the Son.

Two problems appear in Watson's proposal: (1) the identity of God in the OT is taken to be that of P1, and (2) the identification of God in the OT as P1 leads to an isolationist tendency where God in the OT and NT are divided.[39] Seitz's criticism of Watson seems to be a fair assessment. Although Watson's proposal employs the Trinitarian language, it implies that Jesus is different from the God of Israel. It also presents the revelation

---

32. Seitz, "Christological Interpretation of Texts," 218–19.
33. Seitz, "Christological Interpretation of Texts," 220.
34. Seitz, "Christological Interpretation of Texts," 220.
35. Watson, "Triune Divine Identity," 105, 107–8, 113–15. For Dunn's view of Pauline theology, especially his arguments for Paul's view of a Jewish God, see Dunn, *Theology of Paul the Apostle*.
36. Watson, "Triune Divine Identity," 104.
37. Watson, "Triune Divine Identity," 106.
38. Watson, "Triune Divine Identity," 114.
39. This point will be pursued in detail in chapter 3.

in Christ as superseding the OT revelation. A christological reading of the OT here exhibits an isolationist tendency.

Kevin Vanhoozer

"Trinitarian" hermeneutic or interpretation is Kevin Vanhoozer's favorite way of characterizing his advocacy for a distinctly Christian interpretation.[40] In *Is There a Meaning in This Text?*, he argues that every book should be read like the Bible and the Bible should be read like any other text.[41] This idea finds its source in his conviction that God is the author of creation and every text is part of that created order; therefore, every text can be read from a Trinitarian framework.[42] There is more to his rationale. "My appeal to the Trinity arises rather from the perception that the literary crisis about textual meaning is related to the broader philosophical crisis concerning realism, rationality, and right, and that this crisis, summed up by the term 'postmodern,' is in turn explicitly theological."[43] In short, the rise of postmodernity has created a vexing need for reconsidering the advantages modernity has for biblical hermeneutics, however modified that may be.

Concerned with the rise of postmodern philosophies and hermeneutics that have done away with the author's role in ascertaining meaning and relevance, Vanhoozer attempts to restore faith and rationality to the concept of meaning tied up with "authorial interpretation."[44] "The death of God" promoted by Nietzsche is effectively the "death of God put into hermeneutics" in deconstruction, asserts Vanhoozer.[45] To counter the effects of radical postmodern hermeneutics (he presents a monolithic view of postmodernity by referring to Jacques Derrida, Richard Rorty, and Stanley Fish as if they talk about one and the same thing) Vanhoozer turns to E. D. Hirsch's view of the intentionality of the author, and the speech-act

---

40. Vanhoozer, *Is There a Meaning*, 199, 455–58; Vanhoozer, *First Theology*, 12–13, 38n55, 154–58, 231; Vanhoozer, *Remythologizing Theology*, 70, 106; Vanhoozer, *Drama of Doctrine*, 43–44, 65–68, 193–99.

41. Vanhoozer, *Is There a Meaning*, 4, 379, 456.

42. Vanhoozer, *Is There a Meaning*, 46–47.

43. Vanhoozer, *Is There a Meaning*, 456.

44. Vanhoozer's uneasiness with postmodern philosophy—as he understands it to be atheological or antitheistic in origin—explains much of his approach to biblical hermeneutics.

45. Vanhoozer, *Is There a Meaning*, 213, 456.

theory of J. L. Austin *via* John Searle and Nicholas Wolterstorff.[46] Peppered along the way is the phrase Trinitarian interpretation that does not translate into an operative role in his interpretive schema.[47]

Vanhoozer's preference for a Trinitarian hermeneutic is put through the constitutive parts of a speech-act, namely, locution, illocution, and perlocution. He compares the role of God the Father with locution, Son's role with illocution, and the Spirit's role with perlocution.[48] Thus, the Father is the author of the text (word and Word), the Son is the Word or text itself, and the Spirit is the result or the power of reception of that text. Since God is a communicative agent and his communication is revealed in Scripture, God's communication—the Scripture—can be subject to the scrutiny of speech-act theory.[49] Accordingly, language is the most important medium of communication and communion.[50] Language, like mind, is designed by God to be used in certain way. Therefore, the proper function of communicative faculties is to produce true interpretation.[51]

For Vanhoozer, proper interpretation arises from careful attention to complex communicative acts present in a text (locution, illocution, and perlocution in the biblical text).[52] Interpreting a text is ultimately about interpreting the actions of the author. The act is called "locution" and what is done with the act is called "illocution" and the effect of that act is called "perlocution."[53] Yet these acts are not understood apart from

---

46. Chapters 2–4 are his presentation of the problems and chapters 5–7 are his solutions to those problems. He details the malaise and the medicine in these chapters. It is impossible to do full justice to this commendable and programmatic work in this book. His view of Trinitarian hermeneutics is examined to highlight the somewhat incongruous nature of his Trinitarian proposal due to a lack of specificity on how a Trinitarian doctrine of God parallels that of a literary theory and reductionist tendency in his approach to the doctrine of God where Trinity appears to be a mere placeholder for his view of realist hermeneutics articulated via speech-act.

47. Fowl, "Book Review," 261; Vanhoozer, *Is There a Meaning*, 6. In the preface to his revised edition of *Is There a Meaning in This Text?* Vanhoozer acknowledges the gap in his Trinitarian proposal and concedes that his critics are right to point this out.

48. Vanhoozer, *Is There a Meaning*, 199, 456. The presence of Christ in the OT is more in a literary sense than in the literal sense; he is the illocution.

49. Vanhoozer, *Drama of Doctrine*, 176–77. He is more concerned about the relevance of the speech-act theory to the interpretation of Scripture than the concept of Trinitarian interpretation itself.

50. Vanhoozer, *Is There a Meaning*, 205.

51. Vanhoozer, *Is There a Meaning*, 205.

52. Vanhoozer, *Is There a Meaning*, 219.

53. Vanhoozer, *Is There a Meaning*, 221. Vanhoozer interacts with several proponents of the speech-act theory and modifies their conclusions to suit his proposal for a

Trinitarian Correlates in Theological Interpretation 45

certain contexts from which they emerge. Pertinent questions are: What is a context? What do contexts do? How large is the context?[54] These questions are not simply historical in nature, says Vanhoozer, but are also closely related to intention. Since God is understood to be the author of Scripture, his intentions, taken in canonical context, serve as the unifying principle in understanding meaning.[55]

Divine intention does not contravene, but rather supervenes human authorial intention with regard to the Bible, contends Vanhoozer. Yet the texts have a limiting role in that they are not going to reveal just any locution but a particular one, not just any illocution but certain ones controlled by the locution, not just any perlocution but one based on the illocution(s).[56] The role of readers and community in determining meaning is limited because the task of interpretation is primarily to specify "*what, whys, and wherefores of the text considered as communicative action*" and not who, when, and where.[57] His focus on meaning and the status of scriptural authority tied with authorial intention results in the use of Trinitarian correlates as subservient to theories of meaning and interpretive schema (mainly formal and not as much material). This leads to an isolationist tendency.

The isolationist tendency in his works can be best summarized in his own words:

> The thesis underlying the present work takes God's trinitarian communicative action as the paradigm, not merely the illustration, of all genuine message-sending and receiving. God is a speaking God. The Father is the one who, in the words of the creeds, *est locutus per prophetas*. Most of what God does—creating, warning, commanding, promising, forgiving, informing, comforting, etc.—is accomplished by speech acts.... Speech act theory serves as handmaiden to a trinitarian theology of communication. If the Father is the locutor, the Son is his preeminent illocution. Christ is God's definitive Word, the substantive content of his message. And the Holy Spirit—the condition and power of

---

Trinitarian hermeneutic.

54. Vanhoozer, *Is There a Meaning*, 240–59.
55. Vanhoozer, *Is There a Meaning*, 265.
56. Vanhoozer, *Is There a Meaning*, 390–91.
57. Vanhoozer, *Is There a Meaning*, 293. Texts are waiting to be interacted with and understood so that they can reveal their locution, illocution, and perlocution.

receiving the sender's message—is God the perlocutor, the reason that his words do not return to him empty (Isa. 55:11).[58]

For Vanhoozer, speech-act theory provides a realist sense of meaning in texts because authors of texts do intend something with what they write (as opposed to radical hermeneutics). It also allows his hermeneutic to use the triune identity of the Father, Son, and Spirit (speech-act is assigned to all three persons) without necessarily identifying YHWH as T.

Vanhoozer further reveals this isolationist tendency when he argues elsewhere that Christian interpretation has to be christological. In fact, he collapses Trinitarian interpretation into a christological interpretation: "Those who begin with God's self-presentation in the history of Jesus Christ are Trinitarian from the start."[59] He calls christological interpretation "figural" interpretation when the OT is interpreted in light of the Christ event.[60] He writes, "Jesus Christ is the *content* of the Scriptural witness, the one who *interprets* the Old Testament witness, and the one who *commissions* the New Testament witness. Accordingly, *Jesus is both material and the formal principle of the canon: its substance and its hermeneutic.*"[61] However, for Vanhoozer, Jesus is present in the OT only indirectly. Jesus is the Word of the Father and was present in the OT in the form of God's word. But YHWH is identified as P1 in his proposal.

In his joint venture with Daniel Treier, Vanhoozer further evidences his tendency to preempt Christian interpretation with a christological bent. They define "mere evangelical theology" as one anchored to a center and this center is the "light of the gospel of the glory of Christ."[62] The prepositional phrase "in Christ" is emphasized in their proposal (Rom 3:21, 22; Eph 1:11; 2:6; Col 2:3). The Gospels reveal the triune God; yet, it is *in* Christ that this God is revealed. Therefore, theological interpretation must have Christ as the center.[63] Accordingly, "mere evangelical theology" is Trinity-centric (because in the Gospels God is revealed as the

---

58. Vanhoozer, *Is There a Meaning*, 457.

59. Vanhoozer, *Remythologizing Theology*, 70. Craig Bartholomew argues that "any hermeneutic worth its salt must be christocentric." Bartholomew, *Introducing Biblical Hermeneutics*, 5.

60. Vanhoozer, *Drama of Doctrine*, 221–24.

61. Vanhoozer, *Drama of Doctrine*, 195. If Vanhoozer was more ambivalent about his Trinitarian hermeneutics earlier, here he is clear about what he means by a Trinitarian hermeneutic, which is a christological interpretation.

62. Treier and Vanhoozer, *Theology and the Mirror*, 58.

63. Treier and Vanhoozer, *Theology and the Mirror*, 51–63.

triune God) and crucicentric (because the cross is the hinge of history, the decisive turning point in God-world relationship).[64] The goal is to anchor evangelical theology in the Trinity and the cross—namely, in the person and work of Christ.[65]

His repeated use of the term "Trinitarian hermeneutic" gives the impression that Vanhoozer is advocating a thoroughly Trinitarian interpretation. But, if one pays careful attention to his formulation, it becomes evident that he does not attribute speech to all three persons of the Godhead; instead, God the Father is doing the speaking, the Son becomes the speech itself, and the Holy Spirit becomes the one who applies that word/Word to the Church.[66] Vanhoozer's proposal uses language theory and not the identity of YHWH to substantiate the idea of a Trinitarian interpretation. Such concept of a Trinitarian interpretation raises questions regarding the role of the Son and the Spirit in locution (especially in the Gospels). Does not this mean that those who read the OT without recourse to the NT do not necessarily see what Vanhoozer is arguing for? What is the illocution and perlocution for them without the Son and the Spirit? Is it not someone or something other than the Son and the Spirit? If that is the case, then it appears that speech-act theory is only applicable when one approaches the texts from a christological vantage point. If so, his proposal for authorial intention in the OT becomes nullified by his own proposals of divine speech-act because under his paradigm one has to have Christ as the illocution of Scripture—a status OT does not afford on its own right unless one takes YHWH to be T (Vanhoozer has not shown to be advocating YHWH as the triune God). Thus, the "literal meaning" (context-driven authorial intention) is affected by something external to the text under his proposal. If canonical meaning is taken to be the "literal meaning," then "literal" is redefined, which is not very clear from his work. Vanhoozer's proposal is another instance of the isolationist tendency in Trinitarian proposals.

---

64. Treier and Vanhoozer, *Theology and the Mirror*, 79.

65. Treier and Vanhoozer, *Theology and the Mirror*, 80.

66. His later works are more inclusive of this and discuss a christological center for the Scripture.

Christopher Holmes

Christopher Holmes proffers the "prophetic office of Christ" as the integrating aspect in theological interpretation. Holmes describes the prophetic office as Jesus' ongoing presence in and through the Word.[67] He is present in the reading and the hearing of his word. Just as prophets in the past acted as God's mouthpieces, so also God's word, which speaks and acts on behalf of Christ. "Christ speaks as God and man in a form appropriate to his ascended and glorified humanity."[68] Defining revelation as "the history of Jesus Christ," Holmes argues that since the greatest act of God is the reconstitution of the people of Israel around the crucified Son, revelation is best interpreted and understood as the "normative witness to this history."[69]

Drawing on the language of Karl Barth—"what God did in Jesus Christ yesterday is his 'act to-day and to-morrow'"[70]—he argues that Christ as a prophet is present among his people in the reading of this history and Christ attests himself in his word by the power of the Spirit. According to Holmes, the Scripture's center is alive and this has ramifications for reading and interpreting the written word that discloses the risen Word. Interpretation then is not so much about bringing some theory to bear upon the text, but it is about being attentive to the person, whose speech-act it is, present in its reading. Christology, writes Holmes, "governs the doctrine of Scripture."[71] Criticizing J. Todd Billings's proposal for a pneumatological interpretation of Scripture as proper, Holmes argues that Billings's pneumatological reading of Scripture shortchanges a robust Christology that prioritizes Jesus' agency in revelation.[72] Christ is active in the Scripture through his prophetic office. Thus, Christ's prophetic office is central to TIS.[73]

Holmes makes his pitch forcefully for the prophetic office of Christ as the decisive and controlling motif in TIS when he states,

> A rich account of the prophetic office advances the theological interpretation of Scripture by describing Scripture as the place

---

67. Holmes, "Revelation in the Present Tense," 30.
68. Holmes, "Revelation in the Present Tense," 30.
69. Holmes, "Revelation in the Present Tense," 24.
70. Barth, *CD* 4.2, 108.
71. Holmes, "Revelation in the Present Tense," 25.
72. Billings's arguments are presented under "pneumatological interpretation."
73. Holmes, "Revelation in the Present Tense," 25.

> where Jesus discloses himself by the Spirit in such a way that his written Word shines and is given a perspicuity that it would lack in and of itself. Rather than being subject to critical methodologies immune to God's activity, I argue that an account of the prophetic office—of Jesus as One who lives and speaks and as such ministers—has all the bearing for how we read and interpret Scripture.... The prophetic office is what allows us to describe Scripture as the present speech of the Lord. Jesus' prophecy is Scripture.[74]

His counterargument to Billings depends largely on how he defines the Spirit's ministry. Whereas Billings focused on the present ministry of the Spirit as the one who ministers God's word to his people by contemporarizing it to their present situation, Holmes focuses on the particular aspect of the Spirit being "Christ's Spirit"; therefore, Jesus' prophetic ministry should be the starting point.[75] "Christology includes pneumatology" according to Holmes.[76]

Emphasizing the priority of the prophetic office of Christ, Holmes contends, "To argue that it is the Spirit who speaks through Scripture is to confuse the work of the Son and Spirit: the Son speaks in Scripture by the Spirit."[77] Since Scripture is a witness to the history of Christ, it determines how it is to be read and interpreted. Thus, interpretation of Scripture is to be viewed as recognition of its subject matter, it is to be viewed as reception of revelation, and it is to be viewed as a summons for participation, a turning to God as a result of reading. In Scripture, Christ calls, commissions, acts, and appoints. Theological interpretation is bound to this activity of Christ.

Holmes, in conversation with Billings, delineates his case for a christological interpretation of Scripture although the premise of his disagreements with Billings is not fully convincing given the differences in each of their emphasis. Because the history of Israel is centered in Christ, he sees the entire OT as bearing witness to Christ.[78] However, he isolates Jesus from the God of Israel (YHWH). He also does not show how theological interpretation that prioritizes the prophetic office of Christ as the starting point could result in a robust Trinitarian interpretation. Instead,

---

74. Holmes, "Revelation in the Present Tense," 26.
75. Holmes, "Revelation in the Present Tense," 27.
76. Holmes, "Revelation in the Present Tense," 28.
77. Holmes, "Revelation in the Present Tense," 30.
78. Holmes, "Revelation in the Present Tense," 26–27.

he argues whether Christ or the Spirit receives priority in theological interpretation. His proposal neither discusses the identity of God in the OT nor what Trinitarian interpretation should look like.

Phillip Cary

The transition of christological interpretation from its theorizing phase to its practical phase in TIS is embodied in Phillip Carey's theological commentary on Jonah.[79] In his introduction to the commentary on Jonah, Cary writes, "Like the whole Bible, the book of Jonah is about Christ and therefore about all those who find their life in him. It is also about the people of Israel of whom Christ is the king."[80] Jesus is both the king of the Jews and of Christians. Christian reading of Jonah has to begin with the readers identifying themselves with Jews and Jonah in the story as their story.[81] Cary here refers to a typological reading of the OT that encourages such identification.[82]

He charges that Christian interpretation of Jonah has been guilty of a "holier-than-thou attitude" because preachers and teachers often used stories such as this from Scripture to point out how Christians can be better than those Jewish characters in Scripture. This leads to a type of moralistic teaching that shortchanges the intent of the message itself.[83] Instead, Cary reasons that an "Israelogical" reading is what is needed in Christian interpretation of the OT:

> There is no getting around such talk when Christians read the Bible, especially when the Christians are Gentiles convinced, as I am, that an essential step to finding Christ in the Old Testament is what can be called an "Israelogical" reading of the text, one that sees figures like Jonah representing not only Christ, the church, and Christians, but also Israel and Judah. Indeed, I think we cannot see *how* Jonah represents Christ, the church, and Christians without seeing how he represents Israel and Judah.[84]

Here he finds the presence of Christ in the OT typologically.

---

79. Cary, *Jonah*, 17.
80. Cary, *Jonah*, 17.
81. Cary, *Jonah*, 17.
82. Cary, *Jonah*, 18.
83. Cary, *Jonah*, 18–19.
84. Cary, *Jonah*, 19.

Identifying the stories of Israel as Christian stories enables one to read the Scripture as *our* Scripture. This way of reading is not strange, contends Cary, because Christ is the consummation of God's election of both Israel and Gentiles.[85] He suggests that the fourth chapter of Jonah is a clear indication of its need to be read christologically. In the end Jonah is upset with the withered gourd, which—like similar plants in the OT—is an "image of the lineage of David that seems to have died out."[86] He suggests that at the end of the book, Jonah the Jew is without his Messiah and his pain is unspeakable without the Son of David. In Cary's assessment, the book has an open ending that looks forward to the coming of the Messiah. According to Cary, Jesus is that Messiah who comes to answer Jonah's yearning and in the promise-fulfillment, anticipation-reality, type-antitype movement one finds the foundation for a christological interpretation (cf. Matt 12:39–41; 16:4; Luke 11:29–32).

In his verse-by-verse commentary, he reveals even more clearly how Jonah can be and must be read christologically. The word of the LORD (Jon 1:1; cf. John 1:1) that came to Jonah at the beginning of the book has the last word at the end of the book as well (here he sees Jesus as the Word). The LORD commissions Jonah for the mission, his name is revealed to the sailors (Jon 1:10–14) as the LORD (YHWH), and he is worshipped. The name of the LORD is now given to Jesus Christ (Phil 2:9–11) and the Christian interpreters are to make this connection as they read and interpret this book.[87]

Cary takes Jesus and Jonah as examples of substitutionary death. Jonah's disobedience can be taken as his mode of rescuing his people because if he did not preach to the Ninevites, they would continue in their sin and the LORD would punish them. Ninevites were enemies of Israel. Jonah's disobedience was to save his people because he knew that God was a gracious and compassionate God (Jon 4:2). When he asked the sailors to throw him overboard, he was willing to die for his own people. Jonah too was willing to die for the people of Israel. Jesus who accomplishes God's will for his life by dying on the cross is the opposite of the disobedient prophet Jonah.[88] Jesus mirrors the substitutionary nature of Jonah's act, but with one big difference. Jesus obeyed the Father. He was

---

85. Cary, *Jonah*, 19.

86. Cary, *Jonah*, 21.

87. Cary, *Jonah*, 27–28. Cary does not tell us in what sense Jesus is the LORD. It seems he does not see Jesus as YHWH.

88. Cary, *Jonah*, 40.

willing to die for his enemies, unlike Jonah. Thus, Jesus is very similar to Jonah and yet different.[89]

Throughout the commentary, Cary goes back and forth between Jonah and Jesus to find comparisons in almost every verse; sometimes Jesus is similar to Jonah and other times he is different. Finally, in the epilogue, he presents in summary fashion the many comparisons between Jonah, Jesus, church, and Christians.[90]

To suggest that the book of Jonah is about Christ can be taken in at least two different ways. In the first instance, it can suggest that the text has always been about Christ, but that was a mystery to the prophet himself and the original recipients of the book (a typological reading). This can be seen only from the NT perspective. Cary alludes to this sense when he talks about the withering of the gourd in the fourth chapter as a picture of the constant interruption of the Davidic lineage and the prophet's anticipation of a messianic redeemer. A second way to understand it is to suggest that since Jesus Christ has always been part of the identity of YHWH (i.e., YHWH is not identified with P1 alone, but with all three persons of the Godhead) reading Jonah in light of the NT is a legitimate exercise because his presence, which was once not known, is now revealed; thus, Christ is not replacing YHWH, but revealing YHWH because he is YHWH.[91] Cary has not demonstrated the latter option as what drives his interpretation. Instead, Cary seems to have mistaken the identity of YHWH for P1. Throughout the commentary, Cary advances the idea that the book of Jonah is about Christ. Thus, it raises and amplifies the question of the identity of God in the OT, especially the question of how and in what way Jesus was present in the OT. Like other proposals, this one too is of very limited use for a Trinitarian interpretation because of the failure to identify YHWH as the triune God.

Pneumatological Interpretation

Pneumatological interpretation argues that a Trinitarian interpretation must be Spirit-centered. Billings provides a pneumatologically hinged

---

89. Cary, *Jonah*, 66.
90. Cary, *Jonah*, 163–74.
91. "Jesus is YHWH" does not mean YHWH is exclusively identified with Jesus alone. Instead, it is very similar to the statement—"Father is God, Jesus is God, and the Holy Spirit is God," yet not three gods. In the same way it can be argued that Father is YHWH, Jesus is YHWH, and the Holy Spirit is YHWH—a point I pursue in chapter 3.

Trinitarian Correlates in Theological Interpretation 53

example of Trinitarian interpretation. In inviting "readers to the practice of interpreting Scripture in the context of the triune activity of God," Billings expands on the role the Spirit plays in reshaping the church into the image of Christ by applying the words of Scripture in their lives.[92] Initially, he uses Trinitarian and pneumatological language interchangeably.[93] Then he develops his case for a pneumatological interpretation by first paying attention to the character of Christian Scripture as Trinitarian.[94] Before getting to that point, he addresses two important aspects in learning to read Scripture, namely, understanding and explanation.

Understanding involves attention to the basic elements in reading a text. Elements include attention to what type of genre it is (for example, knowing that J. R. R. Tolkien's *Lord of the Rings* trilogy is fiction saves one from mistaking it for real history), presuppositions (they are not inherently bad, but reveal what one brings to reading a text), and tradition (such as *regula fidei*, creeds, and confessions of the church, which provide conditions under which one could take up scriptural interpretation without being in violation of Scripture's intended purpose as understood by church catholic).[95] Explanation involves good attention to various historical-critical elements that are critical to the proper reading of Scripture. Christian reading of Scripture does not have to reject what historical criticism or general hermeneutics offers, writes Billings, because they are within God's gracious providence and gifts to his creation.[96]

Turning to the question of scriptural revelation and its reception, Billings presents the most sustained rationale for his proposal of a pneumatological interpretation. He contends that revelation is either grounded purely on human capacities or on God's action with Israel and Jesus.[97] When Christians receive God's revelation, they enter into a world they did not create. The Bible is God's instrument in the act of redemption, but revelation is not the same as the Bible.[98] He defines revelation as the

---

92. Billings, *Word of God*, xiii.
93. Billings, *Word of God*, 36–37.
94. Billings, *Word of God*, 24–29.
95. Billings, *Word of God*, 39–54.
96. Billings, *Word of God*, 54–67. Billings appropriates Gadamer's and Ricoeur's philosophical hermeneutics, arguing that their proposals are useful for biblical hermeneutics as well because what they propose fall within the purview of God's gift to his creation.
97. Billings, *Word of God*, 75.
98. Billings, *Word of God*, 80.

"self-communicative fellowship of the triune God himself, and the Bible is God's instrument of revelation."[99] The reception of God's revelation in Scripture can be either a deistic hermeneutical exercise or it can be received within a Trinitarian hermeneutic.[100]

Billings maintains that in order to receive Scripture through a Trinitarian framework, one has to be a "Trinitarian Christian" functionally. He describes "Trinitarian Christians" as those who recognize their identity as tied to freedom from bondage in Christ and that they are being filled with the Spirit, having been united into the body Christ. They live in gratitude before the Father.[101] Billings presents his most compelling case for the pneumatological emphasis in this context of the Christian desire to live a faithful and thankful life before the triune God in his own unique life situation.

The pneumatological emphasis is crucial because it is the Spirit who indigenizes (contemporizes) God's word and the message of salvation in different cultures and setting.[102] While theology is culturally conditioned, a properly Christian theology in any culture is the result of the work of the Spirit who applies it in the local setting.[103] Jesus promised that the Spirit would lead Christians to truth (John 14:7–15). It was through the Spirit's indigenizing work on the day of Pentecost that many heard the gospel in their own language. The Spirit critiques, challenges, and transforms cultures in the process of making the Christian message relevant.[104] The Spirit's work in personalizing God's message and making Christ known in different cultures means that there is room for diversity in Christian reception of the message since different cultures employ unique ways of expressing their faith in Christ. It is this particular aspect of the Spirit's work that is the main focus of Billings's argument. He is concerned with an explicit recognition of the work of the Spirit in biblical interpretation. He sees biblical translations as part of the Spirit's interpretation of the truth in various cultures.

---

99. Billings, *Word of God*, 80–81. This does not mean that God excludes human beings in the process of this revelation; instead, God incorporates and empowers humans.

100. Billings, *Word of God*, 86.

101. Billings, *Word of God*, 88–89.

102. Billings, *Word of God*, 104–48. Billings uses "indigenizing" to mean the work of the Holy Spirit in making the word of God known in a person's local language. According to Billings, this indigenizing work of the Spirit includes Bible translation.

103. Billings, *Word of God*, 107.

104. Billings, *Word of God*, 108.

At the Jerusalem Council, the apostles recognized the indigenizing work of the Spirit (Acts 15); they did not require the gentile Christians to follow all the practices of their Jewish counterparts.[105] Not only does the Spirit localize the gospel to many cultures, but the Spirit also criticizes and changes those cultures. The Spirit is a Spirit of discernment.[106] Billings strikes a measured middle ground when it comes to the contemporizing work of the Spirit. He states, "The Spirit generates a bounded diversity as it conforms many peoples to the image of Jesus Christ."[107] The Spirit's work in various cultures and in different times renders a model for theological interpretation. This also helps the church catholic to reckon with the fact that scriptural interpretation in the church does not place itself above the Scripture. On the contrary, this creates a sense of humility among Christians and helps them to be self-critical because the Spirit allows diversity of interpretation as he indigenizes the truths to various cultures.[108]

After establishing his case for a pneumatological starting point for theological interpretation, Billings returns to the language of Trinitarian interpretation in chapter 6 by utilizing the drama metaphor of Vanhoozer; he describes theological interpretation as "participating in the Trinitarian drama of salvation."[109] Billings calls this particular act as "entering into the Spirit's work of being renewed in Christ."[110] The recurring theme throughout the book is that theological interpretation is essentially a participation in the Spirit's work of indigenizing God's word within the framework of the triune drama of salvation. But he does not address the question of how a recognition of the work of the Spirit in interpretation results in a Trinitarian interpretation that attends to the identity of YHWH in the OT.

The interchangeable use of *pneumatological* and Trinitarian interpretation results in ambivalence. This ambivalence is evident in Holmes's criticism of Billings's pneumatological emphasis. "What Billings's account lacks is a robust Christology. Christology governs the doctrine of Scripture. It is Christ who is active as a prophet in Scripture *by* his Spirit. To argue as does Billings that the Spirit uses Scripture shortchanges, I think,

---

105. Billings, *Word of God*, 114–22.
106. Billings, *Word of God*, 124.
107. Billings, *Word of God*, 126.
108. Billings, *Word of God*, 132–33.
109. Billings, *Word of God*, 197–206.
110. Billings, *Word of God*, 208.

Jesus' agency as the One who *by* his Spirit speaks himself in Scripture."[111] Billings's emphasis on a pneumatological interpretation isolates the persons of the Godhead. In doing so, he fails to identify the work of the Father and the Son at the present time. His proposal is weakened by a lack of attention to the identity of God in Scripture. If the identity of YHWH was understood to be Trinitarian, he could have avoided the insistence on a pneumatological interpretation, which suggests that not all three persons are active in the life of the church or in making the message of the gospel relevant in various cultures. This proposal too fails to identify YHWH as the triune God.

Ecclesial Interpretation

Ecclesial interpretation is another proposal for a Trinitarian interpretation. Ecclesial interpretation emphasizes the role of the ecclesial community in interpretation and assumes that such interpretation will be Trinitarian in nature. Some common features include an emphasis on the present ecclesial community's role in determining the meaning of the text, an emphasis on interpretive virtue, and the locus of interpretive authority being with the church and not with the individual interpreter (the emphasis is on church versus individual and not church versus Scripture).

George Lindbeck[112]

Those who favor an ecclesial interpretation model for Trinitarian interpretation follow Lindbeck's arguments for church's grammar. Lindbeck offers his cultural-linguist approach to theology and doctrine in contrast to two other models he identifies, namely, the cognitive model (church doctrines are propositions or truth claims about objective realities) and experiential-expressive model (doctrines as subjective "noninformative and nondiscursive symbols of inner feelings, attitudes, or existential orientations").[113] His cultural-linguistic model focuses on church doctrines as "communally authoritative rules of discourse, attitude, and

---

111. Holmes, "Revelation in the Present Tense," 25.

112. Although Lindbeck is not a prominent advocate of TIS, he has generated much conversation about the role of ecclesial community in shaping biblical interpretation. This has influenced TIS.

113. Lindbeck, *Nature of Doctrine*, 16.

action."[114] The first two models are diametrically opposed to each other and see no possibility of reconciliation (objective vs. subjective).

Lindbeck's proposal is a mediating way to reconcile the objective and the subjective aspects of doctrines based on their use and function in the church. Religion cannot be separated from its particular tradition and community. Thus, Lindbeck is able to argue that theology should first attend to its particular tradition and communal practice.[115] A regulative approach or rules are required. This, he argues, is better suited than propositional or expressivist notions of doctrine because rules retain "an invariant meaning under changing conditions of compatibility and conflict."[116]

The cultural-linguistic model views religion as that which shapes individual beliefs and behavior. In this sense, states Lindbeck, "religion can be viewed as a cultural and/or linguistic framework or medium that shapes the entirety of life and thought."[117] How does this apply to Christianity and Christian theology? If religion shapes individual beliefs and behavior, then learning the story of Israel and Jesus is necessary for one to interpret and experience Christianity and the world.[118] The change in a religious system or thoughts (true of doctrinal developments as well) must be viewed as resulting from a cultural-linguistic system interacting with changing situations.[119] He contrasts this with the experiential-expressivist model that argues that religious experience is prior. Here he critiques Karl Rahner, Bernard J. F. Lonergan, and David Tracy, who

---

114. Lindbeck, *Nature of Doctrine*, 18. The key word here is "rule" or "rules of discourse." Unlike competing propositions, the opposition between rules can be resolved by explaining the contingency that is associated with it. He gives the examples of driving on the left-hand side of the road versus driving on the right. Although both are contradictory rules if applied at the same time and place, but they are meaningful if a bit of the context is provided—driving on the right for Britain and driving on the left for the United States. Propositional claims assume universally biding positions without exception. He prefers "rule" to proposition or expressivist claim. It is important to keep this in mind because he will return to "rule" in chapter 4 to adjudicate between various theories of doctrine.

115. Lindbeck, *Nature of Doctrine*, 25. His theory is called a nontheological study of religion. In other words, the cultural-linguistic model applies to all aspects of life, which includes religion.

116. Lindbeck, *Nature of Doctrine*, 18.

117. Lindbeck, *Nature of Doctrine*, 33.

118. Lindbeck, *Nature of Doctrine*, 34.

119. Lindbeck, *Nature of Doctrine*, 39.

find diverse religions as expressions of the same universal experience or consciousness.[120]

Lindbeck asserts that, for Christians, faith in the God of the Bible is logically prior to and independent of any philosophical concept of God. Christians could argue the uniqueness of their God because a cultural-linguistic model does not subscribe to the idea that all religions share common thread or different emanations of same faith.[121] Similarly, the aspect of interreligious dialogue and the place of propositional claims of Christianity must consider the nonbinding nature of the propositions (he calls dogmatic propositions "second-order discourse of first-intentional uses of religious language").[122]

Lindbeck resumes his presentation with the "rule" theory in the fourth chapter. He asserts that rule theory enables an appropriate concept of doctrines, theology, and the grammar of religion. Church doctrines, writes Lindbeck, are "communally authoritative teachings regarding beliefs and practices that are considered essential to the identity or welfare of the groups in question. They may be formally stated or informally operative, but in any case they indicate what constitutes faithful adherence to a community."[123] According to the rule theory, church doctrines can be categorized as "official," "operational," or "implicit doctrines becoming explicit" as a result of controversy.[124] Doctrines react to changing situations and they adapt to new reality without necessarily losing its indispensability. Doctrines have changing and unchanging aspects to them.[125] Accordingly, the abiding aspects of a religion are not propositionally formulated truths, but "in the story it tells and in the grammar that informs the way the story is told and used."[126] There are unconditionally essential doctrines and conditional doctrines that are either permanent or temporary.[127] Depending on the conceptuality spectrum, one and the

---

120. Rahner, *Spirit in the World*, 132–236; Lonergan, *Method in Theology*, 101–24; Tracy, *Blessed Rage for Order*, 97–103.
121. Lindbeck, *Nature of Doctrine*, 47–52.
122. Lindbeck, *Nature of Doctrine*, 69.
123. Lindbeck, *Nature of Doctrine*, 74.
124. Lindbeck, *Nature of Doctrine*, 74–76.
125. Lindbeck, *Nature of Doctrine*, 80.
126. Lindbeck, *Nature of Doctrine*, 80.
127. Lindbeck, *Nature of Doctrine*, 85.

same grammar can be described differently. But change in conceptuality does not change the truth claim.[128]

Finally, Lindbeck explains the cultural-linguistic model to be concerned with intratextual reality as opposed to extratextual reality that is available in a propositional or expressivist model.[129] He explains intratextual reality as that which emerges from the way words operate in religious grammar. Extratextual reality locates religious meaning outside the text on the objective realities to which they refer.[130] The normative meaning of the text should not be something behind, beneath, and in front of the text, but the "communal language of which the text is an instantiation."[131] Under this rule, what is important in ascertaining meaning is literary consideration rather than historical-critical matters.[132] In doing so, he elevates the church's grammar above the God who is revealed in Scripture.

Lindbeck suggests that faith in the God of the Bible is prior to any philosophical delineations of that God. Can other religious proposals be equally valid for they too can present a particular way of understanding and explicating their theology based on their own grammar? The claim that the Christian God is unique does not answer the question of the very identity of God. Who is he? Is YHWH the triune God? Should that affect theological interpretation? His proposal does not answer these questions, which are critical to a Trinitarian interpretation. As a result, his proposal is rendered ineffective because it still allows isolationist tendency to define the identity of God.

Stephen Fowl

Stephen Fowl presents his view of theological interpretation as one taking place within and with ecclesial community.[133] Christian reading of Scripture is historically conditioned, yet one that takes place in a dialogical and analogical fashion. This is because Scripture is primarily addressed to specific communities and not individuals.[134] Christians do

---

128. Lindbeck, *Nature of Doctrine*, 93.
129. According to Lindbeck, this is foundational for a postliberal theology.
130. Lindbeck, *Nature of Doctrine*, 114.
131. Lindbeck, *Nature of Doctrine*, 120.
132. Lindbeck, *Nature of Doctrine*, 123.
133. Fowl and Jones, *Reading in Communion*, 8, 35–36, 56–80; Fowl, *Engaging Scripture*, 37–38, 60, 75–83; Fowl, *Theological Interpretation*, xiv.
134. Fowl and Jones, *Reading in Communion*, 8.

not read the Bible as Scripture that was addressed to an exclusively past community—a failure of the historical-critical interpretation—but their historical situation finds meaning from the past and, conversely, their present situation sheds light on the past (text) as well.[135]

There are historical continuities and discontinuities when one approaches the Scripture. For example, the earliest Christian communities read the OT in light of Christ's death and resurrection and this reading had social implications for their lives. They did not simply replicate the OT text or the life situations the OT texts were addressed to, but found ways of appropriating it in the new context by interaction and imaginative analogical relation between their condition and the past historical situation. They found a way to navigate between the discontinuities of past and present experiences so that they could live faithfully before God. This was possible because they took communal reading and living seriously, says Fowl.[136]

Key to understanding Fowl's theological interpretation is his emphasis on Christian community as the locus of finding a virtue-driven meaning of Scripture.[137] Fowl highlights this point when he states that the "central interpretive claim here is that our discussions, debates, and arguments about texts will be better served by eliminating claims about textual meaning in favor of more precise accounts of interpretive aims, interests, and practices."[138] Fowl contends that, instead of focusing on the meaning of words or texts, the attempt should be to explicate the author's communicative intentions in using certain words or phrases and how that would

---

135. Fowl and Jones, *Reading in Communion*, 57–58. Fowl and Jones find support in Nicholas Lash who argued that as creatures of history, some understanding of the past is necessary to understand our present predicament and how to respond in the future, just as a self-critical understanding of the present predicament is necessary to read and understand the past. Lash, "Interpretation and Imagination," 24–25.

136. Fowl and Jones, *Reading in Communion*, 58–65. Again Fowl and Jones depend on Lash to help elucidate this point. Lash states that the existence of a hermeneutical gap between the text then and its understanding should not be reduced to what was meant then and what it means today. Instead, the differences are between what was "achieved, intended, or 'shown', and what might be achieved, intended, or 'shown' today." Lash, *Theology on the Way*, 90–91.

137. The main thesis of *Reading in Communion* is the ethical dimension of reading Scripture, which can only be attained in communion with the saints. Reading is not an end in itself, but a means to live faithfully in community before the triune God. See especially chapter 3 of *Engaging Scripture*. Fowl, *Engaging Scripture*, 62–96. Virtue is an important theme in TIS. For example, see Brown, *Character and Scripture*; Briggs, *Virtuous Reader*; Treier, *Virtue and the Voice*.

138. Fowl, *Engaging Scripture*, 56.

have been understood by the hearers. This, he believes, has the potential to answer questions about the text and is verifiable. Choosing explication instead of meaning allows interpreters to surface what the actual disagreements or disputes are about. Often, interpretive disputes are not disputes about the same things, but about interpretive aims.[139] Replacing meaning with explication results in his preferred underdetermined type of interpretation (unlike other types, it is underdetermined by virtue of not having an exhaustive theory of textual meaning). Both the determined (one that follows a historical-critical method, which emphasizes meaning as authorial intention) and the anti-determinate (mainly deconstruction that looks for otherness in a text or in a dominant interpretation as the point of departure) type of interpretations suffer from a focus on meaning unlike his underdetermined type.

His solution is that "theological convictions, ecclesial practices, and communal and social concerns should *shape and be shaped* by biblical interpretation."[140] This approach to biblical interpretation, he argues, will enable the church in its struggle to live and worship faithfully before God.[141] Anticipating objections to his proposal, Fowl offers a preemptive defense by focusing on what it means to be virtuous readers in light of Luke 11:34–36. He focuses on how one could explicate ἁπλοῦς (single) in Luke 11:34 ("when your eye is single") to understand better what the text says and how that serves as a model for reading Scripture.[142] Assisted by Susan Garrett's study on Luke 11:33–36 that concluded ἁπλοῦς does not simply suggest "single," but it points to "integrity, purity of motives, not knowledge or intent of evil."[143] Fowl argues that Jesus is focusing on the whole-hearted and single-minded devotion of those who have had their eyes open to God. Christians are called to be vigilant in their devotion to God. This devotion permeates into all aspects of their lives, including scriptural reading. If their eyes, and for that matter all the faculties of perception, are trained to see Jesus and make judgments based on such a

139. Fowl, *Engaging Scripture*, 58–59.
140. Fowl, *Engaging Scripture*, 60.
141. Fowl, *Engaging Scripture*, 62.
142. Fowl, *Engaging Scripture*, 75.
143. Garrett, "'Lest the Light,'" 93–105. Susan Garrett studied the use of ἁπλοῦς (single eye) in Luke 11:34 in light of the LXX and translations of Aquilla and Symmachus of the Hebrew Scriptures along with its use in the Testaments of the Twelve Patriarchs. She concludes that ἁπλοῦς focuses on *virtue* and that the readers of Luke would have understood that, especially in light of the preceding passage (Luke 11:29–32) where the Jews were seeking signs.

perception, then they would be able to read and embody Scripture well. If not, darkness would be taken to be light and the whole vision would be distorted.[144] Thus, a virtuous reader is the one whose has a single-minded devotion to Christ.

For Christians, practical reasoning is Christ centered. God's activity in Jesus Christ (Phil 2:6–11) animates Paul and provides rules for Christian conduct to live faithfully before their God.[145] The reading of Scripture does not restrict interpretive freedom. "Nevertheless, within this Trinitarian 'freedom of interpretation,' subsequent alternative formulations would have to demonstrate that they maintain continuity with prior christological standards."[146] Fowl does not clarify what he means by a Trinitarian grounding for theological interpretation. Instead, he focuses on the Spirit's role (pneumatological) in reading Scripture.[147] Jesus promised the Spirit (John 14–17) and in Acts 10–15 we see how the Spirit directed the church to respond to various situations appropriately. The Spirit's guidance in reading the text provides a Trinitarian grounding for theological interpretation. His argument is that because the Spirit is God, a Spirit-led interpretation is Trinitarian. Anyone can claim their interpretation to be Spirit-led, but that does not guarantee that all such interpretations are Trinitarian. His proposal does not explicate either the identity of YHWH in the OT or how the OT reading can be Trinitarian.

Figural Interpretation

Figural interpretation is another proposal for a Trinitarian interpretation. Figural interpretation proffers that the God (P1) who raised Jesus from the dead is also the God (P1) who was revealed to Israel in the OT and retains the discrete witness of each testament without one (especially the OT) being surpassed by the other.[148] The direction of thought is from God to Christ and not from Christ to God.[149]

---

144. Fowl, *Engaging Scripture*, 75–79.
145. Fowl, *Engaging Scripture*, 191–97.
146. Fowl, *Engaging Scripture*, 197–98.
147. Fowl, *Engaging Scripture*, 99–127. Fowl is categorized not under a "pneumatological interpretation" but under an "ecclesial interpretation." It is because the major emphasis in his books is on an ecclesially driven interpretation.
148. For an overview of *typology* (*figural* is often identified with or under typological reading) see Treier, "Typology," 823–27.
149. Seitz, *Figured Out*, 6, 32; Seitz, *Word without End*, 6, 51–60; Seitz, *Character of*

Trinitarian Correlates in Theological Interpretation 63

Seitz explains how the discrete voice of the OT can be retained even when it applies to Jesus: "When Christians confess God raised Jesus from the dead 'in accordance with the scriptures,' they do not mean that Isaiah predicted the empty tomb but rather that God's word to Israel was figured in such a way as to accord with God's (P1) wrath and raising vis-à-vis his son."[150] Jesus is said to have risen "according to the scriptures" (1 Cor 15:3–4) and it means that Jesus' identity is tied up with the OT Scriptures because Scriptures here is a reference to the OT Scriptures.[151] In other words, Jesus' resurrection is consistent with the "plain-sense" of the OT.[152] For Seitz, Christ is present in the OT texts in a figural sense.

Childs argues that literal interpretation includes the figural.[153] Figural interpretation does not violate the discrete voice of the OT but rather understands literal sense to be more than its historical sense. If the two Testaments are taken in their canonical context, what then emerges is an exegetical and theological understanding of Scripture in which the purpose of God's revelation controls the attempt to interpret it—both textual witness and the discrete *res* are carefully retained.[154] Childs believes that canonical theology allows the discrete voice of each Testament to be heard while at the same time finding ways to overcome the discrete problems that arise from the differences between the Testaments through dialogue with dogmatic theology. When Christians take the OT with its discrete voice, the interpretation recognizes God's unique witness in the Scriptures of Israel.[155]

Figural interpretation is situated between historical-critical reading of the OT on the one hand and a christological reading of the OT from the NT perspective on the other. To overcome both extremes (as Seitz sees it), the approach to the OT texts is not from the point of "how Israel viewed God" and their relationship to this God (in other words, not from the point of the history of religion), but from the point of "God who chose Israel and the church."[156] This particular approach sees, as Childs

---

Christian Scripture, 154–55. Here "God" stands for YHWH and YHWH is understood to be the first person of the Trinity.

150. Seitz, *Figured Out*, 32.
151. Seitz, *Word without End*, 51.
152. Seitz, *Word without End*, 52.
153. Childs, "Recovering Theological Exegesis," 22–24.
154. Childs, "Recovering Theological Exegesis," 23.
155. Childs, *Old Testament Theology*, 10.
156. Seitz, *Word without End*, 8.

puts it, the *res* of the Testaments as the point of departure and this is theologically driven. For Childs, this does not mean a subjective, "reader-response" interpretation, but a thorough exegetical enterprise, which has its starting point in the doctrine of God, for God himself is the *witness* who evokes and demands such a reading.[157]

How can such an exegetical reading be faithful to the discrete voice of each Testament and be theological at the same time? Childs provides a three-step process as part of a multilevel reading strategy that does not violate the canonical shape of the text. The first step is to retain the literal/plain sense of the OT through a literal and historical interpretation. The second step is to attend to the fact that OT is part of the authoritative collection of sacred writings, which has a unique shape and place in Christian faith and confession allowing the texts to transcend its original historical settings (this is already evident in Christian hymns and liturgy). The third step is to seek a text-oriented hearing that reflects the divine reality emerging from an encounter with the whole Scripture in the community of faith while not projecting a Christian reading on to the texts as its original sense.[158]

A good example of this kind of reading is Childs's reading of Isaiah where he emphasizes figural reading.[159] He finds a rather strong connection between the suffering servant in Isaiah and Jesus Christ. He is critical of Walter Brueggemann's assertion that there is no obvious connection between the OT and the NT and any apparent connection is due to the imaginative construal on the human side.[160] Contra Brueggemann, Childs argues that the Christian reading of Isa 53 by necessity must find

---

157. Childs, *Biblical Theology*, 375–89, 723; MacDonald, "Theological Interpretation," 86–87; Rowe, "Doctrine of God," 155–69.

158. Childs, "Recovering Theological Exegesis," 24–25.

159. Childs, *Struggle to Understand Isaiah*, x. Childs shows the need to rehabilitate allegorical interpretation by removing the pejorative status it has been assigned in the history of interpretation. See also Whitman, *Interpretation and Allegory*; Hanson, *Allegory and Event*.

160. Brueggemann, *Theology of the Old Testament*, 726–35; Childs, *Struggle to Understand Isaiah*, 291–96. Brueggemann contends that OT must be taken in its own right, but with important differences from that of Childs's similar assertion. For Childs, even when the OT is read in its own right, it is still part of the two Testament canon and therefore its interpretation is affected and influenced by the finality of revelation in Jesus. For Brueggemann, the OT NT connection is only on a conceptual level (not ontological) and not in terms of "reality." Brueggemann insists that Christians must recognize the plurality of interpretation and avoid supersessionism. The text's "generative power" evokes and authorizes readings that lie beyond original intention or textual testimony.

Trinitarian Correlates in Theological Interpretation

a morphological connection between Jesus and the suffering servant. The text demands such a reading (he calls it the coercion of the text). Only a multilevel reading (notice, he is not arguing for a multilevel meaning) of the text could resolve the existing interpretive dissonance.[161]

Hans Frei takes an approach to figural interpretation slightly different from that of Childs and Seitz. According to Frei, figural reading is "literalism extended to the whole story or the unitary canon containing it."[162] The emphasis on verbal and historical meaning of the text (understood in the historical critical tradition) challenges the role of figural interpretation, in the opinion of Frei. The solution to retain relevance for figural reading that sought the unity of Scripture was biblical theology.[163] Frei sees it as a problem to be overcome. Instead of pursuing biblical theology to overcome the challenges posed by historical criticism, Frei proposes taking seriously the realistic or history-like (not historical) character of biblical narratives.[164]

Frei sees a distinction between historical-critical interpretation that seeks matters behind the text to ascertain meaning and figural interpretation that sees meaning in the text itself via its narrative character.[165] Frei explains what he means by way of the historicity of miracles in the Gospels. Those who deny miracles dismiss its historicity by assuming that the miracles refer to actual historical events. But historical accuracy is not relevant for realistic reading because realistic reading looks into the indispensability of that particular miracle or event for rendering the particular internals of the story itself.[166] For Frei, figural reading does not necessarily have to follow historical critical reading and there is a clear disjunction between the two types of reading. Contra Frei, Childs sees no such problem in figural interpretation and sees it as a viable alternative to strict historical critical reading. However, Childs is convinced that there has to be some definite relation between the literal (historical) and the figural reading as is evidenced by the first step of his multilevel reading strategy. The historical "does not exhaust the meaning of the text" and a

---

161. Childs, "Recovering Theological Exegesis," 24.
162. Frei, *Eclipse of Biblical Narrative*, 7.
163. Frei, *Eclipse of Biblical Narrative*, 8.
164. Frei, *Eclipse of Biblical Narrative*, 10.
165. Frei, *Eclipse of Biblical Narrative*, 11–12; Frei, *Identity of Jesus Christ*, xiii–xv.
166. Frei, *Eclipse of Biblical Narrative*, 14.

Christian reading at the same time must include figural reading, as in Isa 53, because the texts themselves demand it.[167]

When Seitz, Childs's pupil, talks about Jesus Christ being raised "according to the Scriptures," he is in fact demonstrating what they both mean by figural interpretation. It is clear from Seitz's writings that figural interpretation starts not just with the texts of Scripture (although it is not apart from it), it begins with the God of the Bible.[168] It is not just the world the texts reveal, but much more than that—the texts ultimately take us to the God and his works of which it is a witness, starting with the "first testament."[169] It is important to note how Seitz phrases the aspect of the interpretive movement from OT to NT as configured under figural interpretation:

> It is not that a straight line moves from the Old Testament to Christ in some mechanical fashion. Rather, we comprehend what God is doing in Christ right now and to eternity by returning to the Old Testament and seeking to find within it manifold testimony in accordance with what we are coming to know about God in Christ . . . and the Father has set forth his broader plans for the world in his word to Israel, plans at whose center stands Christ.[170]

Seitz is not hesitant to emphasize a christological center in some places. In fact, Seitz is explicit about it in his exposition of Phil 2:9–11. He states, "To be given a glimpse at the life of YHWH through the lens of Jesus is to see God from within, from inside the relationship, from the standpoint of the Son. The consequence of this is to call God Father and mean by that YHWH, as seen from the standpoint of the Son, to whom has been given the name above every name."[171] Seitz sees it as an opening into the life of the immanent Trinity. Hence, he could make such a statement without being obligated to a christological interpretation. But in places like this, figural interpretation appears quite similar to christological interpretation.

---

167. Childs, *Biblical Theology*, 722–23. Childs is critical of narrative theology as well as ecclesial reading. He is concerned that both readings rob the texts of their determinative meaning and the canon's role as *regula fidei* resulting in the loss of Bible's christological mooring.

168. See also Childs, *Biblical Theology*, 726. Childs describes Scripture as a witness to God's work of redemption in Christ.

169. Seitz, *Word without End*, 56–57.

170. Seitz, *Word without End*, 57.

171. Seitz, *Figured Out*, 143.

Seitz would resist any attempt to reduce figural interpretation into christological interpretation. If so, how are they different?

There are few important differences to be noted between these two approaches to make sense of the distinctions even though both of them have isolating tendencies. The first major difference is the starting point. The starting point for a christological interpretation is the understanding of God presented in the NT, particularly in the Gospels; for a figural reading, the starting point is the doctrine of God found in creedal confessions (there is also a canonical emphasis). As Seitz posits, neither the NT (1 Cor 15:3–4) nor the creeds talk about the rising of Jesus in accordance with the NT texts, but with the OT texts.[172] This fact underlies Seitz's arguments for listening to the "discrete voice" of the OT in biblical interpretation. The second major difference is who "the God who raised Jesus from the dead" is a modifier of—whether it modifies P1, God in the OT (T), or it modifies Jesus Christ through whom P1 is identified in the NT. In other words, the difference consists in whether the move is from Father to the Son (OT–NT) or from Son to the Father (NT–OT). The third difference is between the emphases on economic Trinity (christological interpretation) versus immanent Trinity (figural reading).[173] The last difference to be noted is the age-old question of whether NT interprets OT or OT interprets NT or a mediating position (each of them in its own right within a canonical framework). Christological interpretation seems to assume the proposition that NT interprets OT. Figural interpretation on the other hand assumes the latter proposition of each Testament being interpreted on its own rights, but within a canonical framework, which influences the reading of both Testaments.

In spite of an emphasis on the immanent Trinity in figural interpretation, an isolationist tendency can be observed in this approach as well. The main issue lies in how the identity of YHWH is understood in figural interpretation. Seitz is explicit about the identity of YHWH being P1—a common feature of the isolationist tendency. Christ, in Seitz's view, is related to the OT texts through his relationship to the one who raised Jesus from the dead, God the Father. Thus, the identification of YHWH as P1 in figural interpretation renders the proposal ineffective for a thoroughly Trinitarian interpretation.

---

172. Seitz, *Word without End*, 52.

173. Watson emphasizes the economic Trinity in his interpretive schema, whereas Seitz emphasizes the immanent Trinity. See also Briggs, "Book of Genesis," 48–49.

Trinitarian interpretation

Some works devoted to the renewal of theological interpretation predominantly use phrases such as "divine discourse" (Wolterstorff), "Trinitarian self-revelation" (John Webster), and "divine agency" or "divine-rhetoric" (Mark Bowald) to propose a model for Trinitarian interpretation. Unlike christological interpretation where most of the proponents seem to advance a similar and somewhat coherent position, Wolterstorff, Webster, and Bowald do not offer a coherent vision of what Trinitarian interpretation is like. Instead, they expound quite different proposals that do not seem to advance the same thing. A close examination of these proposals reveals that these too fall short of a robust account of a Trinitarian interpretation.

Nicholas Wolterstorff

Nicholas Wolterstorff attempts to decipher the "divine discourse"—what it means to say "God speaks"—in scriptural interpretation. How can one make sense of the oft-repeated phrase "this is the word of the Lord" in public reading of Scripture?[174] To answer this question and to make sense of divine discourse in Scripture, Wolterstorff divides discourse into two categories, deputized discourse and appropriated discourse, both of which are double-agency discourse[175] Deputized discourse refers to the discourse in which one person (often the superior asking the deputy) requests or commissions another person to perform a locutionary act which then becomes the illocutionary act of the one who requested or commissioned it. An example of deputized discourse is an ambassador speaking on behalf of his head of state in which the speech of the ambassador is taken to be that of the head of state.[176] In this form of discourse,

---

174. Wolterstorff, *Divine Discourse*, 18. He sees a clear distinction between revelation and discourse. Wolterstoff's work had immediate impact on biblical interpretation and many embraced the speech-act theory as a way forward for biblical interpretation. See Wisse, "From Cover to Cover?," 159. Wisse's article sheds light on some of the incongruities of Wolterstorff's proposals, especially with regard to the transitive nature of the double-agency discourse and its shortcomings for biblical hermeneutics.

175. Wolterstorff, *Divine Discourse*, 42–54.

176. Wolterstorff mentions that there is varying degree of superintendence in a deputized discourse. On one end of that continuum is the discourser himself producing the text. Further along the continuum, the discourser dictates to a secretary. The discourser merely communicates the content of the text to the secretary, then the secretary produces the text. On the other end of the continuum is the secretary herself producing

the deputized speech could contain both the words of the deputy as well as the one who deputized it. Biblical prophecy is of this type, says Wolterstorff.[177]

The second type of double-agency discourse is called appropriated discourse. It means that one is appropriating someone else's speech. In the case of the Scripture, humans are the agents of the appropriated discourse and God is the agent of the appropriating discourse. For example, when one says that "I share that commitment" or "I second the motion," he is appropriating the speech of someone else. In such cases, writes Wolterstorff, "one is not just appropriating *the text* of the first person as the medium of one's own discourse; one is appropriating *the discourse* of that other person."[178] Wolterstorff believes that the most natural way to understand the whole Bible to be God's word is to understand it as the appropriated discourse. The Bible contains both deputized speech (prophecy) and appropriated discourse (narratives). The category of appropriated discourse allows Wolterstorff to account for both the diversity and the humanity of the biblical texts because God is the agent of the appropriating discourse and humans are the agents of the appropriated discourse.[179]

According to Wolterstorff, texts may have one locution but multiple illocutions; hence, what one audience takes away from a speech might be different from what another audience takes from the same speech. Wolterstorff gives this example: at the dinner table a mother utters the words, "only two days to Christmas." This one locutionary act has different illocutionary acts for different audiences. For her children it might mean that there are only two more days till Christmas (just what the statement says), but to her husband it could mean that he better get all the shopping done before it is too late (totally different illocutionary act).[180] Similarly, one could write a story for her children to make a point and then later on present the same story in a different context to another audience. Thus, there is a difference between what one is saying by authoring a text and by

---

the text by knowing the mind of the discourser (Wolterstorff, *Divine Discourse*, 41).

177. Wolterstorff, *Divine Discourse*, 45–46. This is also true of apostolic commission. They are sent by God and speak on behalf of God. Because the prophets spoke not of their own, but for God (Deut 18), we are expected to obey the prophecy and in doing so, we are obeying God.

178. Wolterstorff, *Divine Discourse*, 52–53.

179. Wolterstorff, *Divine Discourse*, 53–54.

180. Wolterstorff, *Divine Discourse*, 55.

presenting a text.[181] When applied to Scripture, it makes better sense to read what Paul wrote to the Romans as written to us. Paul's letter was not only a divine discourse when it was written, but also functions the same way when it is presented to us.[182]

Wolterstorff's major concern is not in understanding the presentational discourse, but the authorial discourse. By that he means what God was saying by authoring the text or by appropriating the human text.[183] Interpreting Scripture for divine discourse must begin with interpreting the human discourse—what does the text say? The reason for paying attention to the texts themselves is because God discourses by way of them.[184]

Wolterstorff prescribes five things to bear in mind as one interprets for divine discourse. In order to discern the rhetorical-conceptual structure of divine discourse there is a need to alter the mediating human discourse, especially in places where humans are talking to God or where it makes no sense to attribute such a speech to God. For example, in Rom 1:9, Paul says, "God, whom I serve with my spirit by announcing the gospel of his Son, is my witness." This cannot be understood as God saying it about himself by appropriating what the human discourse is because the rhetorical-conceptual structure is incoherent and wrong.

The next step is to note the point and the main point of the text and to distinguish it from how it is developed. According to Wolterstorff, the psalmist in Ps 93 compares God's steadfastness with the idea of a geocentric cosmology of his time in which the world is considered to be immovable ("He has established the world; it shall never be moved" [Ps 93:1]), but we cannot assume that to be part of God's discourse because he knows that the earth rotates on its axis.[185] Third, one has to recognize that even when God appropriates the texts (literal) of the human discourse he can appropriate it tropically (figuratively), especially when emotions are applied to God. In Ps 137, the psalmist "literally" means the happiness of those who dash the Babylonian infants against the rock, but God could take it tropically in which it could be understood as God opposing whatever opposes God's reign, says Wolterstorff.[186]

181. Wolterstorff, *Divine Discourse*, 55.
182. Wolterstorff, *Divine Discourse*, 56.
183. Wolterstorff, *Divine Discourse*, 188–89.
184. Wolterstorff, *Divine Discourse*, 202.
185. Wolterstorff, *Divine Discourse*, 209.
186. Wolterstorff, *Divine Discourse*, 208–12.

Fourth, one has to pay attention to the transitive discourse, contends Wolterstorff. By this he means that by performing one illocutionary action we perform another illocutionary action. For example, the prophet Nathan used a story to tell David of his act of stealing another man's wife. "I think almost everyone would concede that biblical *narrative* as a whole fits under this category of transitive discourse."[187] The final step is to differentiate the specificity/generality aspect between the appropriated discourse and the appropriating discourse.

Wolterstorff asserts that one interprets for divine discourse in the second hermeneutic and not in the first, which is the academic practice of ascertaining what the text says.[188] This aspect resonates with TIS because the distinction between the first and the second hermeneutics is something that theological interpretation is trying to overcome. Wolterstorff offers ways to apply speech-act theory to biblical interpretation to overcome what he considers to be a major problem in biblical interpretation (in the academy at least), such as how to read the human text of Scripture as God's word.[189]

Wolterstorff acknowledges that the focus of Christian scriptures is Jesus Christ. However, he admits that he did not focus on that aspect in his own work, which Christians consider as central.[190] In fact, he sees no difference in the divine discourse in Judaism, Christianity, and Islam.[191] His concern is primarily with the question of divine discourse and how God can claim to have spoken. Trinitarian interpretation is first and foremost concerned with the Christian understanding of the identity of God in the OT and the NT as triune and how that understanding engenders a particular kind of interpretation. A failure to do that would result in a broad theory that may or may not be of some use to theological interpretation, which is the case with Wolterstorff's proposal. It is noteworthy

187. Wolterstorff, *Divine Discourse*, 214.

188. Wolterstorff, "Promise of Speech-Act Theory," 87; Hesse, "Response," 94–95. Hesse's and Wisse's critical appraisal of the *Divine Discourse* highlight its weaknesses and limited use for theological interpretation.

189. Hesse, "Response," 93–95. Hesse objects to the characterization of the first hermeneutic as something that can be done without some truth-claim in it. For example, the crossing of the Red Sea has to be taken as a metaphor or type of God's deliverance of Israel and for that matter of the whole world. Similarly, she also objects to the assessment that *tropes* (metaphors, irony, metonym, and the like) are illocutions with no truth-value. Wolterstorff's attempt falls short because it undermines aspects such as the propositional character of metaphors.

190. Wolterstorff, *Divine Discourse*, 236–96.

191. Wolterstorff, *Divine Discourse*, 97, 117, 129.

that many in TIS have followed Wolterstorff's appropriation of speech-act theory. His failure to attend to the identity of God in the OT is reflected on their proposals as well.

John Webster

John Webster, influenced by Barth and Wolterstorff, makes a plea to the academy for reconsidering the importance of the Trinitarian nature of Scripture because the texts themselves and their reception history "are subservient to the self-presentation of the triune God."[192] Describing the present state of the doctrine of revelation, he charges that the modern use of revelation became devoid of the "life-giving and loving presence of the God and Father of our Lord Jesus Christ in the Spirit's power among the worshipping and witnessing assembly."[193] Here he describes the God of the OT as God the Father (P1).

Webster addresses two issues concurrently: (1) the dualism (either the Scripture is purely natural/human or it is purely supernatural/divine) that exists in contemporary approach to Scripture and revelation, and (2) the subordination of Scripture to the creaturely act of reception and reading in the church (which dismisses the ontology of Scripture that is closely integrated with the triune identity of God). He constructs his response to the first issue by drawing on Colin Gunton's categorization of revelation as a corollary of soteriology. Gunton argued that the center of Scripture is not God's self-identification, but his saving action.[194] Following Gunton, Webster constructs an account of Scripture from the triune God's self-revelation in the economy of salvation.[195] He turns to sanctification to address the issue of dualism that exists in modern interpretation.

Dualism in the modern concept of revelation can be labeled as either deistic (emphasizes the natural origin of revelation) or docetic (emphasizes supernatural origin of revelation), and the way to overcome that dualism is by paying attention to both the divine and the human agency in revelation.[196] The proper way to discuss the doctrine of revelation and the doctrine of Scripture is the doctrine of God understood within the

---

192. Webster, *Holy Scripture*, 6.
193. Webster, *Holy Scripture*, 12.
194. Gunton, *Brief Theology of Revelation*, 111.
195. Webster, *Holy Scripture*, 16–17.
196. Webster, *Holy Scripture*, 17–41.

framework of the economy of salvation. The church is found within this economy of salvation, and Scripture, and according to Webster, is prior to the church. It is the Scripture and not the church that has priority in biblical interpretation.[197] The reading[198] of Scripture is to be done with an attitude of submission to the Scripture's priority. "Reading Scripture is thus best understood as an aspect of mortification and vivification: to read Scripture is to be slain and made alive."[199] Here, the contrast is between the Scripture's authority versus the church's authority and Webster believes that it is the Scripture that has the ultimate authority in interpretation.

Reading Scripture has to be accompanied by an attitude of humility and virtues of godliness, claims Webster. Scripture reading is inescapably bound to regeneration. This virtue is not just a moral one but more so the resultant effect of soteriological and pneumatological transformation.[200] Reading does not neglect the human aspects of the text, but it acknowledges and pays attention to God's self-explication through the creaturely medium and act.[201] By focusing on reading rather than the preferred term *interpretation* and viewing revelation within a soteriological framework, Webster is able to assume a mediating position between a deistic and a docetic view of Scripture.

Finally, Webster offers an excellent example of how Christian theology can and should be practiced in the academy from Zacharius Ursinus's inaugural address to the Elisabeth-Schule at Bresalu in 1558. Ursinus highlighted the need for catechesis by stating that it is through doctrines that Christ builds his church.[202] Theological schools play an important role in that process of catechizing because theological schools, for Ursinus, exist to train the clergy. By drawing on Ursinus, Webster is

---

197. Webster, *Holy Scripture*, 40–67.

198. Webster prefers *reading* to *interpretation* because it is a low-level term that does not carry all the psychological and philosophical complexities of hermeneutical theories. It is also preferable because reading emphasizes the self-explicating character of divine revelation; whereas, interpretation seems to focus on the immanent aspects of the reader. Webster, *Holy Scripture*, 86.

199. Webster, *Holy Scripture*, 88. Calvin and Bonhoeffer aid his arguments for virtue-driven hermeneutics. The focus is not to dismiss the usefulness of historical-critical reading; on the contrary, the arguments are for an educated reading of the biblical text (that includes all matters pertaining to exegesis) with a childlike submissiveness and dependency.

200. Webster, *Holy Scripture*, 89.

201. Webster, *Holy Scripture*, 92–93.

202. Webster, *Holy Scripture*, 108.

able to show the need for the primacy of the Holy Scripture in academic and church life and offer a dogmatic sketch of why and how the Bible can be called Holy Scripture. Holy Scripture refers to the Bible's origin, function, and end in divine self-communication and the responses that are fitting to that divine character of the texts.[203]

Webster employs Trinitarian language to describe the nature and character of Scripture. He constructs a strong argument for the triune God as the source and content of Scripture. However, he does not mean that all three persons of the Godhead are equal in the process of revelation. The Father is the root or origin of revelation, the Son is the agent of revelation, and the Spirit is the perfection of revelation and the one who makes it effective in the community of the church.[204] This is similar to Vanhoozer's argument in that not all three persons perform the same act of generating the written word. When it comes to the Word of God, there is a shift from the text to the second person of the Trinity. Webster and Vanhoozer first speak of the second person of the Trinity being the Word when they refer to the Son as the agent or illocution in revelation and then making the transition to the written word assuming that the written Word is now P2. The written word is more than P2. Written word is the whole revelation of God spanning two Testaments and the Father, Son, and Spirit speak in it. Thus, making that one-to-one connection between the written word and P2 seems to be missing this point.

When it comes to a Christian reading (interpretation) of Scripture, Webster tends to pivot to a christological center. He writes, "Holy Scripture is a *unified* attestation of Jesus Christ, and so in an important sense a single, coherent text. . . . Jesus Christ guarantees the unity of Scripture, and the propriety of reading it as such, because he is its *auctor primarius* and its *res*."[205] The exalted Christ, who is at the right hand of the Father, continues his unhindered activity of addressing and ministering to the creatures. This address and ministry takes the form of Holy Scripture.[206] Scripture is to be read, writes Webster, "as what it is, a complex though unified set of texts through which the risen Christ interprets himself as the one in whom the entire economy of God's dealing with creatures has its coherence and fulfilment."[207] Reading requires hermeneutical con-

---

203. Webster, *Holy Scripture*, 5.
204. Webster, *Word and Church*, 27–28.
205. Webster, *Domain of the Word*, 17–18.
206. Webster, *Domain of the Word*, 8.
207. Webster, *Domain of the Word*, 32.

version where overcoming sin is the sole work of Christ and the Spirit.[208] Webster sees interpretation as a matter of understanding how Scripture reveals Christ and in that process he undercuts his own search for a Trinitarian interpretation that attends to all three persons of the Godhead.

Webster's turn to a christological center reveals the presence of an isolationist tendency that has marred similar proposals. The oscillation between a Trinitarian and a christological interpretation creates confusion. Christ as the one revealing P1 is not problematic, but identifying YHWH exclusively with P1 is a problem. The identification of YHWH as P1 leads to isolationism; therefore, there is a need to reconsider the identity of YHWH in his proposals without which his proposal becomes unusable for a robust account of Trinitarian interpretation.

Mark Bowald

Mark Bowald addresses a particular kind of isolationist tendency in biblical interpretation. This is influenced by one's view of the agency in scriptural revelation.[209] To mitigate this particular isolationist tendency in biblical hermeneutics, Bowald proposes a reconsideration of the agency of revelation in Scripture and proffers a Trinitarian hermeneutic.[210] To that end he constructs a triangular typology in which the scholars under discussion have been located within a triangle according to their relative proximity toward either the human or the divine agency in revelation. He decries the influence of Enlightenment epistemology in biblical hermeneutics, which leads to deistic tendencies in scriptural interpretation.[211]

One of the implications of the influence of Enlightenment epistemology on scriptural interpretation is that hermeneutics turned to the immanent spheres of agency (or anthropological emphasis) in biblical revelation. Hermeneutical theories and methods dealt with the various aspects of language, speech, and communication without any regard for the divine agency in biblical revelation. This apathy toward divine agency led to, in Bowald's opinion, the replacement of divine supervenience and guidance that existed in precritical interpretation with human beings

---

208. Webster, *Holy Scripture*, 88.
209. Bowald, *Rendering the Word*, 1–2.
210. Bowald, *Rendering the Word*, 32, 41–44.
211. Bowald, *Rendering the Word*, 18, 21–22, 173–75.

assuming that role in interpretation. The attributes and actions once attributed to God were transferred to humans.[212]

Type one and type two in Bowald's typology pertain to human agency either in the production of the biblical texts or its reading and reception. Accordingly, he has Frei (earlier works), Watson, and Vanhoozer as representatives of type 1 who emphasize the author's role in determining meaning.[213] Type 2 is represented by David Kelsey, Frei (later works), Werner Jeanrond, and Fowl, who emphasize the role of the reading or ecclesial community in determining the meaning of the biblical texts.[214] Bowald aligns himself with type three, represented by Barth, Wolterstorff, and James K. A. Smith who emphasize and assign the central role to divine agency in both the production and interpretation of the text.[215]

After explaining the various degrees of proximity toward the human or the divine agency found in various modern works on biblical interpretation, Bowald presses the case that there is an overwhelming tendency in modern hermeneutical methods to create a clear divide between formal principles (the principles generally applicable to any text) and material principles (distinctly related to the content of a specific text).[216] Premodern interpreters, on the other hand, acknowledged and exemplified a close relation between the formal and the material principles.[217]

To overcome the impasse, Bowald proposes a divine-rhetorical hermeneutic after the model of the ancient view of rhetoric as an encounter with the "living and breathing speaker." Bowald follows Aristotle's *Ars Rhetorica* in which he defines three "species" in rhetoric: *ethos*, *logos*, and *pathos*. *Ethos* refers to the character of the speaker embodied in speech. *Logos* is the speech itself and *pathos* is the response produced in the hearers by the speech, which is closely tied to the character of the speaker.[218] Bowald connects the ethos of Scripture with the character of God and logos to the human aspect of the speech, the role of the human author in the production of the text. The study of the logos includes historical-critical elements (more or less as practiced in modern hermeneutics) with

212. Bowald, *Rendering the Word*, 16–19.
213. Bowald, *Rendering the Word*, 45–85.
214. Bowald, *Rendering the Word*, 87–123.
215. Bowald, *Rendering the Word*, 125–62. The ambiguity in his proposal becomes immediately evident from the preceding discussions on Wolterstorff and Webster.
216. Bowald, *Rendering the Word*, 168–70.
217. Bowald, *Rendering the Word*, 169.
218. Bowald, *Rendering the Word*, 175.

one major difference from how modernity handles it—under this rubric logos is subject to divine ethos. Bowald shifts from a triangle typology (because it is insufficient for his purposes) to a circular typology in which logos and pathos are small circles inside the big circle of ethos.[219]

According to Bowald, divine-rhetorical hermeneutics is different in some senses as compared to Aristotle's rhetoric in that it prioritizes divine agency, the ethos of the text, because God the author is ever present in its reading unlike human texts. Bowald does not identify who this "God the author" is, but the language suggests a pneumatological emphasis here given the language of "presence." Similarly, pathos parallels the *missio Dei* of the church, which is influenced by the divine ethos, and this is the telos of reading Scripture.[220] Thus, *rhetoric* can serve to overcome the Enlightenment epistemology prevalent in modern biblical hermeneutics and has the potential to shape theological interpretation.

Bowald's insistence on prioritizing divine agency and proposal of divine-rhetorical hermeneutics gives the impression that his proposal is a thoroughly Trinitarian one (he does not deal with the role of the persons of the Godhead in the production or reading of the texts apart from repeated use of divine agency). His proposal hinges on the conviction that the reading of Scripture is essentially an encounter with the living Christ who speaks through his word.[221] He explains what divine-rhetorical hermeneutics entails: "In this the basic terms for understanding the reading of the Bible emerges from the testament to the givenness of Jesus Christ's ubiquity and clarity as the fulfillment of God's *opera ad extra*. In this model the reading of the Bible begins less as an act of isolated and desperate textual archaeologists but more as spiritually hungry and thirsty creatures who are confronted with the abundant and bountiful gospel in the living speech of the very embodiment of life and truth Himself."[222] Thus, he emphasizes a christological center for theological interpretation.

Throughout the book, Bowald presumes that prioritizing the divine agency naturally leads to a Trinitarian interpretation, which he himself has not proven either with biblical interpretation of certain passages or with necessary explanation as to how his proposal results in a qualitatively different reading from that of the ones who tend to prioritize the

---

219. Bowald, *Rendering the Word*, 177–81.
220. Bowald, *Rendering the Word*, 181–82.
221. Bowald, *Rendering the Word*, 174–75, 183.
222. Bowald, *Rendering the Word*, 174–75.

human agency of revelation.[223] He does not tell us the identity of God, especially in regard to the OT. His emphasis on a christological reading seems to suggest that he views YHWH as P1. This identification of YHWH as P1 needs to be overcome in order for his proposal to have any significant bearing on Trinitarian interpretation.

Conclusion

Much can be learned from these proposals for a Trinitarian interpretation as they are contributing in a significant way to the ongoing exploration of a fully theological interpretation. However, as John Goldingay has pointed out, the tendency to isolate the persons of the Godhead in theological interpretation should be stymied so that the lacunae that exist in the common parlance Trinitarian interpretation can be overcome.[224]

Analysis of the way Trinitarian interpretation is employed reveals considerable ambivalence, leading to confusion and incoherence. Disciplinary and philosophical differences account for some of the disparity in spite of a positive attitude toward Trinitarian interpretation. Those proposals that argue for the priority of the doctrine of God in TIS do not themselves either demonstrate how such proposals could lead to qualitative difference in interpretation or have only a very limited use (as in the case of Wolterstorff) rendering such proposals ineffective.

Inconsistency in current proposals for Trinitarian interpretation and the subsequent isolationist tendency in practice raise the question of the identity of God in the Scripture. Current proposals seem to assume the identity of YHWH in the OT as P1. Chapter 3 analyzes the identity of YHWH in light of the relevant OT and NT passages and the early church's understanding of God to offer a solution to the isolationist tendency by arguing for the identity of YHWH as Trinity.

---

223. It is no surprise that Bowald does not interact with any biblical texts in his proposal. His proposal, in my opinion, is drastically weakened by this lack of treatment of biblical texts to explicate how his proposal would affect TIS.

224. The phrase *isolationist tendency* is mine and I have reached this conclusion independently of Goldingay, although he has pointed out the fact that current models of Trinitarian interpretation tend to identify YHWH as God the Father. Goldingay, *Need the New Testament?*, 165–69.

3

YHWH *Is* Trinity

THIS CHAPTER PRESENTS A case for viewing the identity of YHWH as not just "God the Father" in the sense of the first person of the Trinity, but rather as the one true God, whom the New Testament presents as the triune God. Starting with a word study on יהוה and πατήρ followed by the NT's understanding of YHWH and the identity of God in the church fathers with a special focus on the identity of "God the Father," this chapter will focus on the claim that YHWH *is* Trinity.

A few preliminary remarks are in order. First, an etymological study itself will neither answer the question of the meaning of the words nor their theological significance.[1] Second, this approach does not focus exclusively on ascertaining the meaning of YHWH from its etymological origins; instead, this emphasizes the possibility of discerning plurality of persons in the identity of YHWH. There is less emphasis on the meaning of YHWH in historical context, although some space is devoted to that topic. Instead, the chief focus is whether or not a pattern can be identified within the OT texts that indicate a Trinitarian doctrine of God. In other words, are there evidence within the OT texts that suggest that more than one person is identified by the name YHWH? Can YHWH be identified as the three persons of the Godhead? If these questions can be answered

---

1. Saner, *"Too Much to Grasp,"* 27–31. Saner provides an extensive survey of the literature that deals with the identity of YHWH from etymological and religiohistorical standpoints.

in the positive from biblical and theological evidence, this could help bridge the chasm that exists in Trinitarian interpretation and avoid the isolationist tendency.

Word Study on יהוה and Πατήρ

A word study on יהוה and its meaning to the nation Israel followed by a word study on πατήρ, especially its many occurrences in the NT's reference to P1, highlights two important facts: (1) יהוה is God's personal name and YHWH is identified in the NT as Father, Son, and Spirit and not just as God the Father, (2) πατήρ is used both generically (in the sense of addressing God without specifying the persons of the Godhead) and specifically (as the first person of the Trinity). This word study is not exhaustive, but it is sufficient to make the more substantial point later in the chapter about the identity of YHWH—multiple persons named YHWH, but one YHWH. A comprehensive look at how YHWH revealed himself within the OT provides enough evidence to suggest that there are multiple persons indicated by YHWH. The NT helps specify that identity with clarity.

יהוה

How the identity of יהוה is understood in the Hebrew OT and its corresponding Greek translation κύριος in the Septuagint provides the background to understand the identity of יהוה in the OT and the corresponding identity of God in the NT. These two are related but different ways of looking at the identity of the same God. Together they paint a picture of the identity of the God whom the entirety of Scripture reveals as one.

The Identity of יהוה *in the Hebrew OT*

The following word study focuses first on what various scholars have to say about the origin and meaning of YHWH before making concluding remarks on how best to understand his revelation to Moses in Exod 3:14–15. A fuller explication of the identity of YHWH will be undertaken later in the chapter.

YHWH Is Trinity

Whether or not the Tetragrammaton is the personal name of God in the OT and its etymology have been vexing questions.[2] Etymological studies differ in their conclusions.[3] The Hebrew root הוה (היה) meaning "to fall" (Job 37:6; 2 Sam 11:23) has some similarity with the Arabic root *hwy*, meaning "to blow" or "to fall."[4] Some suggest that יהוה has an Arabic origin. Accordingly, Theophile James Meek suggests that YHWH was a tribal god, most likely a "storm god."[5] He finds support for this argument in such references to YHWH before whom the earth quaked (Judg 5:4; Deut 33:2; Ps 68:7–8). The Hebrew people appropriated the name of this tribal god but did not really know its origin and meaning, contends Meek.

Roland de Vaux disagrees with the suggestion that the similarity with the Arabic root necessarily means YHWH has an Arabic origin; he attributes such misidentification to an improper use of the Arabic root.[6]

---

2. For a detailed bibliography on the treatment of יהוה from within Old Testament research, see Saner, "Too Much to Grasp," 1–58. Saner's argument can best be summarized in his own words: "I argue that the literal sense of Exod 3:13–15, understood within the literary context of the received form of the book of Exodus and the wider Pentateuch, witnesses, in its own idiom, to the identity of the living God, known to Christians as Father, Son and Holy Spirit" (3). He builds his case by depending on Hans Frei's understanding of the literal sense within the narrative context. His contribution is valuable and strengthens my case. My own case is somewhat different. I make a case for the multiplicity or plurality of persons in the identity of YHWH, supported by several OT passages, to advocate that a Trinitarian interpretation must be founded on this identity of YHWH to overcome the isolationist tendency that exists within the proposals for a Trinitarian interpretation. For a historical sketch of the understanding of Tetragrammaton within Western Christendom, see Wilkinson, *Tetragrammaton*. For detailed study on the Hellenistic, Roman, and New Testament understanding of YHWH and its implications for understanding Rev 1:4, see McDonough, *YHWH at Patmos*. For a study on how Jews, pagans, and early Christian understood YHWH, see Kooten, *Revelation of the Name YHWH*.

3. Saner, "Too Much to Grasp," 14. An etymological study alone is not sufficient to explicate either the significance of the name YHWH to the nation Israel or his unique identity. A contextual and theological study is necessary because we are dealing with the theological purpose and meaning of the biblical material and not just its historical or narrative value. Bekkum, "What's in the Divine Name?," 5n4.

4. Köhler and Baumgartner, *Hebrew and Aramaic Lexicon*, 241; Saner, "Too Much to Grasp," 15.

5. Meek, *Hebrew Origins*, 99. See also Knauf, "Yahwe," 467–70; Oesterley and Robinson, *Hebrew Religion*, 137–39. Meek builds his argument based on his view that Israelite religion had a naturalistic origin. Mark Smith proposes that the "oldest biblical tradition places Yahweh originally as a god in southern Edom (possibly in northwestern Saudi Arabia)." Smith, *Origins of Biblical Monotheism*, 140. For a detailed study on the various theories of the etymology of YHWH and the rise of the cult of Yahweh, see Toorn, "Yahweh," 910–19. For a Kenite hypothesis, see Parke-Taylor, *Yahweh*.

6. Vaux, "Divine Name YHWH," 56–59.

Instead, he contends that YHWH comes from the northwestern Semitic root *hwy*, meaning "to be." A. Murtonen reaches similar conclusions as de Vaux's.[7] Even though this root is not found in Amorite and Ugaritic texts, the forms of *hwh, hw', hwy* are found in Aramaic, Nabataean, Palmyrenean, and Syriac texts and inscriptions.[8]

As for the meaning, some suggest that YHWH should be taken as a "causative" (*hiphil*), meaning, "he causes to be" ("he is the creator") instead of the simple form (*qal*), "to be" or "he is."[9] In order for YHWH to be a causative form, de Vaux argues that the construction אֶהְיֶה אֲשֶׁר אֶהְיֶה needs to be amended to אֲשֶׁר אַהְיֶה אַהְיֶה (or אֲשֶׁר יִהְיֶה אַהְיֶה, "I cause to be that which I cause to be, I create that which I create").[10] Bruce Waltke argues that since אֶהְיֶה never occurs in the causative stem, such a reading is unlikely in this context.[11]

Waltke makes a compelling case for taking יהוה as the third person of אֶהְיֶה the first person.[12] According to Waltke, the meaning YHWH depends on the meaning of אֶהְיֶה אֲשֶׁר אֶהְיֶה.[13] In the process of answering Moses' question, God first shortens his "full-sentence name into a single verb" אֶהְיֶה in 3:14 and then reveals his name in the third person (YHWH) in 3:15.[14] Waltke translates אֶהְיֶה אֲשֶׁר אֶהְיֶה as "I AM WHO I AM" and not "I will be who I will be." He takes אֶהְיֶה as the iterative present; for it to be taken as future tense ("I will be what I will be") requires a direct object marker אֶת as in Exod 33:19 ("I will have mercy on whom I will have mercy; and I will have compassion on whom I will have compassion").[15] Seitz thinks that אֶהְיֶה could be taken as a name for God although not

---

7. Murtonen, *Philological and Literary Treatise*, 67.

8. Vaux, "Divine Name YHWH," 59–60.

9. "Yahweh" versus "Yihweh," see Vaux, "Divine Name YHWH," 62. For an argument for the causative form, see Freedman, "Name of the God," 151–56.

10. Vaux, "Divine Name YHWH," 64.

11. Waltke, *Old Testament Theology*, 366.

12. Waltke, *Old Testament Theology*, 359–69. Throughout this book and elsewhere, Waltke uses "I AM" instead of YHWH as God's name. For example, see Waltke, *Book of Proverbs*. For a different view on the relation between אֶהְיֶה and יהוה see Beitzel, "Exodus 3:14 and the Divine Name," 18–19. Beitzel argues that there is no etymological relation between יהוה and היה. He suggests that YHWH is a genuine Tetragrammaton in that the *yod* is intrinsic to the name.

13. Waltke, *Old Testament Theology*, 365.

14. Waltke, *Old Testament Theology*, 365.

15. Waltke, *Old Testament Theology*, 365–66.

in the strictest sense of a proper name.[16] Waltke suggests that the reason God introduced his name in the third person is because "the first person is appropriate only in God's mouth and the third person is appropriate in Israel's mouth when they invoke/mention God's name."[17] There is more to the significance of the meaning of the name in the context.[18] God is reiterating his assurance to Moses that when he goes to Pharaoh and the people, he will be with Moses (see Exod 3:10, 12) because he is a God who does not change.[19] YHWH introduced himself as the God of his fathers in 3:6. That same God who kept his promises to the fathers will also keep his promise to Moses. This assurance could not have been any stronger than to reiterate his character as the promise keeper.

To further understand the significance of the revealing of the name YHWH to Moses, another related issue needs to be addressed. YHWH's declaration in Exod 6:3 that he was not known to Abraham, Isaac, and Jacob by this name requires answers in light of passages such as Gen 12:1, 8; 15:6; 25:21, 25; 28:13; 32:9, where YHWH was known and worshiped by the patriarchs. J. A. Moteyer writes that when God told Moses that he was not known to Abraham, Isaac, and Jacob as YHWH, he was not referring to whether they ever knew or had heard the name YHWH (just a historical knowledge), but that they only knew his nature and did not know it as God's proper name.[20]

Whenever God made a covenant or reiterated it with the patriarchs, he did so not with the name YHWH; instead, to Abraham he was *El Shaddai* (Gen 17:1), to Isaac *Elohim* (Gen 26:24), and to Jacob *El Shaddai* (Gen 35:11; cf. 33:20).[21] In the Mosaic covenant the name of God

---

16. Seitz, "Call of Moses," 154. As for whether YHWH is the proper name, Seitz suggests that *elohim* or *baalim* refers to the genus of the divine beings and YHWH, Marduk, or Asherah refers to the specific (proper) names of the particular deities. He finds support for this argument in the Decalogue (Exod 20:2)—יְהוָה אֱלֹהֶיךָ ("the Lord your God")—"I am YHWH, your Elohim, who brought you up out of the land of Egypt." Seitz, "The Divine Name in Christian Scripture," 25–26.

17. Waltke, *Old Testament Theology*, 365.

18. Gerhard von Rad suggests that the "subject is in the name, and on that account the name carries with it a statement about the nature of its subject or at least about the power appertaining to it. For the cultic life of the ancient East, this idea was of quite fundamental importance." Rad, *Old Testament Theology*, 1:181–82.

19. Waltke, *Old Testament Theology*, 366–67.

20. Motyer, *Revelation of the Divine Name*, 30.

21. Motyer, *Revelation of the Divine Name*, 27. But see Gen 28:13—אֲנִי יְהוָה אֱלֹהֵי אַבְרָהָם אָבִיךָ וֵאלֹהֵי יִצְחָק (I am YHWH, the God of your father Abraham and the God of Isaac).

is YHWH.[22] Hence, it makes sense for God to tell Moses that he was not known by this name to the patriarchs—perhaps a reference to the establishment and reiteration of the Abrahamic covenant. This may well indicate the beginning of a new covenant with Moses, which is different from the ones God had made with the patriarchs. Seitz suggests that the issue in Exod 6:3 is not the name itself, but how God was going to make himself known as YHWH. He understands YHWH's reply to Moses as "I was not known in respect to my name YHWH" meaning in the way he was going to reveal himself to Moses, the nation Israel, and Pharaoh.[23] Conversely, R. W. L. Moberly thinks that the Genesis occurrences of the name YHWH were later additions by the editors because YHWH is explicit that he was not known by this name to the patriarchs. Otherwise, it does not make much sense for God to tell Abraham that, "I am the LORD (YHWH) who brought you from Ur of the Chaldeans" (Gen 15:7) and not allow him to know what that means.[24]

It is obvious from this brief discussion that scholars are divided in their opinion on the root from which YHWH comes, the relation between אֶהְיֶה and יהוה, and the extent to which the patriarchs knew God by the name YHWH. The solution to the question of what God was trying to communicate to Moses has to look beyond any etiological relationships among the words. It is important to look briefly at how the LXX understood Exod 3:14–15 before making observations as to how to understand God's revelation of his name to Moses.

The Identity of יהוה in the Septuagint

The LXX translates יהוה in Exod 3:15 as Κύριος (יְהוָֹה אֱלֹהֵי אֲבֹתֵיכֶם—Κύριος ὁ θεὸς τῶν πατέρων ὑμῶν—"The LORD God of your fathers"). In fact, the LXX frequently replaces יהוה in the MT with κύριος.[25] In the LXX, κύριος is used as an expository equivalent of יהוה. Gottfried Quell writes,

> In the religious sphere, then, κύριος or ὁ κύριος is reserved for the true God, and, apart from unimportant periphrases of the name in figurative speech, it is used regularly, i.e., some 6156

---

22. Payne, "Yahweh." See also Fretheim, "Yahweh."
23. Seitz, "Call of Moses," 158, 161n18.
24. Moberly, *Old Testament*, 65–67.
25. BDAG, 577.

times, for the proper name יהוה in all its pointings and in the צְבָאוֹת יהוה or in the short form יָהּ. Only by way of exception is κύριος used for the other terms for God: 60 times אֱלֹהֵי צְבָאוֹת for אֵל, 23 for אֱלוֹהַּ, 193 for אֱלֹהִים, and 3 for אֱלֹהֵי צְבָאוֹת. The expressions κύριος θεός, κύριος ὁ θεός and ὁ κύριος θεός usually indicate a Mas. יהוה with or without the apposition אֱלֹהִים.[26]

Κύριος often appeared unarticulated except in the case of dative (though not always) that translated the Hebrew *le* preface to יהוה. Thus, the difference between κύριος and ὁ κύριος is dependent on whether the noun is in the "dative case" or not.[27]

Philo uses the LXX translation of κύριος for יהוה.[28] He not only uses κύριος for יהוה, but also frequently interprets it and sees the significance of the name.[29] Despite the inconclusiveness of whether or not Philo used κύριος for יהוה, it is important to note that the critical edition of the LXX today retains κύριος for יהוה.[30] The Septuagint translates אֶהְיֶה אֲשֶׁר אֶהְיֶה as Ἐγώ εἰμι ὁ ὤν ("I am he who is" or "I am the existing one").[31]

Sean McDonough observes that there was no use of ὁ ὤν for the divine Being in Greek literature until long after the LXX translation. It was τό ὤν that was used for the Being of god in Greek. It was an innovation on the part of LXX to use ὁ ὤν for the Being of God, which is repeated in

---

26. Quell, "Old Testament Name for God," 1059.

27. Pietersma, "Kyrios or Tetragram," 93–95.

28. McDonough, *YHWH at Patmos*, 60. Dahl and Segal advance the thesis that Philo and the Rabbis used both YHWH and Elohim for God although they differed in what each name represents. Dahl and Segal, "Philo and the Rabbis," 1.

29. Philo in *Abr.*, 121, explains why and how different designations were attributed to God. Philo, *On Abraham*, 62–63. Not all agree that the Philonic manuscripts are evidence of Philo's own use of κύριος for the Tetragrammaton because, according to Howard, these manuscripts are preserved only by Christians and therefore there is a high degree of probability that Philo was emended to conform to Christian belief. In fact, during Philo's time and in all pre-Christian manuscripts they did not translate the Tetragrammaton; instead, they transliterated it as ΙΑΩ. Howard, "Tetragram and the New Testament," 70–71. Contra Howard, Pietersma argues that there is enough evidence to suggest that Philo used κύριος for יהוה. Pietersma, "Kyrios or Tetragram," 92–93.

30. Wevers, *Exodus*, 85.

31. Wilkinson, *Tetragrammaton*, 7. See also Philo's *Mos.*, 75. Philo also uses ἐγώ εἰμι ὁ ὤν for "I am He who is" in Exod 3:14, which is the same as the LXX translation. Philo, *On Abraham*, 314. McDonough elaborates on the fact that, for Philo, the name of God was not necessarily a name at all. Philo sees ὁ ὤν not strictly a name for God, but a way to know him because God cannot be named. At the same time Philo knew the Tetragrammaton and used κύριος in its place. McDonough, *YHWH at Patmos*, 80–83.

Rev 1:4, 8—ὁ ὢν καὶ ὁ ἦν καὶ ὁ ἐρχόμενος ("who is and who was and who is to come").[32]

Brevard Childs asserts that although it is difficult to assess the extent of the ontological overtones that can be associated with the LXX use, it is interesting to note that Rev 1:8 picked up the LXX rendering. He sees some connection between the OT development of the ἐγώ εἰμι of Exod 3:14 and Rev 1:8:

> Rev. 1.8 refers to God as the one "who is, and who was, and who is to come" (ὁ ὢν καὶ ὁ ἦν καὶ ὁ ἐρχόμενος). Already within the Old Testament a two-member formula for God's name had been developed. He was the "first and the last" (Isa. 44.6). Again, Deut. 32.39 and particularly II Isaiah has used the formula of divine self-address 'anî hû' which the LXX rendered as ἐγώ εἰμι.[33]

The use of the Tetragrammaton in Rev 1:4 and 8 is significant to this discussion and it will be discussed later in this chapter.

According to Quell, יְהוָה אֱלֹהִים (The LORD God) is not only the title for God, but is the only way the nation Israel understood God to be (Deut 4:35; 7:9; 1 Kgs 18:21, 37).[34] The significance of the LXX use of κύριος/κύριος ὁ θεός for YHWH is that in the NT the same title is used for Jesus.[35]

A Closer Look

James Barr reminds us that beyond the etymology of individual words one must examine the semantic structure of the sentence to ascertain the theological data.[36] With regard to understanding the identity of YHWH in Exod 3:13–15, Andrea Saner observes that the "etymological approach

---

32. McDonough, *YHWH at Patmos*, 12. This is significant on multiple levels because Jesus is also identified with the same description. John 1:18 uses ὁ ὤν to describe the preexistence of Jesus—a point to be discussed later.

33. Childs, *Book of Exodus*, 82–83.

34. Quell, "El and Elohim," 80–90. During the Patristic period θεὸς is used for God the Father, the Son, and the Holy Spirit. Lampe, *Patristic Greek Lexicon*, 632–35.

35. Κύριοςὁ θεὸς (יְהוָה אֱלֹהִים) of Gen 2:8 (LXX) is found twenty-four times in the NT. Ten occurrences are in the book of Revelation. In Revelation κύριος ὁ θεός is used interchangeably for Christ and YHWH. Witherington, *Revelation*, 78. McDonough concludes that Christians in general and Jewish Christians in particular used κύριος for YHWH in the NT. McDonough, *YHWH at Patmos*, 98. The use of κύριος for יהוה is significant when it comes to the identity of Jesus Christ who is also called κύριος.

36. Barr, *Semantics of Biblical Language*, 115–19.

is specifically limited because it separates the history of the name from that of those who worshiped the God so named."[37] The name and what is associated with that name in history are both important.

Moses was terrified when God addressed him from the burning bush saying that he was the God of Abraham, Isaac, and Jacob (3:6). But soon Moses became very defensive when he heard the mission to which God was calling him. He began to make excuses (vv. 11, 13). When Moses asked God, "Who am I that I should go to Pharaoh or that I should bring Israel out?" (NET) suggesting he himself was weak, YHWH promises that he will be with Moses ("Surely, I will be with you"). He even gives a sign, which was that the people would come to worship him on this very mountain at a later stage (v. 12). YHWH gave further signs to Moses to prove to the people if they asked to see evidence for Moses' encounter with YHWH (4:2–9).

Moses' next excuse was that he did not know the name of God (v. 13), although YHWH had just told him that he was the God of his fathers. Could it be because God revealed himself to the fathers under different names as mentioned earlier and that Moses knew about it and now he is not sure which of those names to associate with the God who was speaking to him? Otherwise, who did he think the God of the fathers was? We can only guess whether or not Moses already knew the name of the God of Abraham, Isaac, and Jacob. It makes little sense if Moses already knew the identity of God as YHWH that he would ask that question. Had that been the case, we would expect some response from YHWH, similar to that of 4:14. Later we read that Moses and Aaron went to the people and performed the signs in front of them and they believed that it was YHWH who sent Moses (4:29–31). Moses is justified in asking YHWH his name because the people needed both the name and the evidence to prove that it was indeed YHWH who sent Moses to them.

In the following verses God addressed himself as the God of the fathers, he did so by prefacing it with YHWH: "YHWH, the God of your fathers" (3:16). Similarly, in 3:18, God is addressed as "YHWH, the God of the Hebrews." But that is not the case in 3:6 where the address begins with "I am the God of your father, the God of Abraham, the God of Isaac, and the God of Jacob." It may be concluded that, concerning Moses, this is the beginning of his knowledge of this name in an explicit sense. Henceforth, the name of the God of Israel will be known as אָנֹכִי

---

37. Saner, *"Too Much to Grasp,"* 30. See also Beitzel, "Exodus 3:14."

יְהוָה אֱלֹהֶיךָ "I am YHWH, your Elohim" (Exod 20:2, 5).[38] From this time on, YHWH spoke to the people of Israel, Pharaoh, and other nations through his messengers. This was quite different than the way God spoke individually with the patriarchs. It is the beginning of a new epoch in the history of Israel where their God was going to be known by this name YHWH.

In the passages that introduce God as "YHWH, the God of Israel" all such instances are either a call to action (Exod 5:1; 32:27; Jer 11:3; 25:25) or a declaration (both reassurance and warning: 1 Sam 2:30; 25:32; 1 Kgs 11:9; Jer 13:13–15; 21:4; 24:5; Ezek 44:2). Both are also seen in Exod 3:13–15 where God revealed himself to Moses and assured him of his presence. The association of his name with what he does makes even more sense if Exod 3:14–15 is taken in conjunction with Exod 20:24b—"In every place where I cause My name to be remembered, I will come to you and bless you" (NASB).[39] It is not man but YHWH himself who will make his name be remembered—a guarantee of his future action in and for the nation Israel.[40] Similar sense can be found in Exod 3:6–15 where YHWH heard the cry of the Israelites and was going to intervene on their behalf.[41] Further discussion on the identity of YHWH follows later.

YHWH not only identified himself to Moses by this name as his name forever (Exod 3:15), but also that he jealously guards his name and his reputation, both of which are known by who he is and what he does (2 Kgs 19:34; 20:6; Ps 23:3; Isa 48:9; 66:5; Ezek 20:9, 14, 22, 44; 36:22). His name reveals who YHWH is *en se* and how what he does is inherently associated with how he revealed himself to Moses.

---

38. Or "I, YHWH, am your God." It is worth noting that in the Decalogue YHWH is addressing each one of them individually as indicated by the singular suffix (אֱלֹהֶיךָ). He is not just the God of Israel, but each of their God. See chapters 3 and 4 of Saner's *"Too Much to Grasp"* for a detailed study to understand the revelation of YHWH to Moses.

39. Childs, *Book of Exodus*, 447. Childs suggests that it is better to take the *hifʿil* form here in the denominative meaning "to proclaim" in the sense of giving praises to YHWH.

40. Soulen, *Divine Name(s)*, 132–35.

41. Childs concludes that the paronomasia here does not mean indecisiveness; instead, it emphasizes the actuality of God in that he will be there where he is expected to be. Childs, *Book of Exodus*, 69.

Πατήρ

An answer to whether or not God was called πατήρ is not sufficient to adjudicate between the significance of the NT's use of πατήρ (on the lips of Jesus and in the NT writings) and "Father" as a reference to P1. A diachronic study of πατήρ is limited in its scope to answer satisfactorily the relationship between God as Father in the OT and Jesus' reference to God as Father in the ontological sense, and if any differences exist between these two addresses to God as Father (OT and NT).

Πατήρ in Jewish and Christian Contexts

Πατήρ is used in a number of ways in biblical and extrabiblical sources.[42] Πατήρ is used for the supreme deity who stands behind the origin and sustenance of all that exists (Job 38:28; Mal 2:10).[43] In the OT God is called "Father" to indicate God's care for the nation Israel (Exod 4:22; 18:4; 2 Sam 7:14). On few occasions during the intertestamental period God was called the "Father" of individuals (Sir 23:1, 4; Tob 13:4; Wis 2:16).[44] In LXX, πατήρ is used for God as the Father and creator of the nation Israel (Deut 32:6). Πατήρ in the NT was used for the Father of Jesus Christ (Matt 7:21) and as the Father of human beings (Matt 6:8).[45] During the patristic period, πατήρ was used generally and theologically. Generally, πατήρ was used for respectable men, Apostles, Fathers of the church, spiritual fathers, OT patriarchs, and Popes. Theologically, πατήρ was used for God the Father, God as the universal Father of all creation, Father of Christians, first person of the Trinity in relation to the second person, Christ as the Father of truth.[46] Theophilus of Antioch ascribes πατήρ to the Son—"But his Logos, through whom he made all things, who is his *Power and Wisdom* [1 Cor. 1:24], assuming the role of the

---

42. Lewis Sperry Chafer suggests that there are at least four different ways of understanding divine "Fatherhood" in the Bible: (1) Fatherhood over creation, (2) Fatherhood by intimate relationship with Israel, (3) the Father of the Lord Jesus Christ, and (4) Fatherhood over all who believe. Chafer, *Systematic Theology*, 311–17.

43. BDAG, 787. For a comprehensive treatment on Jesus' use and understanding of "Father" language in the NT, see Jeremias, *Jesus and the Message*; Hamerton-Kelly, *God the Father*; Thompson, *Promise of the Father*; Lee, *From Messiah to Preexistent Son*; Grindheim, *God's Equal*.

44. BDAG, 787.

45. LSJ, 1348.

46. Lampe, *Patristic Greek Lexicon*, 1050–51.

Father and Lord of the universe, was present in paradise in the role of God and conversed with Adam."[47]

Quell and Gottlob Schrenk interpret Jesus' use of "my Father in heaven" in Matt 18:19 and the Lord's Prayer in Matt 6:9 as a term of deeper personal designation, not as a substitute for the name of God.[48] They suggest that πατήρ was used for God in Hellenistic Judaism before the time of Christ and was always used for God's covenantal relationship with his people.[49] They contend that God was commonly addressed as "Father" in first century BC due to Platonic influence who called God the "Father of the universe."[50] "Father in heaven" was a common phrase in Palestinian synagogues (though it became common parlance during AD first century) and the address to God as "Father in heaven" was to distinguish him from earthly fathers.[51]

Jesus Did Not Call God **Father**

Joachim Jeremias suggests based on his reading of Sumerian and Akkadian hymns from Ur that the title "Father" was applied to God to indicate his status as both the creator and the sustainer. The ANE reference to God's "Father" figure meant what "Mother" signifies for our times.[52] It is in this sense of being the creator and the sustainer that God was called "Father" in the OT, argues Jeremias. Yet, there is one unique difference in the way God was called "Father" in the OT compared to the ANE concept—he was not thought of as "ancestor or progenitor," says Jeremias.[53]

47. *Autol.* 2.22. Théophile d'Antioche, *Trois livres à Autolycus*. English translation is from Grant, trans., *Theophilus of Antioch*, 63. Brackets in the original. Reference to his works follows standard abbreviations.

48. *TDNT*, 987.

49. *TDNT*, 5:979.

50. *TDNT*, 5:978.

51. *TDNT*, 5:980–81. The same is said about Jesus' use of "Abba Father" and "Father in heaven." Accordingly, Jesus was not necessarily identifying the first person of the Trinity; instead, he was addressing God as Father who is in heaven as opposed to the earthly fathers. However, a closer look at John 5:17–18 reveals that Jesus' address to God as Father had more connotation than just to distinguish him from earthly fathers. This point will be pursued in this chapter.

52. Jeremias, *Prayers of Jesus*, 11.

53. Jeremias, *Prayers of Jesus*, 12. Jeremias contends that Ps 2:7 refers to an act of adoption of the king as his son and not a reference to procreation. He makes a similar observation regarding the nation Israel being the "firstborn son"—this refers to Israel's unique relationship to God, which was grounded in his act of salvation on their behalf (Exod 4:22; Jer 31:9).

Jeremias suggests that the NT writers such as Matthew may have been influenced by rabbinic literature (Palestinian Judaism) of their time, especially that of Johanan B. Zakkai (c. AD 50–80) who first used the phrase "heavenly Father" for Israel's God.[54] According to this view, Matthew was the contemporary of Johanan and must have been influenced by his reference to God as " our heavenly Father" because Jesus certainly had not called God by that name.[55] His preferred address to God was *Abba*.[56] Jeremias contends that Jesus in fact considered this title for God so sacred he forbade his disciples from using it as a courtesy title in everyday use except for God (Matt 23:9). Jeremias attributes the differences in the Lord's Prayer in Matthew (Matthew uses "our Father in heaven") and Luke (earliest Lucan manuscripts do not have "our Father in heaven") to their respective Jewish and Gentile church backgrounds where they have heard these prayers being recited in catechumenal settings.[57]

Robert Hamerton-Kelly, following Paul Ricoeur's idea of symbols and criticism of Sigmund Freud's Oedipus (myth) view of the father (he views the rise of the father figure negatively), takes the father language for God in the Bible as a symbol.[58] It stands to reveal more of his relation-

54. Jeremias, *Prayers of Jesus*, 16–18.

55. Jeremias, *Prayers of Jesus*, 32–35.

56. Jeremias, *Prayers of Jesus*, 35–65. He believes that the first century addresses to God as "heavenly Father" in Palestinian Judaism supplies the necessary tradition for the Gospels' use of the title for God on Jesus' lips. Jesus overwhelmingly uses *Abba* in addressing God, according to Jeremias. This was something new that Jesus introduced because in Palestinian Judaism they did not address God as *Abba*. He suggests that Matthew added "our Father" in the Lord's Prayer and Lucan omission of it is considered original because the earliest manuscripts do not have ἡμῶν ὁ ἐν τοῖς οὐρανοῖς (39). The earliest Christians picked up this vocabulary (Rom 8:15–16; Gal 4:6) and continued Jesus' tradition. It emerges from this argument that much of the father language for God on Jesus' lips is suspect, at least, in its employment in the Gospels, especially in the Gospel of John. Jeremias does not see any ontological connection between the Father and the Son in the Trinitarian sense. Jesus was called God's Son because he called God his father. Such a conclusion is not only against the orthodox Christian tradition, but also against the very identity of the Christian God in the Bible. Jeremias has been a leading proponent of the view that Jesus called God *Abba*. Many follow suit and often cite his work as the authoritative source for this view. See also *TDNT*, 5:984.

57. Jeremias, *Prayers of Jesus*, 89. See also his discussion on which version of the Lord's prayer may have been original (89–95). In a sweeping conclusion, Jeremias attributes Johannine use of "Father" on Jesus' lips to what he calls the "retrospective" tradition in the Gospels, which came about due to the influence of the early Christian traditions about Christ (108). While it is hard to ascertain the *ipsissima verba*, it can certainly be attributed to the *ipsissima vox Jesu* (108–12).

58. Hamerton-Kelly, *God the Father*, 20–51. He suggests that there were both indirect and direct symbols for God in the OT. Until the time of Moses, it is the indirect

ship (often in redemptive settings) with the people (for example, Deut 32:1–43). He suggests that the father symbol is used both for God's anger (Jer 3:4–5, 19–20) and the basis of his pardon (Isa 63:16–17). Hamerton-Kelly believes that as a carpenter's son, Jesus found it easy to incorporate the language of father for God because he himself had seen how a son obeys his father and its place in family setting.[59] However, Jesus broke the patriarchal hierarchy of his time by assimilating women into his entourage and required his disciples to sever ties with their earthly fathers to be in the family of God just as he himself had done (Mark 3:31–35; cf. Matt 10:37; Mark 10:28–30; Luke 14:26). Jesus' use of the appellation "Father" for God is in the context of the kingdom. Because he called God his Father, he was called the Son.[60] Hamerton-Kelly also follows Jeremias conclusion that Jesus called God *Abba*. Accordingly, the reason Mark and Paul, writing to the gentiles who have no knowledge of the Aramaic title *Abba*, use this appellation for God is because Jesus himself must have used it.[61]

Discoveries from the Qumran texts show evidence for the first century use of "my father" and "father" for God. This evidence challenges the claims of Jeremias and Hamerton-Kelly, as the following section makes clear.

Jesus Called God **Father**

Recent scholarship, in light of Qumran texts, has questioned Jeremias's claim that "there is as yet no evidence in the literature of ancient Palestine Judaism that 'my Father' is used as a personal address to God."[62] This claim is based on Jeremias conclusion that any mention of the personal type—"you are my Father" or "our Father"—is a statement and not a vocative.[63] However, Qumran texts 4Q372 and 4Q460 attest to the fact that "my Father" was used for God before the time of Christ.[64] Eileen

---

father symbol that is ascribed to God. With Moses the story of the direct symbol begins in the history of Israel and Jesus is cognizant of this tradition of his fathers.

59. Hamerton-Kelly, *God the Father*, 55.
60. Hamerton-Kelly, *God the Father*, 71.
61. Hamerton-Kelly, *God the Father*, 72.
62. Jeremias, *Prayers of Jesus*, 29. For a summary of recent criticism of Jeremias's position, see Doering, "God as Father," 107–35.
63. Doering, "God as Father," 107.
64. Schuller and Bernstein, "372. 4QNarrative and Poetic Composition," 165–97;

Schuller presents a case against Jeremias's explication of *abba* as a child's address to his or her father from 4Q372 1 in which she points out that the appellation "my Father" for God clearly existed at least couple of centuries before the birth of Christ.[65] Barr and Géza Vermes similarly conclude that *abba* was not a childish language for God (something that Jeremias has alluded to), but it was the same word used for God by both adults and children. Children were trained to speak the language of the adults.[66]

While these Qumran texts in themselves do not prove that Jesus called God "my Father," it nevertheless casts doubts on Jeremias' argument that Jesus could not have called God "my Father" because such a precedent was nonexistent in Palestinian Judaism before Christ. Marianne Meye Thompson suggests, contrary to the claims of Jeremias and others (including the feminist arguments for an inclusive language for God that avoids the fatherhood), that it is reasonable to believe that Jesus did call God his Father.[67]

It is common among those who follow Jeremias's view to avoid placing the Johannine presentation of "my Father" or "the Father who sent me" upon Jesus' lips. Yet, Thompson devotes a chapter to John's Gospel and observes that Jesus' address to God as his Father in John needs to be understood functionally.[68] Jesus' affirmation of God as his Father cannot be divorced from God as the source of life and it is in this sense Jesus makes the claim, "For as the Father has life in himself, so he has granted the Son also to have life in himself" (John 5:26).[69] She concludes that there are at least two trajectories, namely, creedal and eschatological (or three if ecclesial trajectory is taken as independent of eschatological trajectory).

Larson, "460. 4QNarrative Work and Prayer," 369–86; Popovic, "God the Father," 125–30; Doering, "God as Father," 125–30.

65. Schuller, "372. Psalm of 4Q372 1," 75–79. Line 16 of 4Q372 reads, "He called to God the Mighty to save him from their hands and said, 'My father, my God, do not abandon me into the hands of the nations.'" This translation is taken from Schuller, "372. 4Q372 1: A Text," 355. According to Schuller, this Psalm about Joseph is not a reference to biblical Joseph in Genesis, but rather Joseph stands as a figure for the northern tribes. According to this assessment, this Psalm sets the Jerusalem community against the community centered at Mt. Gerizim, see Schuller, "372. Psalm of 4Q372 1," 69. Josephus similarly uses the appellation "Father" for God. Mladen Popovic suggests that Josephus was influenced by his ancestral traditions contrary to the claim that Josephus was heavily influenced by Stoic thought. Popovic, "God the Father," 193, 96.

66. Barr, "'Abbā Isn't 'Daddy,'" 28–47; Vermès, *Jesus and the World*.

67. Thompson, *Promise of the Father*, 67.

68. Thompson, *Promise of the Father*, 135–37.

69. Thompson, *Promise of the Father*, 141–44.

The creedal trajectory starts with the creeds of the church, mainly based on the NT. The eschatological trajectory begins with God's dealing with Israel in the OT and ends in the eschaton when God's promises to be the Father of the faithful will be realized.[70]

It is important to note some of her observations with regard to whether "Father" is a metaphor for God's love and care or a name for God. For Thompson, Jesus' references and addresses to God do not present a new name for God or understanding about him. In fact, "the historical contexts of Jesus' own day, as well as the New Testament data themselves, mitigate against the claim that the name of God is Father or Father, Son, and Holy Spirit."[71] The NT authors did not take Father to be a name for God. "There is little evidence to justify the assertion that in the New Testament Father or even Father, Son and Holy Spirit, is the new name for God, or a name that precluded address to God in any other form."[72] She concludes that Father can be ascribed to God without it assuming the status as "the new or revealed name" of God.[73] Here, she follows Jeremias.

Missing in her treatment is a discussion on *perichoresis* (John 17:21) and its significance for Jesus' identity, or in what sense Jesus made himself equal to God by calling him his Father (John 5:18), or what Jesus meant by "so now, Father, glorify me in your own presence with the glory that I had in your presence before the world existed" (John 17:5 NRSV). Aquila Lee concludes in critiquing Jeremias and Thompson that although there have been attempts to place Jesus' use of "Father" for God within the OT and early Jewish framework, there is enough evidence to suggest that Jesus' address to God did not emerge primarily from such a background; instead, Jesus' view emerges from his personal conviction and unique position as the Son of God.[74] Had this not been the case, the Jewish leaders' reaction would be unfounded because they were particularly agitated by the fact that Jesus made himself equal to God when he called God his Father. That was not the case when the appellation Father was applied to God in the canonical texts of the OT and in the extrabiblical instances. This could be because he sees an ontological difference in both of these addresses to God.[75]

70. Thompson, *Promise of the Father*, 155–64.
71. Thompson, *Promise of the Father*, 176.
72. Thompson, *Promise of the Father*, 177.
73. Thompson, *Promise of the Father*, 177.
74. Lee, *From Messiah to Preexistent Son*, 179–80.
75. Lee, *From Messiah to Preexistent Son*, 129. "To his mind the oneness of Godhead is principally and foundationally established in the proper perception that God

It can be reasonably argued that the appellation "my Father" or "Father" for God was known in first century Judaism. However, a closer look at Jesus' own use of the "Father" for God is necessary to establish the various ways in which the appellation "Father" was used for God in the NT.

A Closer Look

The argument against Jesus' designation of God as his Father was based on the idea that there was no historical precedence, and it is hardly a viable option.[76] *Abba*, instead, was the popular title for fathers and Jesus must have followed that convention. Findings from Qumran challenge that view, and the idea of Jesus calling God his Father is now taken to be quite possible because there is evidence, even if scant, to such designation for God.

A treatment on the ontological aspect of the Fatherhood of God is seriously lacking in these studies. Did Jesus simply call God his Father in the same sense God was called the Father of Israel? Or, did Jesus reveal a Trinitarian ontological aspect in the sense that when he called God his Father he was addressing the first person of the Trinity? How one views the identity of YHWH largely depends on the answers to these questions. Jesus' reference to God as his Father needs to be taken in the ontological sense. He was referring to the first person of the Trinity in most of those occurrences. An exception appears when he makes a general statement such as in Matt 6:9 and John 8:41–42.[77]

In John 5:17 Jesus claims, "My Father is working until now, and I too am working." Upon hearing this, the Jewish leaders wanted to kill

---

is ontologically the Father and the Son is ontologically God, and the one God is the Father begetting the Son" (Weinandy, *Athanasius*, 73). Athanasius sees the Fatherhood of God as eternal; therefore, God in that economy must also be Father, Son, and Spirit just as he is so *en se*.

76. Two preliminary observations are in order. First, the discussion on the OT development of the idea of the fatherhood of God follows the basic arguments of documentary hypothesis. See, for example, Hamerton-Kelly, *God the Father*, 40, 50. Second, the discussion on the NT idea of Fatherhood, whether that is from Jesus or his followers, appropriates source criticism and redaction criticism. Hence, Jeremias was able to argue for Mark's use of *abba* as original and Matthew's use of "our Father in heaven" at the beginning of the Lord's Prayer as being influenced by the theology of his particular Christian community. See, for example, Jeremias, *Prayers of Jesus*, 37–38.

77. *TDNT*, 5:978–81. See also, Lowery, "God as Father," 157–58, 177–79, 361–67. Lowery suggests that Matthew uses "Father" in 6:7–15 as a surrogate for the Tetragrammaton. Also, Matthew sometimes uses "Father" in the OT sense of God's covenantal relationship and caring character.

Jesus. In v. 18, John tells us the specific reason they wanted to kill Jesus: "For this reason the Jews were seeking all the more to kill him, because he was not only breaking the sabbath, but was also calling God his own Father, thereby making himself equal to God" (NRSV). It is important to note how the present active participle ποιῶν is translated here. It is translated as a "participle of result"[78] and this is significant theologically. But commentators like Marianne Meye Thompson overlook its significance in exposition.[79]

If the participial force is retained in translation, it shows something more in the text than what Thompson shows. Her interpretation of John 5:16–18 concludes that Jesus was making himself equal to God by working (healing) on the Sabbath, which according to Philo and the rabbis was God's prerogative alone.[80] If breaking the Sabbath alone constituted their anger, John did not have to mention the additional reason for their anger because he had already mentioned it at the beginning of v. 18 ("he not only was breaking the Sabbath"). It is clear from the passage that there were two reasons for them wanting to kill Jesus: (1) Jesus broke the Sabbath by healing the paralytic, and (2) he called God his own Father, thereby he made himself equal to God.[81]

In John 5:19–30, Jesus further explicates his equality with God, but with one decisive difference—in these verses Jesus was revealing more of why his healing of the man on the Sabbath did not amount to breaking the Sabbath. These verses explicate v. 17 in which Jesus provides the rationale for healing on the Sabbath, that is, the Father has been working until now and I too am working. In vv. 19–30, Jesus continues to emphasize that what he does is in accordance with the Father's will and direction. Although these verses could also reveal how Jesus is still equal to the Father even in incarnation, they do not necessarily explain why Jewish leaders took offense at Jesus calling God his own Father because they must have been familiar with such appellation for God on the lips of pious Jews. They sensed something inherently different here because this was not the first time God was called Father (as seen in biblical and extrabiblical

---

78. Wallace, *Greek Grammar Beyond the Basics*, 638. See also Köstenberger, *John*, 186n52.

79. Thompson, *John*, 119, 123–25. See also Barrett, *Gospel according to St. John*, 256. Although the translation "making" can bring out the internal or logical result participle, it is better to state it explicitly.

80. Thompson, *John*, 123–25.

81. Grindheim, *God's Equal*, 1.

sources). They must have understood it to be more than merely calling God Father because elsewhere they say, "We have only one Father, God himself" (John 8:41–42). Jesus' healing on the Sabbath, which to the Jewish leaders showed utter disregard for Sabbath observance (thus breaking the law), coupled with his address of God as his own Father must have convinced them that Jesus was alluding to an ontological relation—an incomprehensible and blasphemous statement for a Jew.[82] It is safe to say that in Jesus' use of the appellation "Father" for God, he introduced a new kind of understanding about God. Jesus' equality with the Father became a contentious matter for the Jewish leaders.[83]

When Jesus forgave the sin of the paralytic in Mark 2:5, the Jewish leaders immediately labeled it a blasphemy because God alone forgave sin (v. 7); in their eyes, Jesus had wrongfully usurped such an authority.[84] Jesus' prerogative to forgive sin differentiated from that of his disciples by the addition that whatever they forgive on earth will be forgiven in heaven as well (cf. Matt 16:19; 18:18).[85] The disciples did not appear to be offering forgiveness on their own, but forgiveness of sin is attributed to God (Acts 8:22; 13:38; 26:18).[86] Only God can forgive sins and Jesus, by virtue of forgiving the paralytic his sins, claimed equality with God. When Jesus called God Father, he was not only revealing that equality with the Father, but also addressing the first person of the Trinity as he was doing what only God could do.

The differences in our relationship to God the Father becomes even more apparent in Jesus' interaction with Philip in John 14. Jesus tells the disciples that, "There are many dwelling places in my Father's house" (v. 2) and he was going to prepare a place for them in his Father's house. Once he prepares the house, Jesus says, "I will come again to take you to be with me" (v. 3). Then Jesus says, "And you know the way" (v. 4). Hearing Jesus'

82. Köstenberger, *John*, 185–86. Jesus was later accused of this very thing in that he called God his Father (John 10:33; 19:7). The ontological aspect (intra-Trinitarian language) becomes clearer when we read John 1:1, 14, 18; 8:58; 10:30; 14:10–11; 17:5, 21; cf. Matt 3:17; 17:5; 2 Pet 1:17.

83. For a comparison of Jesus' identity and claims to authority with the Mosaic law and what it does to the OT Scriptures, see Bockmuehl, *Jewish Law*, 23–48; Bockmuehl, "God's Life as a Jew," 60–78.

84. For a detailed study on how the OT and extrabiblical Jewish literature understand forgiveness of sin, see Grindheim, *God's Equal*, 65–76. God has been the explicit or implicit subject whenever סלח is used in the OT because God alone can forgive sin. Olivier, "סלח," 259–63; Kaiser, "סלח," 627. See also Milgrom, *Leviticus 1–16*, 245.

85. Grindheim, *God's Equal*, 67.

86. Grindheim, *God's Equal*, 68.

statement that they already know the way, Thomas responds by saying in effect, "Contrary to what you just said, we do not in fact know the way" (v. 5). To which Jesus answers, "I am the way, and the truth, and the life. No one comes to the Father except through me. If you have known me, you will know my Father too. And from now on you do know him and have seen him" (vv. 6–7). The phrase "from now on" is worth noting. The particular knowledge concerning the Father that the disciples are given is something new. They did not possess this knowledge before. The statement "from now on you know him and have seen him" also reveals the fact that the disciples' knowledge of the Father is intimately tied to their knowledge of Jesus—not only theirs, but also the knowledge of everyone else. This is quite different from Jesus' own access to the Father. He and the Father are one (John 10:30).

The fact that their only access to the Father is through the Son becomes even clearer in Jesus' reply to Philip's request to "show us the Father" (v. 8). Jesus insists that his words and deeds were not his own; instead "the Father residing in me performs his miraculous deeds" (v. 10). After mentioning the mutual indwelling of the Father and the Son (v. 11), Jesus reveals something very important regarding our access to the Father. First, he states that he will do whatever we ask in *his name* for the Father's glory (v. 13). He reiterates that in v. 14, again emphasizing the phrase "in my name." Second, he states that, "If anyone loves me, he will keep my word, and my Father will love him, and we will come to him and will make our dwelling place with him" (v. 23).[87] The Father and the Son indwell a believer just as the Holy Spirit does (cf. 1 Cor 3:16).

In light of John 14, it can be deduced that (1) the knowledge of God the Father is available only through the Son, but (2) the Son knows the Father filially, therefore (3) any human knowledge and relation to the Father is different from that of the Son. Even when Christians address P1, they do so on a different level from that of the Son.[88] They are encouraged

---

87. The significance of this passage cannot be overstated. It reveals the fact that the Father, Son, and Spirit indwell a believer (cf. 1 Cor 3:16). It also tells us that our knowledge of God the Father (P1) and access to him is only through Jesus and it continues to be so. Even when we address the Father (P1), we do so through the Son. It may be deduced from this that a prayer to the Son is as good as a prayer to the Father, Son, and Spirit because one is not without the other two; there is a mutual indwelling.

88. Lashier, *Irenaeus on the Trinity*, 58. Lashier observes that the "writers of the Gospels, for example, had used the title 'Father' not to discuss God's creative function, or any other function for that matter, but to discuss his unique, filial relationship to the Second Person and, his analogous, salvific relationship to human beings as a result of this filial relationship."

to pray to P1 through Jesus. Christian prayer to Jesus or worship of Jesus, according to this passage, is not the worship of just one person, but all three persons. The prayer is addressed to the Son and the Son answers the prayer to glorify the Father (vv. 13–14; cf. Phil 2:11).

In John 17:5, 21, Jesus makes even more explicit what he meant when he called God his Father. In v. 5 Jesus talks about the glory he had with the Father before incarnation. Some see it as John's appropriation of a formula found in paganism,[89] while others see it as a legitimate reference to Jesus' preincarnate state.[90] The argument that this is a reference to Jesus' preincarnate state of glory makes better sense if one takes into consideration John's stated objective in the Gospel—"so that you may believe that Jesus is the Christ, the Son of God" (20:31). When John 17:5 with 17:21 are compared, the picture that emerges is even clearer. There is oneness between the Father and the Son, and this was not a new phenomenon.[91]

The emphasis on the mutual indwelling (*perichoresis*) of the Father and the Son also explains the basis for Jesus' claim that "the Father and I are one." Jesus wanted his disciples and the world to know that the Father has sent him.[92] Jesus makes it clear to his disciples that no one knows the Son except the Father and no one knows the Father except the Son and those to whom the Son reveals P1 (Matt 11:27). If it were just about God in the OT, then it would not have made much sense, for God had already revealed himself to Moses (Exod 3:14–15; 6:2–3) and to the nation Israel through him and the prophets after him (for example, Isa 45:21–23). Thus, Jesus' appellation "Father" for God must certainly include the new revelation—God the Father as the Father of the Son.[93]

---

89. Haenchen, *John*, 2:151–52.

90. Carson, *John*, 557; Thompson, *John*, 350–51; Köstenberger, *John*, 489–90.

91. Carson, *John*, 568.

92. Haenchen, *John*, 2:155; Thompson, *John*, 356. The world may not have understood what Jesus meant when he called God his Father, but the disciples are told that they have been given this unique revelation (Matt 16:17).

93. Robert Jenson writes, "There are also, to be sure, numerous candidates to be 'Father' or 'Spirit', but within the Trinitarian name, 'the Father' is not primarily *our* Father, but the Father of the immediately next-named Son, that is, of Jesus." Jenson, *Triune Identity*, 17. See also chapter 4 of his book for a detailed argument for the uniqueness of "Father" in the NT.

New Testament Understanding of YHWH

The focus in this section is on the few crucial passages that explain the identity of YHWH from the NT perspective and the NT appropriation of OT passages that have YHWH as the referent. The selection of passages is limited to those I consider important to explain my point and strengthen my argument for the triune identity of YHWH.

A Closer Look at Some NT Texts

The New Testament argues that Jesus reveals the one true God of the Old Testament and he reveals him as the Father, Son, and Spirit—"he who has seen me has seen the Father" (John 1:18; 10:30; 14:7–11; 17:21; 1 Cor 8:6; Eph 4:4–6; Phil 2:9–11; cf. Isa 45:18–25).[94] John 1:18 unmistakably presents Jesus as the one revealing the identity of YHWH. Once the textual variants and syntactical problems of this verse are sorted out, a picture emerges of the same God who was revealed in Exod 3:14 (ὁ ὤν) as the one revealing himself in John 1:18 (ὁ ὤν). John states it is the μονογενὴς θεός who is revealing the only God (here God is a reference to the triune God) and he was in the Father's (P1) bosom.[95] John's appropriation of ὁ ὤν of Exod 3:14 needs to be viewed as a deliberate allusion to YHWH given the telos of his Gospel to make a strong case for Jesus as the Christ and the Son of God (20:31). Paul McReynolds translates John 1:18 as "No one has ever seen God (*YHWH*); the only begotten (P2), God (P2), the

---

94. Father is YHWH, Jesus is YHWH, and Holy Spirit is YHWH.

95. καὶ εἶπεν ὁ θεὸς πρὸς Μωυσῆν Ἐγώ εἰμι ὁ ὤν· καὶ εἶπεν Οὕτως ἐρεῖς τοῖς υἱοῖς Ισραηλ Ὁ ὢν ἀπέσταλκέν με πρὸς ὑμᾶς (Exod 3:14) versus Θεὸν οὐδεὶς ἑώρακεν πώποτε· μονογενὴς θεὸς ὁ ὢν εἰς τὸν κόλπον τοῦ πατρὸς ἐκεῖνος ἐξηγήσατο (John 1:18). John 1:18 has three textual variants: ὁ μονογενὴς υἱός, ὁ μονογενὴς θεός, and μονογενὴς θεός. NA[28], 293. From internal evidence it can be concluded that the scribal tendency would be to use ὁ μονογενὴς υἱός because it is already part of Johannine Christology (3:16, 18; 4:9) and substituting θεός for υἱός is uncharacteristic of this tendency. ὁ μονογενὴς θεός (with the article) is smoother reading compared to μονογενὴς θεός and the scribal tendency is to smooth things out rather than to opt for a difficult and hard reading. μονογενὴς θεός is supported by the earliest and best sources. It is the harder and unnatural reading. Given the scribal tendency to smoothen out a reading, the harder reading is preferred. Anarthrous use of θεός is not uncommon in John (1:1c, 6, 12; 3:2, 21; 9:16). See also Köstenberger, *John*, 50. Morris thinks there should be a comma after μονογενής; thus, "giving three titles of Christ: Only begotten, God, he who is in the bosom of the Father," Morris, *John*, 101. Morris believes that the copula "is" expresses a continuing union between the Father and the Son.

one (P2) in the Bosom of the Father (P1), that one (P2) has explained him (*YHWH*)" (italics mine).[96] No one except God could reveal himself.[97]

Paul, alluding to the Shema, writes that there is only one God and he identifies this God as the Father, Son, and Spirit (Rom 3:30; Gal 3:20 cf. Rom 5:1, 5; 1 Cor 8:6; Eph 4:4–6).[98] The "story that undergirds the references to the Fatherhood of God in Paul's letters is the story of Jesus, and the Father's relationship to him, not the story of Israel as a nation and God's relationship to Israel."[99] The NT is not presenting a different God but a new way of understanding the one true God who was revealed in the OT.[100]

Concerning Jesus, Paul writes in Phil 2:9–11, "For this reason also, God highly exalted Him, and bestowed on Him the name which is above every name, so that at the name of Jesus every knee will bow, of those who are in heaven and on earth and under the earth, and that every tongue will confess that Jesus Christ is Lord, to the glory of God the Father"

---

96. This indicates my interpretation of this verse and not McReynolds's. McReynolds, "John 1:18," 115. McReynolds presents a very detailed study on the history of the textual variants and concludes that both external and internal evidence are in support of μονογενὴς θεός.

97. Similarly, Exod 23:20–23 and Mal 3:1 speak of an angel/messenger of YHWH sent ahead of him to prepare the way, which in the NT is applied to Jesus (Mal 3:1; Exod 23:20; Isa 40:3–5; cf. Matt 11:10; Mark 1:2). Mal 4:5 identifies the messenger who is sent ahead of the LORD as Elijah whom Jesus identifies as John the Baptist (Matt 11:10; Luke 1:17). See Cassuto, *Exodus*, 305–6. Cassuto identifies the angel of God with YHWH himself.

98. Dunn, *Christology in the Making*, 179. Dunn opines that Paul had Deut 6:4 as the background in 1 Cor 8:6. Cf. MacDonald, *Deuteronomy*, 95–96. MacDonald suggests that Paul's reflections in 1 Cor 8:6 may be a better frame of reference to understand Deut 6:4b as opposed to the view that Deut 6:4b is about "monotheism." Hurtado comments that in Paul's understanding of Jesus' Sonship there is an understanding of God's direct involvement with the Son in accordance with the Christian and Jewish traditions. Hurtado, *Lord Jesus Christ*, 22. Commenting on 1 Cor 8:5–6 Hurtado writes, "Paul's easy inclusion of devotion to Christ within his emphatically monotheistic posture nicely illustrated the intriguing nature of early Christ-devotion. For Paul and for many other Jewish and Gentile Christians of the time, it appears devotion to Christ was compatible with a vigorously monotheistic faith and practice." Hurtado, *Lord Jesus Christ*, 48–49.

99. Witherington and Ice, *Shadow of the Almighty*, 34.

100. Gunton, *Father, Son, and Holy Spirit*, 6–7. Gunton writes, "The New Testament shows quite clearly that the first Christians, who were almost universally Jews also, had no difficulty in believing that the God they worshipped through Jesus was the same as the one they had always known. They did not find a new God, but a new and living way of knowing him." Gunton, *Father, Son, and Holy Spirit*, 4.

(NASB).¹⁰¹ This is almost exactly the same as what is said of YHWH in Isa 45:21–23:

> Declare and set forth your case; Indeed, let them consult together. Who has announced this from of old? Who has long since declared it? Is it not I, the LORD? And there is no other God besides Me, A righteous God and a Savior; There is none except Me. Turn to Me and be saved, all the ends of the earth; For I am God, and there is no other. I have sworn by Myself, The word has gone forth from My mouth in righteousness And will not turn back, That to Me every knee will bow, every tongue will swear allegiance. (NASB)¹⁰²

By attributing to Jesus what was once exclusively referred to YHWH, Paul is revealing the New Testament conviction that this Jesus is one with YHWH and is identified in the identity of the one true God of Israel.¹⁰³ Richard Bauckham argues that "with the inclusion of Jesus in the unique identity of YHWH, the faith of the *Shema* is affirmed and maintained, but everything the *Shema* requires of God's people is now focused on Jesus."¹⁰⁴ This association of Jesus with YHWH makes even more sense when we observe how the NT attributes OT passages to Jesus that were once attributed to YHWH.¹⁰⁵

In 1 Cor 10:9, Paul argues that the Israelites tested Christ in the wilderness (cf. Jude vv. 4–5 and Num 21:5–9). If the original reading is

---

101. N. T. Wright comments that Phil 2:9–11 reveals what was rightfully Jesus' all along. "For consider: if the God who will not share his glory with another has now shared it with Jesus (the position asserted in 2:9ff.), then there are only three possible conclusions that can be drawn. It might be the case that there are now two Gods. Or Jesus—who up until then had been a man and nothing but a man—might now have been totally absorbed into the one God without remainder (so to speak). Or there might be a sense—requiring fuller investigation, exploration, and clarification, no doubt—in which Jesus, in being exalted to the rank described in 2:9ff., is receiving no more than that which was always, from before the beginning of time, his by right." Wright, *Climax of the Covenant*, 94.

102. Yeago, "New Testament," 153. Yeago argues that "the ancient theologians were right to hold that the Nicene *homoousion* is neither imposed *on* the New Testament, nor distantly deduced *from* the texts, but rather describes a pattern of judgements present *in* the texts, in the texture of scriptural discourse concerning Jesus and the God of Israel."

103. Aageson, *Written Also for Our Sake*, 22. Aageson argues that, for Paul, God is one and this one God is the God of Israel.

104. Bauckham, *Jesus and the God*, 106.

105. McDonough, *YHWH at Patmos*, 126–28. Note especially McDonough's observations regarding why Jesus is given the name above every name because the highest name in the OT was that of YHWH.

Χριστόν, it has theological significance.[106] After analyzing the internal and the external evidence of 1 Cor 10:9, Carroll D. Osburn concludes that,

> While the external evidence is certainly in favour of Χριστόν as far as weight and diversity are concerned, Χριστόν can also be demonstrated as preferable on internal grounds. A good and reasonable claim can be made that κύριον, which has every appearance of being a theologically motivated alteration to the text, is of Eastern origin in the later third century.[107]

If the harder reading (Christ) is original, then a good case can be made that for Paul the identity of Christ is inseparably tied to the identity of YHWH. This makes even better sense because he has already asserted that Christ was present during the wilderness journey (1 Cor 10:4).[108] The NT references such as these necessitate a reconsideration of the dominant way of thinking of YHWH in the OT as P1.

Jude 5 opens another window on the NT understanding of the deliverance of Israel from Egypt, thus the identity of YHWH. Scholars are conflicted as to what the best reading of Jude 5 might be and this is evident in the choices between NA[27] and NA[28]. NA[27] reads Ὑπομνῆσαι δὲ ὑμᾶς βούλομαι, εἰδότας [ὑμᾶς] πάντα, ὅτι [ὁ] κύριος ἅπαξ λαὸν ἐκ γῆς Αἰγύπτου σώσας τὸ δεύτερον τοὺς μὴ πιστεύσαντας ἀπώλεσεν ("you have known all things once for all that the Lord after saving people from the land of Egypt, later destroyed those who did not believe").[109] But, subsequently, NA[28] replaced κύριος with Ἰησοῦς and the text reads

106. Two variant readings appear in some sources: κύριον is found in ℵ B C P 33. 104. 326. 365. 1175. 2464 sy[hmg]. θεόν is found in A 81. The text of NA[28] Χριστόν is found in 𝔓[46] D F G K L Ψ 630. 1241. 1505. 1739. 1881. 𝔐 latt sy co; Ir[lat] Or[1739mg] and enjoys earliest and best support with wider geographical distribution. It is also the harder reading. The scribal tendency is to prefer a smoother reading.

107. Osburn, "Text of 1 Corinthians 10:9," 212. Paul's interpretation seems to emerge from his strong conviction of the inseparability of the identity of YHWH and Jesus Christ. In Deut 6:16, Moses reminds the Israelites not to test the Lord as they did at Massah. One can see why scribes want to make the reading compatible with the OT text of Num 21:5–9 and Deut 6:16. For a detailed analysis of the textual variants here, see Zuntz, *Text of the Epistles*; McReynolds, "John 1:18." Comparing Jude 5 (textual variants are also found, but NA[28] makes a compelling statement by preferring to use Ἰησοῦς instead of κύριος as found in NA[27]) with Paul's statement makes a similar claim that Jesus saved the people out of the land of Egypt.

108. See chapter 4 for a theological interpretation of this passage.

109. See the text-critical notes in NA[27] and NA[28] for the supporting evidence for each of the readings. Since NA[28] has determined Ἰησοῦς to be the original reading, I have spared the space to do critical evaluation of the different readings because I simply want to acknowledge the move as important contextually and theologically.

Ὑπομνῆσαι δὲ ὑμᾶς βούλομαι, εἰδότας ὑμᾶς ἅπαξ πάντα ὅτι Ἰησοῦς λαὸν ἐκ γῆς Αἰγύπτου σώσας τὸ δεύτερον τοὺς μὴ πιστεύσαντας ἀπώλεσεν ("you have known these facts/things once-for-all that Jesus having saved/after saving the people from the land of Egypt, later/subsequently destroyed those who did not believe").[110]

If Ἰησοῦς in NA[28] is the original reading (if the original text claims that Jesus rescued the people of Israel from Egypt, then some scribes might have found it to be too difficult a claim, especially if the scribes were of Jewish background), then it is theologically significant as it further clarifies the NT's understanding of the identity of YHWH. This reading makes better sense too because in v. 4 Jude had warned about those who deny "our only Master[111] and Lord, Jesus Christ" who had already infiltrated their group. In v. 5, he is making the case even stronger by pointing to the subsequent destruction of those who rebelled against Jesus after he had delivered them from Egypt. Similar misfortune will befall those who now deny Jesus Christ because they are already marked out for destruction. So they must beware that they too do not fall into their deception. If this is the original reading, then this is significant from the point of the NT in that there is no difference between YHWH and Ἰησοῦς—both are said to have delivered the people of Israel from Egypt. It is possible only if Jesus is identified with YHWH himself, something Phil 2:9–11 also suggests.

Revelation 1:4 and 8 present another case for the inclusion of Jesus Christ in the identity of YHWH. McDonough presents a compelling study on Rev 1:4. He concludes that this passage is referring to YHWH and that John could not speak of YHWH without also mentioning Jesus.[112] In 1:8 "who is and who was and who is to come" is prefaced with "I am the Alpha and the Omega," which is to say that he is the first and the last. Then in 1:17, the "one like the Son of man" who was speaking to John addressed himself to John as the "first and the last," an echo of 1:8, which is made even clearer in 22:13. John could easily make the connection here between 1:8 and 1:17. Moreover, if it was the same John who wrote John 1:18, then it was quite possible for him to make the connection between the ὁ ὤν of Exod 3:14, John 1:18, and Rev 1:4, 8. This is further evident in John's quote of Zech 12:10 in Rev 1:7. It is YHWH who is the referent

---

110. My own translation.

111. Some later sources have θεὸν (P ¥ 5. 88. 1175. 1448. 1611. 1735. 2492 Å sy) after δεσπότην, although this reading does not enjoy much external support.

112. McDonough, *YHWH at Patmos*, 195–233.

in Zech 12:8–10 and now John is applying the same to Jesus, making the implicit connection explicit—in the identity of YHWH one sees the presence and identity of Jesus and the Spirit (cf. Isa 63:10–14).

OT Quotations in the NT

The question of how to view the OT quotations in the NT divides scholars.[113] For this study, the need is to identify NT examples to illustrate that what was once said of YHWH is now said of Jesus. The reason for this change in referent from YHWH to Jesus is due to the fact that the identity of Jesus is inseparably tied to the identity of YHWH as the triune God.[114] Generally, in quotations from the OT, where MT reads יהוה, the NT has κύριος.[115] In the NT, many of these quotations directly apply to Jesus although the original context had YHWH as the referent.[116] From the NT's perspective, it was not an infraction on the identity of YHWH because Jesus himself had made several claims to that effect (Luke 24:44–45; John 5:38–47, etc.).[117]

---

113. Cf. Kaiser, *Uses of the Old Testament*; Porter, *Hearing the Old Testament*; Moyise, *Old Testament in the New*.

114. For a detailed look at the christological reading of YHWH texts, see Bauckham, *God of Israel*, 186–232.

115. McDonough, *YHWH at Patmos*, 97. Cf. McDonough with Howard. Howard, "Tetragram," 63, 65–66, 74–83. Howard hypothesizes that the NT quotations and allusions to the OT originally contained YHWH before they were replaced with κύριος in AD second century (Howard's claim that the Christian OT [LXX] originally had יהוה instead of κύριος is labeled a hypothesis without any manuscript evidence). McDonough, *YHWH at Patmos*, 97n205.

116. There are also implicit and indirect references to Jesus' equality with YHWH in the NT. For example, see Geddert, "Implied YHWH Christology," 325–40. Geddert believes that "Mark deliberately embedded an exceedingly high Christology (Jesus is God; Jesus is, in fact, the embodiment YHWH) within his narrative but did so only by implication, attested to only by hints and pointers, so that those who want to resist this conclusion are able to do so." Geddert, "Implied YHWH Christology," 327.

117. How one understands Jesus' claim to the OT influences one's view of how the NT uses OT quotations. Luke reports Jesus' conversation with the two people on the Emmaus road (Luke 24:13–31). Notice that instead of beginning with himself, Jesus begins with the Scripture (the authority is the very OT Scriptures that present YHWH as the only God). During the conversation, Jesus explains to them the things written concerning himself in all Scriptures, beginning with Moses (v. 27). Afterwards, Jesus appears in their midst and reminds them what he had told them earlier concerning Christ's suffering according to the Scriptures (vv. 44–47). Luke provides a commentary on what was happening to the disciples in v. 45: "Then He opened their minds to understand the Scriptures" (NASB; "Scriptures" here is a reference to the OT Scriptures).

A few examples are in order to substantiate this point. Matthew 3:3 makes a statement concerning the identity of Jesus and John the Baptist by quoting Isa 40:3 ("A voice is calling, 'Clear the way for the Lord in the wilderness; Make smooth in the desert a highway for our God'" [NASB]). The Isaiah passage has YHWH as the referent of "the way of the LORD" and Matthew has Jesus Christ as the referent of "the way of the Lord" (cf. Matt 11:10; Mark 1:3; Luke 3:4–6; John 1:23). Later, Jesus confirms John's identity: "This is the one about whom it is written, 'Behold, I send My messenger ahead of You, Who will prepare Your way before You'" (Matt 11:10 NASB cf. Isa 40:3; Mal 3:1). In Isaiah and Malachi, YHWH (the LORD of hosts) was the referent before whom a messenger would be sent. By ascribing to Jesus what was said concerning YHWH, the NT is making it clear that Jesus is YHWH (Jesus means YHWH saves).

On the day of Pentecost (Acts 2:21), Peter declared that everyone who calls on the name of the Lord will be saved. This is a quotation from Joel 2:32 where the referent is בְּשֵׁם יְהוָה ("on the name of YHWH"). Compare this with Peter's comments concerning salvation in the name of Jesus (Acts 4:12): "And there is salvation in no one else; for there is no other name under heaven that has been given among men by which we must be saved" (NASB). Peter makes the explicit connection between YHWH and Jesus when he juxtaposed the name of YHWH and the name of Jesus in whose name alone there is salvation.[118]

Romans 10:9–13 is another succinct example of Jesus occupying the space once YHWH occupied.[119] In v. 9, Paul says, "If you confess with your mouth Jesus as Lord, and believe in your heart that God raised Him from the dead, you will be saved" (NASB). By observing the object-complement construction in Rom 10:9 as equivalent to subject-predicate clause, Daniel B. Wallace argues that Ἰησοῦν is the object and κύριον is the complement here. He concludes, "The confession would be that Jesus

---

They no longer look at those Scriptures the same way they used to but a new kind of understanding has dawned. The life, death, and resurrection of Christ significantly affect the understanding of the very OT Scriptures with which the disciples were already familiar, and which testified to him. See also Murray, "Christ in/and the Old Testament," 1–22. Each of the five scholars who contributed to this article makes the central claim that the NT's understanding of Christ as an interpretation of the OT's terminus and telos is theologically appropriate because in the identity of YHWH we see the identity of the Father, Son, and Spirit.

118. Marshall, "Acts," 536.

119. Wallace, *Greek Grammar beyond the Basics*, 187–88; Wallace, "Semantics and Exegetical Significance," 91–112.

is *the* Lord, that is, *Yahweh*."[120] In v. 13, Paul repeats the identity of the referent "Lord" again—it is Jesus who is YHWH (Isa 28:16; Joel 2:32). Paul is explicitly clear that in the confession of "Jesus as Lord" one is confessing "Jesus as YHWH," and salvation is contingent on this particular confession.

These few examples are representative of most similar OT quotes in NT. They are sufficient to establish the fact the NT equates the identity of Jesus with the identity of YHWH. The reason NT writers did not find the application of the OT passages to Jesus problematic was because to them, the identity of Jesus is included in the identity of YHWH himself.[121] They did not find Jesus' claims of equality with the Father (first person of the Trinity) or YHWH himself preposterous. Identifying Jesus with YHWH also substantiates Jesus' own claims that the OT was about him. In other words, Jesus was saying that when the OT bears witness to YHWH, it is essentially witnessing to him because Jesus is YHWH just as much the Father and the Spirit are also YHWH. From this viewpoint, it is possible for the NT writers and the early church to find the presence of Christ in the OT. Such a conclusion was not pure naivete but grounded in clear and decisive understanding *of* and belief *in* who Jesus claimed to be. To overcome the isolationist tendency in Trinitarian interpretation it is necessary to view the Father, Son, and Spirit as YHWH.

The Identity of God in the Church Fathers

The church fathers use the title "God the Father" in diverse ways. For example, the apologists use "God the Father" to mean the creator God and not necessarily the first person of the Trinity (although occasionally they use it that way as well), because they mounted their arguments against those from outside Christianity. From the time of Irenaeus onward, the identity of God began to crystallize around Father, Son, and Spirit. Given the brevity of this section and the breadth of the works of the fathers and patristic scholarship, this section will be highly eclectic to highlight one important point—church fathers invariably use the appellation "God the Father" in

---

120. Wallace, *Greek Grammar beyond the Basics*, 188.

121. Bates, *Apostolic Proclamation*, 2. Bates writes that Paul "received, utilized, and extended" the apostolic, kerygmatic narrative tradition around the person of Christ, which became the interpretive lens through which he read OT scriptures. Bates' first chapter gives a good overview of scholarly opinions about Paul's hermeneutical method and his use of the OT.

quite different and diverse ways. Therefore, their use of "God the Father" or "Father" cannot be viewed as conclusive evidence of the church's belief in the identity of YHWH in the OT as God the Father (P1).[122]

The Apologists

The apologists such as Justin, Athenagoras, and Theophilus argued for Christian belief in one creator God.[123] Some have shown that the apologists often refer to God as "Father," not in the New Testament sense of him being the Father of Jesus, but in the Platonic sense as the creator of the universe.[124] Plato calls God "Maker and Father of this Universe" (*Tim.* 28c).[125] Justin, in fact, begins much of his first apology before the Roman Emperor Antonius Pius by making comparisons between Christian and pagan belief in God, especially with the philosophers' concept of God.[126] He details why Jesus alone is God's Son and why the truth presented in Jesus is superior, while also defending Christians against the charge of atheism (*1 Apol.* 22.1–24.1).

In *Dialogue with Trypho*, Justin explains that "he who appeared to Abraham under the oak tree of Mamre was God, sent, with two accompanying angels, to judge Sodom by another, who forever abides in supercelestial regions, who has never been seen by any man, and with whom no man has ever conversed, and whom we call Creator of all and Father."[127]

---

122. Here I follow Jackson Lashier and Peter Widdicombe on how the church fathers understood God's Fatherhood. Lashier, *Irenaeus on the Trinity*; Widdicombe, *Fatherhood of God*.

123. Lashier, *Irenaeus on the Trinity*, 54–70.

124. Lashier, *Irenaeus on the Trinity*, 57.

125. "Now to discover the Maker and Father of this Universe were a task indeed; and having discovered Him, to declare Him unto all men were a thing impossible." Plato, *Timaeus*, 51.

126. Justin, *Apologie pour les chrétiens*; Justin, *Dialogue avec le Tryphon*. English translation of the *Apology* is from Justin Martyr, *Justin, Philosopher and Martyr*. English translation of the *Dialogue* is from Justin Martyr, *Dialogue with Trypho*. Reference to his works follows standard abbreviations. "For in our saying that all things were fashioned and came into being through God we will seem to speak the opinion of Plato. . . . And when we say that the Logos, which is the first offering of God, was born without sexual intercourse as Jesus Christ our teacher, and that after his crucifixion, death, and resurrection he went up to heaven, we introduce nothing stranger than those you call the son of Zeus" (*1 Apol.* 20.4–21.1). Justin calls God "Creator of all and Father."

127. *Dial.* 56.1. Justin takes the angel of the Lord as the preincarnate Christ himself (*Dial.* 56.23; 58.3, 9–10; 59.1; 60.2–3).

Later, Justin asserts that "he who is said to have appeared to Abraham, Jacob, and Moses, and is called God, is distinct from God, the Creator; distinct, that, is number, but not in mind. For I state that he never did or said anything other than what the Creator—above whom there is no other God—desired that he do or say."[128] In all the appearances of God to humans, it was the second person of the Trinity and not God the Father who appeared to them; for Justin contends—"even if there were two persons, as you claim, both an angel and God, yet no one with even the slightest intelligence would dare to assert that the Creator of all things left his super-celestial realms to make himself visible in a little spot on earth."[129]

Athenagoras uses the title "Father" for God in the sense of God as the author of all creation.[130] Concerning the persons of the Godhead, Athenagoras writes, "We say that there is God and the Son, his Word, and the Holy Spirit, united in power yet distinguished in rank as the Father, the Son, and the Spirit, since the Son is mind, reason [word], and wisdom of the Father and the Spirit an effluence like light from fire."[131]

Theophilus often uses "Father" in the sense of the creator God and not as an appellation for the first person of the Trinity.[132] Concerning the nature of God, he writes, "He is Lord because he is master of the universe, Father because he is before the universe, Most High because he is above

---

128. *Dial.* 56.11. Cf. 56.14-23.

129. *Dial.* 60.2. See also 61.1. But, concerning the Spirit he says that "Moses, the aforementioned prophet, signified that it is not proper to consider the Spirit and the Power which is from God as anything other than the Logos who is also first-born of God" (*1Apol.* 33.6). There is clear ambivalence in Justin's identification of the persons of the Godhead in the OT, but it is very clear to him that the angel of the LORD and YHWH who appeared in the OT was Jesus Christ. Moreover, he assumes that God the Father did not appear on earth. The one who spoke with Moses from the burning bush was Jesus, and not the Father.

130. Athenagoras, *Supplique au sujet des chrétiens*. English translation is from Athenagoras, *Legatio and De Resurrectione*. Reference to his works follows standard abbreviations. *Leg.* xviii. In the introduction, William Schoedel observes that Athenagoras declares, "There is one God, the Maker of this universe" (*Leg.* 4.2).

131. *Leg.* 24.2. Brackets in the original. Similar language is found in *Leg.* 4.2; 6.2; 10.2-5; 12.3; 18.2.

132. *Autol.* 1.3. "Hear me, O man: the form of God is ineffable and inexpressible, since it cannot be seen with merely human eyes. . . . For if I call him Light, I speak of his creature; if I call him Logos, I speak of his beginning; if I call him Mind, I speak of his intelligence; if I call him Spirit, I speak of his breath; if I call him Sophia (Wisdom), I speak of his offspring; . . . if I call him Lord, I speak of him as judge. If I call him judge, I speak of him as just; if I call him Father, I speak of him as all things."

everything, Almighty because he controls and surrounds everything."[133] Concerning God as the creator he says that this God is the Lord of the universe. He heals and gives life through God's Logos and Sophia (*Autol.* 1.7). God had his Logos in his own bowels before the Logos was generated along with Sophia. Logos and Sophia were always part of the Father; therefore, John 1:1 could claim that the Word was with God and the Word was God (*Autol.* 2.10).[134] When Adam heard the voice of God, it was indeed the Logos whom he heard. Whenever God decided to create things, he generated the Logos, "making him external, as the *firstborn of all creation* [Col. 1:15]" (*Autol.* 2.22). Echoing Justin's conclusion that it was Jesus who appeared to Moses and the Patriarchs, Theophilus writes, "Whenever the Father of the universe wills to do so he sends him into some place where he is present and is heard and seen. He is sent by God and is present in a place" (*Autol.* 2.22).

Comparing and contrasting the apologists' view of God the Father, Jackson Lashier concludes that their use of the "Father" did not carry any "Trinitarian significance. In other words, 'Father' says nothing about the nature of God, which would have entailed reference to the Son. 'Father' only describes what God does, he creates and rules."[135]

From Irenaeus to Augustine

Irenaeus, Athanasius, and Augustine develop a more fully Trinitarian view of the doctrine of God found in the apologists. This development is gradual and against a particular background.[136] Remembering the settings for their arguments is very important as it helps nuance their choice of particular language to explain the doctrine of God.

Irenaeus develops the idea of God in the apologists.[137] His view of God the Father is often in relation to the Son as opposed to the apologists'

133. *Autol.* 1.4.

134. Theophilus proposes that "let Us make man in our own image" of Gen 1:26 was addressed to the Logos and the Sophia of God (*Autol.* 2.18).

135. Lashier, *Irenaeus on the Trinity*, 62. It is important to keep in mind that the Apologists were defending their faith against pagans and often appropriated languages that the pagans could relate to, just as Paul did on Mars Hill (Acts 17:22–34). Their use of the appellation "Father" for God is quite ambivalent and inharmonious.

136. Plantinga, "Trinity," 913–21.

137. For the critical edition of Irenaeus' work, see Irenaeus, *Contre Les Hérésies*. English translation is from Roberts and Donaldson, ANF01. Reference to his works follows standard abbreviations.

middle Platonist concept.[138] Irenaeus employs λόγος to mean creator and revealer in referring to the preincarnate Christ (clear development from that of the apologists) and uses υἱός for the incarnate Christ.[139] Irenaeus calls God (P1) creator, only God, only Lord, only Father.[140] He calls Logos (P2) the Mind of God (P1), then later states that the Father himself is the Mind that comprehends everything (*Haer.* 2.28.5). He calls the Son and the Spirit as God's (P1) two hands through whom he created the world and to whom the Father said, "Let us make man" (*Haer.* 4.preface.4). The apostles preached one God, the creator of heaven and earth, and one Christ, the Son of God. If anyone does not believe this, he despises the Father and the Son (*Haer.* 3.1.2) whom he calls the Maker of heaven and earth (*Haer.* 4.4.4). The same God (P1) authored both testaments (*Haer.* 4.32.1–2) and the Son is the Revealer of the Father and the manifestation of the Son is conversely the manifestation of the Father (*Haer.* 4.4.3). Therefore, Moses, Elijah, and Ezekiel saw the preincarnate Christ and not the Father (P1) himself (*Haer.* 4.20.8–11).[141] Unlike the apologists, Irenaeus calls the God who spoke to Moses the Father of Christ (*Haer.* 4.2.1–8). Here we find an early clear reference to YHWH as the Father of Jesus Christ, although Irenaean language is fluid because Irenaeus himself sees the presence of the preincarnate Christ in the OT and takes the Logos as the Mind of God.

Athanasius focuses on the aspect that P1 has always been Father and there was no time when P1 was not the Father (*C. Ar.* 1.14–29; *Decr.* 6, 22; *Syn.* 34).[142] His purpose is not to identify whether YHWH was P1 in the OT; instead, his concern is about the eternity of the Godhead before any creation. Unlike the apologists and Irenaeus, Athanasius deliberately did not appropriate the understanding of God found in Greek philosophy and mythology precisely because he charged Arius with understanding God from such categories (*C. Ar.* 1.30; *Decr.* 32).[143] Arius

138. Rusch, *Trinitarian Controversy*, 7.

139. Lashier, *Irenaeus on the Trinity*, 92n1, 119. For further study on Irenaeus's view of the Son, see Osborn, *Irenaeus of Lyons*. The brevity of this project does not allow in-depth analysis of Irenaeus's theology and his particular language for the Father, Son, and Spirit. Only a few examples from his works are cited to present his understanding of the "Fatherhood" of God.

140. *Haer.* 2.1.1

141. This is similar to Justin and Theophilus.

142. Athanasius, *Orationes contra Arianos*; Athanasius, *De synodis* 13,3; Athanasius, *De decretis Nicaenae synodi*. The English translation is from NPNF², vol. 4.

143. Hanson, *Christian Doctrine of God*, 432–33. Hanson argues that Athanasius

applies ἀγένητος (ingenerate/uncreated) and ἀγέννητος (unbegotten), an appellation for God in Greek philosophers, to propose that the Father alone was uncreated and the Son was a creature.[144] Therefore, Athanasius chose to use the biblical titles of Father and Son to refer to the first and second persons of the Trinity respectively because that would allow him to reason on biblical ground and not philosophical.[145] He maintained that the Son is the wisdom and the word of the Father who always existed with the Father (*Decr.* 28–30; *Syn.* 47; cf. *C. Ar.* 1.32, 58).[146] Athanasius contends for the eternality of the Father in order to prove the eternality of the Son, and to refute the claim that the Son was created. He uses Father for the first person of the Trinity, but does not identify him with YHWH. Instead, Athanasius' focus was on God *en se* and not the economy.

Augustine is conscious of the limits of language.[147] He writes that the Scripture uses words and imageries drawn from nature to explain the things of God so that even babies can understand the truth (*Trin.* 1.1.2), but it is difficult to know the substance of God (*Trin.* 1.1.3). Father is God, the Son is God, and the Holy Spirit is God, but there are not three Gods, but one (*Trin.* 1.5.8). From John's Gospel, Augustine argues that the Son was the very Word that was with the Father and he was of the same substance as the Father (*Trin.* 1.6.9).

In books 5–7, Augustine explains what the Nicene "God from God" means in relation to the Father, Son, and Spirit to refute the Arian position.[148] He argues that the Father is not God without the Son and the Son

---

could have made a case from the Greek descriptions for God if he wanted to because such a case could be made, but he chose to turn to scriptural categories because he had already labeled Arius's use as unscriptural and would undermine his own argument by doing that.

144. *C. Ar.* 1.30. Anatolios, *Athanasius*, 212–13. For a word study on Athanasius's understanding of ἀγένητος and ἀγέννητος, see Prestige, "ΑΓΕΝ[Ν]ΗΤΟΣ," 258–65; Morales, *Théologie trinitaire d'Athanase d'Alexandrie*, 211–18; Behr, *Nicene Faith*, 212–14; DelCogliano, "Influence of Athanasius," 197–223.

145. Weinandy, *Athanasius*, 73.

146. "Athanasius employs a technical metaphysical grammar in order to establish that scriptural language about God as Father and Lord tells us something about the very essence of God, about what it means to be God. And if 'Father' is part of what we mean by God, and 'Father' necessarily implies relation with a 'Son', then in fact the relation of Father and Son is part of what we mean by 'God'. Yet, for Athanasius, this is an utterly incomposite relation. Being God is not other than being Father; hence it is not other than being Father and Son." Radde-Gallwitz, *Divine Simplicity*, 86.

147. Augustine, *De Trinitate*. The English translation is from Augustine, *Trinity*.

148. Ayres, *Augustine and the Trinity*, 199. "If the Son of God is the power and wisdom of God, and God was never without power and wisdom, then the Son is co-eternal

is not God without the Father, but they together are God (*Trin.* 6.2.3). The Father and the Son are equal because the Scripture says that they are one (*Trin.* 6.3.4). Similarly, the Holy Spirit is of the same unity of substance and equality (*Trin.* 6.5.7). In the middle of this discussion, he makes an important claim regarding the identity of YHWH in the Shema, "Hear, O, Israel: The Lord our God is one Lord" does not exclude the Son and the Spirit (*Trin.* 5.11.12). Augustine is right to make that claim in light of Pauline explication of the Shema in 1 Cor 8:6. The identification of YHWH with the Father, Son, and Spirit is a significant claim for Trinitarian theology.

This very brief survey of the appellation "Father" in the writings of the Fathers of the church reveals that there is ambiguity in their use of the appellation for God. The appellation "Father" for God was used at least in three different ways: (1) in the generic sense of him as the Father of the universe, (2) as a reference to P1 in the specific sense of him being the Father of the Son, and (3) as the God who revealed to Moses (here too they see the Son and the Spirit present). It should be noted that the apologists, because of their disputations with non-Christians, focused mainly on establishing why their faith in the one true God was a reasonable and faithful reflection on the revelation given through Moses and Jesus Christ. Others whose debates were with those who claimed to be Christians (Arius, et al.) or have faith in the Christian God (Marcion, et al.), focused their refutations on unorthodox positions on the oneness of God and equality of persons in the Godhead. These reasons may explain their choice of appellations for God.

We cannot be certain when YHWH or God in the OT came to be viewed as the first person of the Trinity in the history of the church.[149] However, Gregory of Nazianzus uses this clear distinction in his fifth theological oration.[150] He writes, "The Old Testament proclaimed the Father openly, and the Son more obscurely. The New manifested the Son, and suggested the Deity of the Spirit."[151] The identity of God as Father, Son, and Spirit (coequal and coeternal in every sense) became the dominant way of referring to God since the time of Irenaeus.[152] Because of the

---

with God the Father" (*Trin.* 6.1.1).

149. Some attribute the identification of YHWH as the first person of the Trinity to the idea of supersessionism in Christian thought. See for example, Soulen, "YHWH the Triune God," 25–54; Soulen, "Supersessionism"; Soulen, *Divine Name(s)*, 1:258n9.

150. NPNF², vol. 7, 326; Pelikan, *Catholic Tradition*, 211.

151. NPNF², vol. 7, 326.

152. For a different view of the Trinitarian identity in the early church, see Bates,

OT's lack of explicit reference to the triune identity, coupled with Jesus' use of the appellation "Father" for the first person of the Trinity, YHWH came to be viewed as the first person of the Trinity.

To correct this tendency of misidentifying YHWH as the first person of the Trinity, a careful observation of various OT passages that indicate the possibility of plurality of persons in the identity of YHWH is necessary. If the presence of a plurality of persons in the identity of YHWH can be established, then an argument can be made that the Trinitarian identity of the one true God in the NT as the Father, Son, and Spirit is biblically accurate and should be foundational in Trinitarian interpretation.

YHWH as the Triune God

How do we understand the identity of YHWH in light of the word study on יהוה and πατήρ, the NT's understanding of the one true God, and the church fathers' perception of the persons of the Godhead? Are there clues in the Scripture that might help explain the identity of YHWH to be more than "God the Father"? The answers given here are neither exhaustive nor a thorough analysis of every passage in which YHWH appears. The rest of the this chapter will make three points:

1. There are evidence in the OT texts that suggest multiplicity of persons in the identity of YHWH.
2. The explication of the identity of YHWH in the NT as Father, Son, and Spirit helps explain not only the identity of YHWH in the OT, but also why the NT applies OT passages to Jesus that were once ascribed to YHWH.
3. The identity of YHWH as Father, Son, and Spirit aids in mitigating the isolationist tendency so prevalent in Trinitarian interpretation because this identification allows the OT texts to be read through a Trinitarian lens.

The following discussion will present evidence from the OT for a plurality of persons in the identity of YHWH, which can be understood from the NT distillation of the identity of God as the Father, Son, and Spirit. There is no attempt to discuss the identity of preincarnate Christ,

---

Birth of the Trinity. Bates suggests prosopological exegesis as the cradle of early development of the Trinitarian dogma.

Plurality of Persons in the Identity of YHWH

The question of the identity of YHWH is significant to the study, primarily in the OT texts and then by extension in the NT. Deuteronomy 6:4b plays an indispensable role in defining the identity of YHWH for Israel and for the Christian Scriptures. It is necessary to briefly look at how to understand Deut 6:4b before discussing the possibility of plurality of persons in the identity of YHWH.[153]

Deuteronomy 6:4b and Monotheism

One of the major difficulties concerning the identity of YHWH since the nineteenth century has been the question of "monotheism" and how it is defined based on Deut 6:4b.[154] Nathan MacDonald presents the history of monotheism through its developmental stages and how it is understood in modern times. Drawing on Gerard von Rad, he proposes that the earliest Israelite religion was defined by the first commandment, and not by "monotheism" versus "polytheism."[155] After surveying the first use (Henry More) of monotheism to its latest iteration (James A. Sanders) to define Israelite religion, he argues that most of the modern studies on monotheism took a diachronic approach to the question and dealt often

---

153. For a biblical argument for fluidity in the identity (multiple identities) of YHWH in the OT, see Sommer, *Bodies of God*, 38–79. For example, he argues that מלאך יהוה in Exod 23:20–21 "carries something of Yhwh's own essence or self; it is not an entirely separate entity" (42).

154. MacDonald, *Deuteronomy*. For counterarguments to MacDonald's position, see Janzen, "Most Important Word," 280–300. Janzen argues that at the heart of Deut 6:4b is the "oneness" of YHWH and not just his uniqueness. He builds his case in light of the first commandment, similar to that of MacDonald, but with one decisive difference. For Janzen, Deut 6:4b is further explication of the first commandment, but for MacDonald, the first commandment establishes the uniqueness of YHWH in the sense that "you shall not have any other gods." The emphasis is not so much on number (one) but on YHWH being the only God. I find MacDonald's arguments compelling, in light of my own study on the plurality of persons in the identity of YHWH, and his study is instrumental in my own conclusion on Deut 6:4b. Richard Bauckham concurs with this judgment although he develops MacDonald's idea further. Bauckham, *Jesus and the God*, 61–94.

155. MacDonald, *Deuteronomy*, 1:40–41.

with the various developmental stages. He prefers a synchronic approach to the task of understanding what Deut 6:4b meant and how that would help overcome the modern definition of "monotheism."[156]

MacDonald discusses the merits of four possible ways of translating Deut 6:4b: (יְהוָה אֱלֹהֵינוּ ׀ יְהוָה אֶחָד) (1) YHWH is our God; YHWH is one, (2) YHWH, our God, YHWH is one, (3) YHWH, our God, is one YHWH, and (4) YHWH is our God, YHWH alone.[157] With regard to the translation "YHWH is our God; YHWH is one," MacDonald states it is not to be taken as a statement about the nature of YHWH, but as a statement about the relationship between YHWH and Israel.[158] "YHWH, our God, YHWH is one" is understood to be a statement about YHWH's nature, integrity of his will, a statement of his uniqueness.[159] Third option—"YHWH, our God, is one YHWH"—is explained as a statement about "mono-Yehwism."[160] The fourth option—"YHWH is our God, YHWH alone"[161]—is MacDonald's preferred reading. This translation of Deut 6:4b understands this verse to be about Israel's allegiance to YHWH alone and none else.[162]

As seen earlier in the study of Exod 3:14–15, YHWH was going to be known by his works.[163] From the time the Israelites left Egypt, YHWH was trying to prove to them that he alone was God. If Moses was the author of the book of Genesis, then the creation account makes better sense because his audience would have been the exodus generation who were quite familiar with the Egyptian gods. YHWH wanted to remind these people that he was not like the demigods of Egypt who were believed to have very limited power (not one god controlled everything; hence, the need to appease all gods). Rather, he made the heaven and the earth and everything in it. So for YHWH to require allegiance to himself

156. MacDonald, *Deuteronomy*, 1:55.

157. MacDonald, *Deuteronomy*, 1:64.

158. MacDonald, *Deuteronomy*, 1:65. See also Vervenne, "Phraseology," 467–92.

159. MacDonald, *Deuteronomy*, 1:66.

160. MacDonald, *Deuteronomy*, 1:67.

161. Christensen, *Deuteronomy 1:1—21:9*, 141–42. MacDonald, *Deuteronomy*, 1:67. Christensen and MacDonald agree on this translation.

162. MacDonald, *Deuteronomy*, 1:68. See also Mayes, *Deuteronomy*, 176. Mayes concurs with MacDonald's choice of translation in light of Deut 6:5 where the emphasis is on single-minded devotion to YHWH.

163. "If YHWH lets himself be known *in what he does*, however, then his intervention has actual value in itself. The recognition of YHWH *takes place* in what he does." Vervenne, "Phraseology," 492.

did not arise out of a vacuum, but against a particular religious milieu. Perhaps, that is the reason YHWH reminds the people toward the end of Deuteronomy (32:37–39) that he alone is God and other so-called gods are not gods at all.

The fact that Exod 20:3 commands Israel to not have any other gods before them acknowledges that there are "so-called" gods that the Israelites were aware of and would have a tendency to follow. The history of Israel, especially during the times of the prophets, is a story of Israel's wandering after other gods. This is also important in light of Josh 24:14 where Joshua reminds the people that their ancestors worshiped other gods beyond the Euphrates. When the Shema is placed against the background of Deut 4:35–39 and what immediately follows 6:4b, it becomes clearer that YHWH continues to recount what he had done for them to require their allegiance toward him and none other.[164] He wants their wholehearted devotion (6:5).

Elijah declares to the people, אִם־יְהוָה הָאֱלֹהִים לְכוּ אַחֲרָיו וְאִם־הַבַּעַל לְכוּ אַחֲרָיו ("If YHWH is God, follow him, but if Baal [is God], then follow him"—1 Kgs 18:21). Clearly, the emphasis is not on one God versus many, but the fact that YHWH alone is God and none else (cf. Song 6:8–9—there are other women, but this one is unique).

MacDonald summarizes how the Shema is supposed to be understood in light of the immediate theological reason:

> The significance of the *Shema* (Deut. 6.4–9) is strongly indicated by a number of factors, including its place in the structure of Deuteronomy and its emphatic call for wholehearted devotion. Its opening lines make declaration that YHWH is one. As the following verse indicates this has personal and relational import: YHWH is the only god for Israel, they are to have no others. This may be viewed as a positive restatement of the first commandment. Both Deut. 6.4 and the first commandment assume the existence of other gods and that they present a genuine temptation to Israel.[165]

---

164. YHWH kept reminding the people that they should not have any other gods because people had a tendency to go after other gods.

165. MacDonald, *Deuteronomy*, 1:95. Saner agrees with MacDonald's argument for a relational understanding of YHWH in Deuteronomy and for that reason the entire OT. In his own study of Exod 3:13–15, Saner proposed a very similar position. Saner asks whether the relational aspect negates the possibility of ontology, meaning whether it also rules out the fact that there is only one God. He thinks that it can be answered in the positive. Saner, *"Too Much to Grasp,"* 207–19.

Labeling the Shema as a statement on monotheism resulted in a misconstrual of YHWH's identity. If Deut 6:4b is understood as an emphasis on the uniqueness of YHWH in that he alone is God and not construed as a statement about the establishing of monotheism, then the discussion of the identity of YHWH can be pursued more positively.[166] It is true that there is only one God for the Jews and for the Christians, but for many, Deut 6:4b created a chasm between YHWH and the Father, Son, and Spirit.

Bauckham presents a strong case for the compatibility of early Christology and Jewish monotheism from the NT perspective. As a refutation of the suggestions that the NT Christology is dependent on the Second Temple Jewish concept of divine intermediaries,[167] he writes,

> I show that early Judaism had clear and consistent ways of characterizing the unique identity of one God and thus distinguishing the one God absolutely from all other reality. When New Testament Christology is read with this Jewish theological context in mind, it becomes clear that, from the earliest post-Easter beginnings of Christology onwards, early Christians included Jesus, precisely and unambiguously, within the unique identity of the one God of Israel. They did so by including Jesus in the unique, defining characteristics by which Jewish monotheism identified God as unique. They did not have to break with Jewish monotheism in order to do this, since monotheism, as Second Temple Judaism understood it, was structurally open to the development of the christological monotheism that we find in the New Testament texts.[168]

Bauckham develops this idea further in *Jesus and the God of Israel* and argues that part of the reason for the confusion concerning Jewish monotheism (*monotheism* versus *monolatry*) is a lack of clarity on what counts as "divine" in Jewish understanding of God.[169]

Bauckham focuses on the identity of YHWH and not his nature.[170] The unique identity of YHWH is what leads to the demand of exclusive worship of him. The emphasis is on monolatry, the exclusive worship

---

166. MacDonald, *Deuteronomy*, 1:16–58.

167. For an understanding of the concept of various intermediaries in Second Temple Judaism, see Hurtado, *One God, One Lord*.

168. Bauckham, *God Crucified*, vii–viii.

169. Bauckham, *Jesus and the God*, 4.

170. Bauckham, *Jesus and the God*, 7–11. He distinguishes two ways in which the identity of YHWH was construed in the OT: (1) in relation to Israel, and (2) in relation to all reality.

YHWH Is Trinity

of one God and not created beings.[171] Working through many OT and NT passages (Exod 33–34; Ps 110:1; Isa 44–55; John 3:14–15; 4:26; 6:20; 8:28; Rom 3; Eph 1:21–22; Phil 2:6–11; Rev 4–5), Bauckham states it is amply clear the NT writers understood they were worshiping the one true God when they worshiped Jesus because such a knowledge predated these writings since it is found in all of them.[172] Worship, prayer, doxology, exorcism, commission, were addressed to Jesus; in doing so the NT proclaims the identity of Jesus with the identity of YHWH.[173]

Bauckham categorizes early Jewish monotheism as creational (God alone created all things without any assistance), eschatological (in the future YHWH will reveal his deity to the nations and make his name known to them), and cultic (only the sole creator and Lord over all things is worthy of worship).[174] He contends that from many texts it can be argued that the NT presents the eschatological coming of YHWH. He summarizes how Jewish monotheism was understood by and continued in the NT:

> Early Christian interest was primarily in soteriology and eschatology.... But early Christian reflection could not consistently leave it at that. Jewish eschatological monotheism was founded in creational monotheism. If Jesus was integral to the identity of God, he must have been so eternally. To include Jesus also in the unique creative activity of God and in the uniquely divine eternity was a necessary corollary of his inclusion in the eschatological identity of God. This was the early Christians' Jewish way of preserving monotheism against the ditheism that any kind of adoptionist Christology was bound to involve. Not by adding Jesus to the unique identity of the God of Israel, but only by including Jesus in that unique identity, could monotheism be maintained.[175]

He differentiates "including" from "adding" to make the point that Jesus has always been part of the identity of YHWH.

---

171. So Second Temple Judaism knew well and maintained a strict adherence to the prohibition of worshiping any created reality. Given this background, it would have been impossible for Jewish Christians to worship Jesus if he was understood to fall within the realm of created reality. Bauckham, *Jesus and the God*, 12–13.

172. Bauckham, *Jesus and the God*, 18–59.

173. Hurtado, *Lord Jesus Christ*, 176–206; Bauckham, *Jesus and the God*, 128–39.

174. Bauckham, *Jesus and the God*, 184.

175. Bauckham, *Jesus and the God*, 184–85.

Bauckham's conclusion is possible and makes sense when one considers the meaning of Deut 6:4b and that this has been misunderstood in modern scholarship. A reconsideration of the identity of YHWH is necessary for TIS to overcome the impasse created by the earlier understanding of monotheism in Israel.

It becomes clear from the analysis of Jewish monotheism above that a monotheistic idea does not exclude the possibility of multiple persons because the emphasis is not on number, but on the uniqueness of YHWH as the only God. This does not mean that there are multiple gods, but at the same time, it does not rule out the possibility of multiple persons in that identity. Christian faith, similarly, does not argue for multiple gods, but multiple persons in the identity of one God—three persons, but one God. Although the identity of Jesus, as already included in the identity of YHWH, can only be realized fully in the NT, there are hints in the OT to that effect (multiple persons in the identity of YHWH) to which we now turn.

Multiple Persons but One YHWH

From Exod 3:14–15 on, the identity of the God of Israel (Israel as a nation) is inextricably tied to his personal name YHWH. Exodus 4:1–2 reiterates that it was God's self-identifying name to Moses and to the nation Israel. In Exod 5:1, Moses and Aaron tell Pharaoh that YHWH, the God of Israel, sent them to him. Exodus 6:3 clearly indicates that he was not known to the patriarchs by this particular name ("but by my name YHWH I was not known to them"). As observed earlier, the Abrahamic covenant and its reiterations were directed to individuals, but from the time of Moses, the covenant is with the nation Israel. Hence, the phrase יְהוָה אֱלֹהֵי יִשְׂרָאֵל—the LORD, the God of Israel—and not just Moses or Aaron's God like "the God of Abraham, Isaac, and Jacob." The Decalogue clearly states that Israel shall not have any other god apart from YHWH (Exod 20:2–5).

Establishing whether or not YHWH was God's personal name alone cannot resolve the question of the identity of YHWH. A canonical view is required here.[176] In Exod 3:2, it is stated that מלאך יהוה (the angel of the

---

176. Jenson, *Ezekiel*, 27–30. Jenson argues in this commentary that YHWH in Ezekiel has to be understood through the Trinitarian structure given the presence of "the glory of the Lord," "the name of the Lord," and "the angel of the Lord." YHWH was not only God's self-identification, but also that the nation Israel will know him through his

YHWH Is Trinity

LORD) appeared to Moses in the burning bush.[177] But in v. 4 the language simply changes to יהוה.[178] Do we see here two persons at the same time or do we simply see מלאך יהוה and יהוה as one and the same? Some suggest that there is no difference between the identity of מלאך יהוה and יהוה in Scripture, especially in light of Exod 23:20–23 (cf. Ps 78:35–40; Dan 9:8–10).[179] A recap of Exod 23:20–23, Judg 2:1–5 reminds the people that they sinned against מלאך יהוה (Judg 2:2). It was he who delivered them from Egypt. But elsewhere we read that when the people sinned, they sinned against יהוה (Exod 32:33; Num 21:7; Deut 9:6). Even if it is conceded that the מלאך יהוה here is יהוה himself (or his representative), it still does not resolve all such appearances of the angel of the LORD where there is clear evidence that מלאך יהוה and יהוה are different (Judg 6:11–24).

Just as in Exod 3:2, it is מלאך יהוה who first appears to Gideon in Judg 6:11–24. In v. 11, the text says that מלאך יהוה appeared to Gideon. However, in v. 14, the text makes the transition to "YHWH himself" and it was not the angel of the LORD who turned to Gideon and spoke, but YHWH himself.[180] Now, both יהוה and מלאך יהוה are present at the same time.[181] How do we know it? The text says that, Gideon later on realized that he had seen מלאך יהוה and was afraid to have seen him (v. 22 cf. Gen 32:30; Exod 33:11–23; Deut 34:10),[182] but יהוה (the text reads אֲדֹנָי יְהוִֹה "the LORD God") reassures Gideon that he would not die as a result of seeing מלאך יהוה (v. 23). It seems Gideon is not as much concerned with seeing and talking to יהוה himself who appeared along with the מלאך יהוה (cf. Num 22:34–35—did Balaam sin against מלאך יהוה? It seems to be so). Normally, one would not expect such mannerisms from Gideon

---

actions (then you/they shall know that I am YHWH, Ezek 6:13; 7:4, 9; 11:10).

177. Justin in Dialogue with Trypho argues that the angel of the LORD who appeared to Moses and Abraham was the preincarnate Son (*Dial.* 59–62). Also see earlier references to Justin's work where he makes such explicit connections.

178. Concerning the identity of the angel of the LORD, see Fossum, *Name of God*.

179. Cassuto, *Exodus*, 305–6; Ausloos, "'Angel of YHWH,'" 9. Ausloos suggests that in light of the evidence within the text of Exod 23:20–23, the מלאך יהוה is a substitute of YHWH himself and not a human or angelic messenger.

180. Sasson, *Judges 1–12*, 331. Daniel Block calls the angel of the LORD his alter ego. Block, *Judges, Ruth*, 259. Concerning the appearance of the angel of the LORD, Barry Webb writes that וַיֵּרָא is often used for theophanies in the Scripture where God appeared in human or other material forms. Webb, *Book of Judges*, 229.

181. Trent Butler suggests that sometimes the angel of YHWH appears as YHWH himself. Butler, *Judges*, 200. Cf. Gen 16:7–14.

182. In v. 20 the title changes to מלאך אלהים from מלאך יהוה. Sasson thinks that these two titles could be interchangeable. Sasson, *Judges 1–12*, 335.

because he should have known who יהוה was.[183] Could it be that Gideon understood מלאך יהוה to be equal to יהוה himself? The text does not say, but that seems a possibility.[184]

The possibility of seeing more than one person in the identity of YHWH becomes even more apparent when it is related to the Spirit of the LORD in Judg 13:24—16:20. Samson received great strength when the Spirit of the LORD came upon him (Judg 13:25; 14:6, 19; 15:14). But when the Spirit of the LORD left him after his hair was cut, it is written in 16:20 that YHWH left him.[185] The significance of this passage cannot be overstated. Clearly, these texts show that the Spirit of the LORD is equated with YHWH. It can be posited that in the person of YHWH one could see the identity of the angel of the LORD and the Spirit of the LORD. Thus, the angel of the LORD is YHWH[186] and the Spirit of the LORD is YHWH.

Another important perspective into the identity of YHWH can be ascertained from Isa 45:18–25. It is written that he is the one who made the heaven and the earth (v. 18) and that there is no God beside him (vv. 21–22). He declares that there is no peer to him—no other God who could claim what is rightfully his. Every knee will bow to him and every tongue will confess allegiance to him (v. 23). A quick glance at Phil 2:9–11 reveals that the same thing is attributed to Jesus that was once said to be YHWH's alone. Does it mean that YHWH relinquished what was rightfully his? Probably not. A better way to interpret this is Jesus has always been part of the identity of YHWH and it can rightfully be ascribed to him. If so, then it would be correct to say that Jesus has been given what once belonged to YHWH. It is also true of YHWH being the creator God

---

183. Block writes that it did not make much of a difference for Gideon whether he saw YHWH or the angel of the LORD. Block, *Judges, Ruth*, 264. Webb suggests that Gideon may have understood the angel of YHWH to be YHWH himself given his fear for life. Webb, *Book of Judges*, 232–33. It is worth noting that Gideon was still speaking with YHWH even after the מלאך יהוה had left the scene and he was not afraid of that conversation. Could it be that Gideon did not recognize the identity of both persons, but came to know one of them as מלאך יהוה because the food that Gideon offered him was consumed, and it is the narrator who is making the identity of the other person explicit to the readers? We do not know the answer to that. Nonetheless, we are still left with the question as to who Gideon thought he was talking to after the מלאך יהוה had left.

184. Even if Gideon did not see or understand it that way, we are supposed to read it that way, especially given the NT understanding of God.

185. See Block, *Judges, Ruth*, 459–60.

186. This may explain why church fathers interpreted angel of the LORD as the pre-incarnate Christ.

because Jesus and the Spirit too are called creators (Col 1:15–19; John 1:3–7; Job 33:4).

Israel's deliverance from Egypt is often attributed to YHWH (Exod 13:3, 9, 14, 16; 14:25; 16:6), but Isa 63:14 tells that it is the Spirit of the Lord (רוח יהוה) who granted them rest.[187] According to Isa 63:10, they sinned against his Holy Spirit (רוח קדשו), but in Exod 16:8; Num 11:1; Deut 1:26; 9:23; Jer 3:25, it is said that they sinned against יהוה. Isaiah says that they sinned against the Holy Spirit who was placed among them (63:11).[188] Because they sinned against the Holy Spirit, YHWH turned against them (63:10). Joseph Blenkinsopp suggests that the association of the Spirit of YHWH with the presence or the face of God (Ps 139:7) is to be seen as the object of theological reflection, "a kind of hypostasis similar in that respect to the Face (*panîm*), the Angel (*mal'ak*) and, later in the Targum, the Word (*memra'*). We are at the beginning of the development that will eventuate in the Christian doctrine of the Holy Spirit and the rabbinic concept of the *rûah haqqodes* as the spirit of prophecy (*rûah hannebû'â*)."[189] When Jesus warned about sinning against the Holy Spirit (Matt 12:32; Mark 3:29; Luke 12:10), he made a statement similar to YHWH's statement in Isa 63:11 concerning the Israelites sinning against the Holy Spirit.

Just as the OT refers to the Holy Spirit as the Spirit of YHWH (1 Sam 10:6; Isa 61:1; 63:10–11, 14) the NT also calls the Holy Spirit the Spirit of the Lord (Acts 5:9; 8:39; 2 Cor 3:17), Spirit of God (Matt 3:16; 12:28; Rom 8:14; 15:9; 1 Cor 2:11, 14), Spirit of Jesus (Phil 1:19 cf. Acts 16:7; Rom 8:9; Gal 4:6; 1 Pet 1:11) or the Spirit of the one who raised Jesus from the dead (Rom 8:11). The description of the Holy Spirit as the "Spirit of YHWH" in Isa 63:10–11 and 14 matches similar descriptions of him in the NT. One could make the connection that the referent in these OT and NT passages is the same Holy Spirit who is identified as the third person of the Trinity in the NT and in the creeds. If this is a reasonable conclusion, what emerges from the many OT passages concerning the identity of YHWH is that there are clear biblical evidence of more than one person being identified as YHWH in the OT, which when

---

187. In this passage (Isa 63:10–14) the Spirit of the Lord and the Holy Spirit are used interchangeably.

188. Watts, *Isaiah 34–66*, 901–2. Watts writes that "his Holy Spirit" is a rare use in the OT (cf. Ps 51:13) and he concurs with the idea that it was the Holy Spirit whom the Israelites offended.

189. Blenkinsopp, *Isaiah 56–66*, 261.

taken together with the NT, paints the portrait of the triune identity of God—who he has always been.

The NT presents the identity of YHWH as encompassing the triune Godhead and not just God the Father. The particular NT understanding of Israel's redemption from Egypt reveals a larger point in that the NT can attribute to Jesus the OT passages that were once ascribed to YHWH because to the disciples and the early followers of Jesus the identity of YHWH clearly included the person of Christ. If this is true, many of the NT quotations of the OT can also be understood as stemming from this new kind of understanding like the one that happened to the disciples in Luke 24:45.

These observations lead to another important point in this book. If multiple persons can be identified as YHWH, are there three YHWH's? The simple answer is no, there are not three YHWH's. If multiple persons can be identified as YHWH and the NT clarifies those identities as the Father, Son, and Spirit, then it is reasonable to state the Father is YHWH, the Son is YHWH, and the Spirit is YHWH just the Father is God, the Son is God, and the Spirit is God. This statement makes the point that YHWH refers to what the creeds mean when they name the Father, Son, and Spirit as one God; it points to the essence of God. Whatever the Father is in his essence, the Son and the Spirit are also. So if the Father is YHWH (Matt 28:19; John 1:14, 18; 6:27–29, 37–40; Rom 4:24; 8:11; 2 Cor 4:14; Rev 1:4, 8; 4:9—5:10), then the Son (cf. Isa 45:21–23 with Phil 2:9–11 and Exod 3:15; 20:2; 13:3; 14:25; Deut 6:4b with 1 Cor 10:4, 9; Jude 5; Rev 1:4, 8, 17; 22:13) and the Spirit are also YHWH (cf. Judg 13:25, 14:6, 19; 15:14 with 16:20 and Exod 13:3; 14:25 with Isa 63:10–14).

The Westminster Confession of Faith defines the Godhead this way: "In the unity of the Godhead there be three persons, of one substance, power, and eternity; God the Father, God the Son, and God the Holy Ghost. The Father is of none, neither begotten nor proceeding; the Son is eternally begotten of the Father; the Holy Ghost eternally proceeding from the Father and the Son."[190] According to the Confession "the Father is of none" means that he has being in himself. He does not proceed from anyone else. But the Son and the Spirit eternally receive their being from the Father, but all three persons are equally God and the same in essence. Similarly, the Father is YHWH in himself, but the Son and the Spirit eternally receive that name from the Father and yet all three are

---

190. Leith, *Creeds of the Churches*, 197.

equally YHWH. The claim "the Father is YHWH," "the Son is YHWH," and "the Spirit is YHWH" does not appear to be problematic in light of the Christian understanding of the divine essence.

John Goldingay offers help in explaining this idea, although a little differently. Using theological reasoning, he demonstrates that YHWH in the OT can be understood as the Father, Son, and Spirit.[191] He starts with the premise that "YHWH is God" and "God is YHWH."[192] If YHWH is God and God is YHWH, then it follows from this that YHWH and God has the same referent, but different meaning.[193] From this conclusion, he moves onto God as Father, Son, and Spirit. He explains that this is not a statement the Scripture makes, but a legitimate inference from the NT. Conversely, the Father, Son, and Holy Spirit are God. This too is not a statement of Scripture but a legitimate inference. In Christian conviction "God" and "Father, Son, and Holy Spirit" have "different meanings but the same reference, different connotations but the same denotation."[194] He combines these two rationales and concludes, "Since YHWH is God, and Father, Son, and Holy Spirit are God, it follows that in Christian conviction YHWH is the God who is Father, Son, and Holy Spirit. It then follows that whenever you read about YHWH in the OT, you are reading about God the Father, the Son, and the Holy Spirit."[195] Goldingay takes a theological approach to arrive at this conclusion; however, he reaches the same conclusion that can also be reached exegetically, as has been proposed by Saner and MacDonald.

In light of the evidence presented here and of the clear teachings of the NT, I propose that when Christians approach the OT, they must approach it from a Trinitarian perspective since they are equipped with the knowledge of the one true God—YHWH as triune. A Christian reading of the OT from this perspective does not violate the OT presentation of YHWH's identity because the OT texts themselves make room for such a reading. The onus is on Christian readers to be faithful to this understanding in their reading. If the particular identity of YHWH that

---

191. Murray, "Christ in/and the Old Testament," 7–11. He especially focuses on how to justify a christological interpretation of the OT.

192. Murray, "Christ in/and the Old Testament," 9.

193. Murray, "Christ in/and the Old Testament." To substantiate this point, he gives the example of John Goldingay and "David Allan Hubbard Professor of Old Testament," both of which have the same referent but different connotations (9).

194. Murray, "Christ in/and the Old Testament."

195. Murray, "Christ in/and the Old Testament." For Goldingay, this conclusion is a theological and not an exegetical one.

is advocated here is a reasonable one, that does not mean that one could come up with any kind of interpretation, but only the ones that do not violate the clear teachings of Scripture. As Stephen Fowl reminds us, we are expected to be virtuous readers—readers who are conscious of the history of Christian interpretation and the orthodox teachings of historic Christianity and who have a sincere desire to continue to uphold the historic Christian faith. These (history of interpretation and orthodox beliefs) must be taken as limiting factors in our quest to hear God speak afresh to our context today because our cultural expressions of Christian faith must always be regulated by the clear teachings of Scripture.

Further Observations

The identity of YHWH, the God of Israel, has been understood as triune by the early church and is reflected in its liturgy.[196] David Yeago argues that the early Christians were vigorous monotheists who were determined to worship no other God apart from YHWH. From the very beginning, Christian worship of this one true God was concentrated in and through Jesus—by addressing prayer, thanksgiving, and worship in his name—always assuming that in their worship of Jesus they were worshiping YHWH.[197]

Karl Barth argues that the doctrine of the Trinity is nothing other than the explanation of the name Yahweh-Kyrios:

> In our demonstration of the root of the doctrine of the Trinity in the biblical revelation we began with and continually returned to the revealed name of Yahweh-Kyrios which embraces both the Old Testament and the New. *The doctrine of the Trinity is not and does not seek to be anything but an explanatory confirmation of this name* [italics mine]. This name is the name of a single being, of the one and only Willer and Doer whom the Bible calls God.[198]

His explication of the Fatherhood of God (T) is consistent with this particular reading of the identity of YHWH. He argues that the Fatherhood of God is not related to the creation at all (as had been argued by Plato or some of the apologists), but is exclusively in relation to the Son and this

---

196. Soulen, "YHWH the Triune God"; Klappert, "NAMENs des Gottes Israels," 54–72.
197. Yeago, "New Testament," 154–58.
198. Barth, *CD* 1.1, 348.

YHWH Is Trinity

predates creation.[199] When Jesus calls God Father, it was a reference to the intratrinitarian name of Father and not God as the Father of creation or as Father in the OT sense (Father of the nation Israel).[200] He further explains, "Not the Father alone, then, is God the Creator, but also the Son and the Spirit with Him. And the Father is not only God the Creator, but with the Son and the Spirit He is also God the Reconciler and God the Redeemer."[201] Not to confuse his statement with modalism or patripassianism, he writes that the Father was not conceived or was born as the Son did, nor did he die on the cross, although that does not make him less of a redeemer or reconciler.[202]

Robert Jenson believes YHWH is the proper name of Israel's God.[203] Concerning the identity of God in the NT, he writes, "The gospel of the New Testament is the provision of a new identifying description for this same God. . . . Identification of God by the resurrection did not replace identification by the Exodus, for it is essential to the God who raised Jesus that he is the same who freed Israel."[204] He states, "'Father, Son, and Holy Spirit' in fact occupies in the church the place occupied in Israel by 'Yahweh' even hasty observation of the church's life must discover."[205]

Jenson contends that the new identifying description of God—Father, Son, and Spirit—is also God's proper name and that the name Yahweh does not reappear because it was buried too deeply under the appellative "Lord." The church needed a proper name to identify God in her missionary reality. The name of Jesus became the name that served that purpose. The appearance of God's name as Father, Son, and Spirit was dependent on the invoking of God by naming Jesus.[206] Countering the temptation to say that Israel's God was superseded by the Christian God, Jenson argues that such suppositions are simply false because the church's triune mission depended on Israel's eschatological mission.[207] Therefore, Jesus could say, "Whoever has seen me has seen the Father" (John 14:9 ESV). Jenson's arguments are persuasive and his contention that YHWH

199. Barth, *CD* 1.1, 390–98.
200. Barth, *CD* 1.1, 393.
201. Barth, *CD* 1.1, 394–95.
202. Barth, *CD* 1.1, 396–97.
203. Jenson, *Triune Identity*, 4–5; Jenson, *Systematic Theology*, 44–46.
204. Jenson, *Triune Identity*, 7–8.
205. Jenson, *Triune Identity*, 10.
206. Jenson, *Triune Identity*, 8–10.
207. Jenson, *Triune Identity*, 34.

was buried under the appellative "Lord" seem to be a plausible explanation for NT's understanding of the identity of YHWH. The NT calls Jesus and the Spirit "Lord"; in the NT the occurrences of the "Lord" make the identity of YHWH even more explicit.

Kendall Soulen proposes YHWH as the eternal identity of the immanent Trinity.[208] The name of YHWH, argues Soulen, was replaced by the individual identity of the Father, Son, and Spirit in the Trinitarian formularies of the early church. He suggests that the main reason for this shift in attitude is due to the ancient Christian teaching of supersessionism—church replaced Israel; therefore, the New Covenant is superior to the Old Covenant.[209] This attitude resulted in replacing "YHWH" with the persons of the Godhead.[210] Soulen argues that YHWH is the name

---

208. Soulen, "YHWH the Triune God." See also Soulen, *God of Israel*; Soulen, *Divine Name(s)*. For a similar view, see Klappert, "NAMENs des Gottes Israels," 70–72. Klappert argues that a biblically sound doctrine of the Trinity should orient itself to the name of YHWH as revealed in the Old Testament because the Trinitarian doctrine is an explication of this one true God. He thinks that the background against which the doctrine of the Trinity is developed is not necessarily in defense against the Jews, but against the Neoplatonic philosophy and the teachings that philosophy engendered. There is room to reconsider the triune identity of God in light of the identity of YHWH.

209. Soulen, "YHWH the Triune God," 26–31. Soulen believes the hermeneutical tendency of viewing the relationship between Old and New Testaments in a type/antitype, shadow fulfillment relationship that leads to undermining the important aspect of God's revelation and dealings in the history of Israel. Because the OT was viewed only as a type or shadow the fulfillment of which is found in the NT, the former gradually receded to oblivion in Trinitarian thoughts. He suggests that the only way to reclaim biblical Trinitarianism (contra Neoplatonic) is by reclaiming the identity of YHWH as the triune God. God *is* YHWH both *en se* and in the economy.

210. Soulen maintains that there was a move from YHWH to *ousia*, also seen in the church fathers, that treats the important aspect of YHWH as God's identity to be subservient (supersessionism) to the identity of God as Father, Son, and Spirit. Soulen, "YHWH the Triune God," 36–41. Soulen's postulation of the lack of treatment of the Trinitarian identity of YHWH as due to supersessionism is too strong a claim although he does raise the importance of reconsidering the identity of YHWH in Christian theology. Part of the problem with his supersessionist view is that the church fathers, or for that reason Christian theologians in general, do not think that the God of the OT is less important and is trumped by the God of the NT. On the contrary, church, from very early on, did simply adopt the Father language for God in the OT and understood that to be the referent in Jesus' own reference to God as his Father. A better assessment of the traditional understanding of God the Father in the OT to be the first person of the Trinity would be to think that in the process of establishing the triune identity along with the eternality and the equality of the Son with the Father, the church did not always make a careful distinction between the immanent trinity and the economic trinity even though the creeds make it amply clear that the Father has always been the Father and the Son has always been the Son. They appropriated Jesus' own address to God as Father assuming that Jesus' "Father" language meant that the God in the OT was God

YHWH Is Trinity

of the immanent Trinity and the use of Father, Son, and Spirit shows discontinuity in Christian thought. Soulen's conclusion differs from Jenson's findings as seen earlier because Jenson sees continuity between the name of YHWH and the triune God.

Unlike Soulen, Saner observes that אֶהְיֶה אֲשֶׁר אֶהְיֶה in Exod 3:14 suggests that YHWH can only be identified through his self-reference and identification with Israel and he cannot be fully described. When the NT describes God as Father, Son, and Spirit, it is not an aberration of YHWH's identity; rather, as the NT argues, only God can truly reveal himself, which is what we see in Jesus. We know God through his actions. The nation Israel knew him thus and the NT church knows him as Father, Son, and Spirit or specifically in Paul's language, "but if the Spirit of Him who raised Jesus from the dead dwells in you, He who raised Christ Jesus from the dead will also give life to your mortal bodies through His Spirit who dwells in you" (Rom 8:11 NASB). He makes the important observation that the identity of YHWH necessarily makes room for the identity of the triune God and they are not incompatible or superseding—ontological and relational are not antithetical concepts.[211]

It is evident in the NT that the Son takes up a central role in redemptive history, but that does not mean that the Father and the Spirit are absent or passive. In the same way, YHWH in the OT cannot be viewed as God the Father alone. YHWH must be understood as Father, Son, and Spirit. We know it through the NT's explication of this one true God who was revealed to Moses and to the patriarchs. Although not clearly stated, it becomes obvious from the OT and NT references to YHWH that in the

---

the Father in the intra-Trinitarian sense (again, not everyone thought so). This conclusion is supported by the fact that the Apologists and many of the early church Fathers used the OT scriptures to argue for the eternality and equality of the Son although such assertions were made in light of the incarnation, death, and resurrection of Jesus. For them, Jesus was not a new God, but a new way of understanding YHWH, the one true God (see the earlier quote from, Gunton, *Father, Son, and Holy Spirit*, 4). Although there have been anti-Semitic sentiments in some quarters of Christian thinking that could have influenced the view of the OT for some people, that cannot be generalized because most Christians in the history of the church did regard the OT revelation as indispensable and foundational to Christian understanding of God and consider it integral to the identity of Jesus himself because he revealed the one true God of Israel. To suggest otherwise is misleading. For a critique of Soulen's position, see Saner, "*Too Much to Grasp*," 219–28.

211. Saner, "*Too Much to Grasp*," 228–30.

identity of YHWH we see the Trinitarian identity of the Father, Son, and Spirit. Hiddenness does not mean absence.[212]

Conclusion

As has been shown, there are evidence within the OT texts to suggest the presence of multiple persons in the identity of YHWH, even though there is ambiguity within those texts as to the precise identities of those persons who bear the name YHWH. The NT clarifies that ambiguity by identifying the Father, Son, and the Spirit as YHWH (1 Cor 8:6). Another important point this chapter presents is that Jesus' appellation for God as "my Father" is ontologically different from the appellation "Father" for God in the OT. YHWH not only means that it is God's identifying name to the nation Israel, but also a name that clearly states the relational aspect—he is known through his actions. In the NT, "Father" is used as an appellation for God in the generic sense (more or less in the OT sense of God as Father) and in the specific (ontological) sense as the first person of the Trinity. The NT's use of the OT quotations for Jesus whose referent in the OT was YHWH himself indicates that the new way of understanding God in the NT did not replace YHWH but simply explains who YHWH has always been.

The apologists and other church Fathers understood the appellation "Father" for God in the OT, often in conflicting ways, leading to more confusion. In the process, they sometimes referred to God in the OT as the first person of the Trinity although they often went back and forth between a generic and a specific identity. Jesus' reference to God as his Father might have influenced such an identification. However, Jesus used the appellation "Father" for God in the generic sense (John 8:41–42) and in the specific sense (John 14:9–11; 17:5). This shift in Jesus' use of "Father" for God has not always been carefully analyzed. This resulted in a kind of isolationism where the interpretation of the OT tended to exclude any reference to Jesus or to the Spirit.

As has already been discussed, the isolationist tendency that resulted from identifying YHWH as the first person of the Trinity led to conflicting interpretive proposals and conclusions. In this chapter, I offer a solution to overcome the isolationist tendency in biblical interpretation,

---

212. Saner, "*Too Much to Grasp*," 231. For a helpful survey on the hiddenness of YHWH, see Brueggemann, *Theology of the Old Testament*, 333–59.

especially a theological interpretation of Scripture, and that solution is to reconsider the identity of YHWH in the OT as triune. In order to do that, we need to first distinguish the two senses in which the appellation "Father" is used. Second, we need to recognize the presence of multiple persons in the identity of YHWH as evident in the many OT texts. Third, we need to carefully analyze how and why the NT ascribes to Jesus what was once ascribed exclusively to YHWH in the OT. Fourth, we need to get used to the language of "Father is YHWH," "Jesus is YHWH," and "the Spirit is YHWH" just as the Father is God, the Son is God, and the Spirit is God. Finally, we need to reevaluate our understanding of monotheism in light of the wider context of the Shema, particularly in relation to the many times the nation of Israel went after other "so-called" gods.

Theological interpretation must pay careful attention to the *sameness* of God in the OT and in the NT. The reconsideration of the identity of YHWH in the OT and that of the Father, Son, and Spirit in the NT demands a kind of reading that is faithful to that identity, vis-à-vis Trinitarian interpretation. As has been shown in chapter 2, current models of christological, pneumatological, ecclesial, and figural interpretations seem to misconstrue the identity of YHWH as P1. As a result, the phrase "Trinitarian interpretation" today functions practically as a placeholder in those proposals, resulting in considerable lacunae in the practice of Trinitarian interpretation. The reason for identifying YHWH with P1 lies in the misunderstanding of the appellation "Father" for God in the OT. As has been explicated, there is a difference between calling God "Father" in the OT and Jesus' reference to God the Father. To a great extent the problem is not about God the Father being YHWH because he is, but that he alone is YHWH.

If Trinitarian interpretation can embrace the triune identity of YHWH, then it will engender a kind of reading that is faithful to this identity. Such an identification of YHWH as the triune God helps one make better sense of the NT uses of the OT texts and can enjoy interpretive freedom that allows for the entire Scripture to be interpreted in light of this triune identity. In chapter 4, I demonstrate how such an understanding of the identity of YHWH could result in a robust kind of Trinitarian interpretation that is lacking today.

4

Bridging the Gap

JOHN GOLDINGAY ASSERTS THAT "theological interpretation is proper exegesis."[1] Therefore, Goldingay takes particular issue with the dominant position within historical critical interpretation that undermines a theological emphasis: "It is not merely that historical-critical study is influenced by evolutionism, Hegelianism, rationalism, and romanticism, though the study is so influenced. It is that the very focus on historical questions has a decisive effect on what interpreters find in the books, with the problem that it corresponds only partially to the book's own interests."[2] When we read William Shakespeare and Plato, they tell us something about their time. Goldingay states that if we were to study Shakespeare's *Anthony and Cleopatra* only to understand something more about the Roman Empire or seventeenth-century England and not about the play itself (its plot development, characters, structure, and how it all contribute to a single story), that would undermine the objective of the whole work.[3] Similarly, biblical interpretation must look beyond the historical matters, although they are important, to what they communicate about the God the Bible presents.

The OT Scriptures center on the question "about God and Israel and life. They are religious literature, not merely history or sociology.

1. Goldingay, *Need the New Testament?*, 160.
2. Goldingay, *Need the New Testament?*, 158–59.
3. Goldingay, *Need the New Testament?*, 159.

Exegetes need not agree with what the texts have to say on these matters, or even on whether these questions are important, but if they are aiming to do exegesis, one would expect that they would give major attention to these questions," states Goldingay.[4] This is what theological interpretation is emphasizing and the theological nature of these texts should be self-evident.[5]

Exegesis defined as a historical critical exercise is a narrow, questionable concept. A broader definition of exegesis is necessary as Kent Clarke and Stanley Porter advocate. After discussing the numerous ways the term "exegesis" has been defined, Clarke and Porter conclude that exegesis cannot be defined in monolithic terms:

> Exegesis is no one single thing, but rather a complex and multifaceted collection of disciplines. The approach or orientation one takes to exegesis, which is most often determined by the particular interest of the interpreter and the questions brought to the text, may only constitute one part of the whole exegetical task. For a linguist, exegesis becomes an analysis of lexis and grammar. For the historical critic, exegesis concerns itself with uncovering ancient backgrounds and original intentions. The theologian embraces exegesis in order to aid in the contemporization of traditions and doctrines that will continually speak in a new and vital way to present believers. The fact is that there are various aspects of a text's meaning and different types of exegesis can address these various aspects. For this reason, the exegete can never hope to present *the* exegesis of a passage as if it were the final word. Rather, one does an exegesis of a passage in which a coherent and informed interpretation is presented, based upon that interpreter's encounter with and investigation of a text at a given point in time.[6]

They understand exegesis to be quite diverse; thus, not giving one party monopoly over its definition.

James Dunn concurs with this conclusion: "Without the theological dimension to the task of interpretation, a historical or literary approach, no matter how insightful, will never get to the heart of the text as Scripture, to the heart of its theology."[7] Theological interpretation can also make a legitimate claim to exegesis.

4. Goldingay, *Need the New Testament?*, 159–60.
5. Goldingay, *Need the New Testament?*, 160.
6. Clarke and Porter, "What Is Exegesis?," 17–18.
7. Dunn, "Ex Akoēs Pisteōs," 35.

R. R. Reno reminds us concerning the role of doctrine in interpretation:

> Doctrine, then, is not a moldering scrim of antique prejudice obscuring the meaning of the Bible. It is a crucial aspect of the divine pedagogy, a clarifying agent for our minds fogged by self-deceptions, a challenge to our languid intellectual apathy that will too often rest in false truisms and the easy spiritual nostrums of the present age rather than search more deeply and widely for the dispersed keys to the many doors of scripture.[8]

If heeded, his timely words of wisdom will be of much benefit to theological interpretation. Turning to the question of various kinds of proposals for theological interpretation, especially Trinitarian interpretation, Goldingay makes some important observations that are pertinent to my criticism of the current models of christological, pneumatological, ecclesial, figural, and Trinitarian interpretations. Critiquing the arguments of Francis Watson, Phillip Cary, and Craig Bartholomew for a christological interpretation, Goldingay writes that Christ himself was theocentric.[9] Unlike Matthew, Paul sees the fulfillment of the OT prophecies in the church and not in the person of Christ. Therefore, it is better to say that the NT is ecclesiocentric rather than christocentric.[10] Goldingay argues that Jesus came to reveal God, to speak of his reign, and to bring him glory so that God may be all in all.[11]

Goldingay's objection to christological interpretation is shaped mainly on two points. First, the concept that the OT cannot be understood apart from Christ misconstrues the fact that there was no OT but just Scriptures when Jesus came. Second, the misidentification of YHWH in the OT as P1.[12] OT interpretation mostly from a christological perspective undermines the messages of the OT because the OT is more than about Christ. In order to hear the message of the OT clearly, a proper understanding of the Godhead in Scripture is necessary because Christ has always been YHWH.

---

8. Reno, *Genesis*, 12.

9. Goldingay, *Need the New Testament?*, 161–62. Cf. Watson, *Text and Truth*, 185; Cary, *Jonah*, 17; Bartholomew, "Listening for God's Address," 3.

10. Hays, *Echoes of Scripture*, xiii; Hays, "'No Lasting City,'" 151–52.

11. Cf. Phil 2:11; 1 Cor 15:24, 28; Goldingay, *Need the New Testament?*, 162.

12. Goldingay, *Need the New Testament?*, 163, 167. For him, the concept of the OT developed only after the writings of the NT.

Goldingay subjects current proposals for a Trinitarian interpretation to similar criticism. For example, Richard Schultz states that the Major Prophets can be interpreted in a Trinitarian fashion because we can find references to the Father, Son, and Spirit in these books:

> The Major Prophets ... are strikingly trinitarian. First of all, their message is christocentric, repeatedly looking beyond the ongoing series of political and military crises and the spiritual malaise that marked the Israelite monarchy, as well as the devastating humiliation of exile, to the coming of a Davidic heir and just ruler who would succeed where his predecessors had failed and would therefore enable Israel to experience the covenantal blessings that they frequently forfeited through disobedience....
> Second, the Major Prophets refer more frequently to God as "Father" than other sections of the Old Testament (e.g., Isa. 9:6; 63:16; 64:8; Jer. 3:4, 19; cf. Mal. 1:6; 2:10). Finally, the Spirit is instrumentally involved in the ministries of the prophets and the future Davidic king (e.g., Isa. 11:2; 32:15; 34:16; 42:1; 44:3; 48:16; 59:21; 61:1; 63:10, 11, 14; Ezek. 2:2; 3:12, 14, 24; 8:3; 11:1, 5, 24; 36:27; 37:1, 14; 39:39; 43:5). The Major Prophets should be heard as a message regarding the triune God's will and plan for humanity—with a special focus on Israel.[13]

Craig Bartholomew argues similarly, "Precisely because a theological hermeneutic is Christocentric it will be trinitarian."[14] It is evident that these proposals that advocate a Trinitarian interpretation also misconstrue the identity of YHWH. As I indicated in the last chapter, "Father" in the OT does not necessarily mean the first person of the Trinity (P1). Moreover, a case has already been made that YHWH in the OT is the Father, Son, and Spirit.

Goldingay concludes his critique of the proposal for a so-called Trinitarian interpretation, "Christian theological interpretation will be trinitarian in the sense that it knows that Yahweh the God of Israel is the God who is Trinity. It will not be Trinitarian in the sense that it looks for reference to the Trinity in Isaiah or Genesis."[15] Goldingay points out an important gap in the current models of Trinitarian interpretation, the misconstrual of the identity of YHWH.

---

13. Schultz, "Hearing the Major Prophets," 335–36.
14. Bartholomew, "Listening for God's Address," 4.
15. Goldingay, *Need the New Testament?*, 169.

For the most part, I agree with Goldingay's observations about the shortcomings of these proposals. His criticism of the christological and the Trinitarian interpretation also applies to ecclesial, pneumatological, and figural interpretation because they too make the same mistake of identifying YHWH in the OT as P1. Consequently, these proposals exhibit an overwhelming tendency to isolate the persons of the Godhead in their economic manifestations. He is justified in pointing out that these works are not truly Trinitarian because they fail to embrace the Trinitarian identity of YHWH in the OT. To mitigate the isolating tendency in Trinitarian interpretation, a reconsideration of the identity of YHWH in conjunction with making proper distinctions between the generic and the specific uses of the appellation "Father" for God are necessary, as proposed in the last chapter.

As indicated in the introduction, there is a chasm between proposals and practices in Trinitarian interpretation. A common tendency among the practitioners of TIS is to theorize the need for Trinitarian interpretation and leave it at that, without demonstrating how such a theory affects the reading itself. There is a need to demonstrate how a Trinitarian reading that is founded upon the triune identity of YHWH impacts biblical interpretation; otherwise, my own proposal would fall short and come under the same criticism that I level at others.

Now that the identity of YHWH has been established as Father, Son, and Spirit, it should facilitate a more fully Trinitarian reading of the whole Scripture by escaping Marcion's straitjacket. It would also help bridge the chasm that exists between Trinitarian proposals and practice. Because YHWH is the triune God, one can see the presence of all three persons of the Godhead beginning with the first chapter of Genesis even though the Father, Son, and Spirit are not identified individually. It is also incumbent for exegetes to remember that since the Father is YHWH, the Son is YHWH, and the Spirit is YHWH, the words and actions of YHWH in the OT can later be attributed to any one person of the Godhead without contradiction.

The following case studies on Gen 3:22 and 1 Cor 10:4 demonstrate how the identity of YHWH as the triune God affects Trinitarian interpretation. Since the identity of YHWH is taken to be Trinitarian, the reading of these passages exhibits a free movement between the OT and the NT passages where the transition from YHWH to any one person of the Godhead is undertaken without providing the necessary rationale for such a move in every instance. These examples are but one way of undertaking a Trinitarian interpretation.

"Eat and Live Forever"—Gen 3:22

The immediate background to Gen 3:22 highlights the important role this verse plays both in what follows immediately and in the ensuing story of redemption and eternal life. Earlier in Gen 3 we see human disobedience by eating from the tree of the knowledge of good and evil (3:1–6). As a result, YHWH declared the consequences of that action on the woman, the serpent, and the man (3:13–19). Genesis 3:22 appears at the end of YHWH's pronouncement of judgment and before Adam and Eve were expelled from the Garden of Eden.[16] It provides one of the reasons for their expulsion from the garden.[17]

---

16. The historical character and purpose of Gen 3:22 and 24 and chapters 2–3 in general divide scholarly opinion. Westermann, *Genesis*, 272–73. Westermann discusses the new motif ("and live forever") introduced in v. 22 in relation to the tree of life, which is absent in its earlier mention (2:9), and observes its correspondence with the Gilgamesh Epic to suggest that the primeval narrative in Gen 2–3 is not unique to Hebrew tradition. He also suggests that 3:22 and 24 originate from a separate tradition and v. 22 has a faint similarity with the "motif of the envy of the Gods" as found in other ANE traditions (273). Contrary to the "motif of the envy of the Gods," Hamilton argues that there was nothing sinister to suggest that God was being jealous because he had not forbidden their right to the tree of life before. Hamilton, *Genesis*, 209. For a detailed critical introduction to Genesis, see Wenham, *Genesis 1–15*. Wenham argues that the theological theme of Genesis presents an alternative worldview to the presuppositions of the ancient Near East (xlv). See also Aitken, "Divine Will and Providence," 282–302; Lanfer, *Remembering Eden*. According to Westermann, the thrust of Gen 2–3 is not to present a history of the "fall" (a term he disagrees with), but to answer the question "why is a person who is created by God limited by death, suffering, toil and sin?" Westermann, *Genesis*, 277. Walter Brueggemann posits that the Genesis account of creation deals with the "reality of God" and not merely an account of the fall. As such it presents something more than a hopeless analysis of the human predicament, it is a call to live in his world on his terms as obedient creatures. Brueggemann, *Genesis*, 44. Brueggemann presents an exposition of the creation account that diverges from Paul's interpretation of it (Rom 5:12–21) as a historical account of the fall and the dominant dogmatic position influenced by Paul's reading. Instead, he links Gen 2–3 in the lectionary with Mark 3:20–35 and 2 Cor 4:13—5:1 (42–44). Abraham Kuruvilla, using the language of the fall contends that the main focus of this book is on divine blessing. Kuruvilla, *Genesis*, 6. Kuruvilla sees a temple imagery in the creation narrative and connects it with the rest of the OT to argue that man was created to serve God and worship him in his temple—a desire the Psalmist often revealed (Pss 23:6; 27:4–6; 42:1–2; 63:1–4; 84:1–4, 10). Kuruvilla writes, "It is probably not coincidental that the Hebrew Bible begins with an account of God's creation of heaven and earth (Gen 1:1) and ends with a command from God to build a temple in Jerusalem (2 Chr 36:23; 2 Chronicles is the last book of the Hebrew Bible in Jewish reckoning): in twenty-four books, biblical history goes from creation (Temple) to Temple (creation)" (48).

17. Mathews, *Genesis*, 256.

This verse starts with יְהוָה אֱלֹהִים discussing an urgent situation in which he has to act in a certain way. Man is now in a position to take from the tree of life and eat.[18] The problem is not with man eating from the tree of life, but him eating from it after what had happened earlier. Even though God had forbidden man from eating from the tree of the knowledge of good and evil, he still had the capacity to choose to eat or not to eat from that tree. Mankind exercised their capacity and chose to eat from the tree of the knowledge of good and evil. They are now in a similar position where they are able to make another decision, whether to eat from the tree of life or not to eat from it.

Twice in chapters 2–3 we read that God forbade man from eating from a certain tree. At first, it was about eating from the tree of the knowledge of good and evil (2:17—לֹא תֹאכַל) and the second time it was from the tree of life (3:22—וְאָכַל . . . פֶּן). The first eating results in death and the second eating results in life forever. While "life forever" is desirable, that is not the case in man's present condition of disobedience and fall.[19] יהוה does not want them to take from the tree of life, eat, and live forever because the first act of eating resulted in death. The second act of eating would have resulted in man's life in that state forever.[20] God did not

---

18. H. Obbink states that Adam had indeed eaten from the tree of life before this because God did not forbid man from eating from the tree of life in Gen 2:16–17. In fact, the way man was able to live forever was by eating from the tree of life (Obbink thinks that this was the way Adam was immortal). To substantiate his claim, he argues that the פֶּן in 3:22 should be translated not as "lest" but as "lest further" or "lest more" (Exod 1:17; 1 Sam 13:19). By sending man out of the garden of Eden, he was denied access to the tree of life in order to eat and continue to live forever. Obbink, "Tree of Life in Eden," 475. Contra Obbink, Cassuto feels that man had not eaten from the tree of life before. His argument hinges on the presence of פֶּן (lest) in 3:22, which suggests that man had not eaten before from the tree of life. His access to the tree of life was conditional in that if he had continued in his simplicity by keeping God's command, he could have even achieved immortality by eating the fruit of the tree of life. Cassuto, *Genesis*, 123–24, 172–73.

19. *Pseudo-Jonathan* reads: "Then the Lord said to the angels who were serving before Him, 'Behold, Adam is alone on earth just as I am alone in the high heaven. There will come from him those who know how to distinguish between good and evil. If he had kept the rule which I commanded him, he would have lived and endured just as the tree of life, forever. . . .For, if he eats from it, he will live and endure forever.'" Drazin and Wagner, trans., *Onkelos on the Torah: Genesis*, 407.

20. Whybray, "Genesis," 44. Whybray suggests that v. 22 echoes the Mesopotamian myth that mankind fails to attain immortality. According to Whybray, chapters 2–3 do not indicate that mankind was intended for immortality. But after the fall, God did not want man to obtain immortality in his state of disobedience. Hence, v. 22 suggests that through man's expulsion from the garden, God could prevent man from reaching that state of immortality.

want man to attain eternal life on his own. He wanted man to depend on him for life.²¹ If they reach out and take from the tree of life, they have a chance to live in the state of rebellion forever.²² So he expels them from the garden (v. 24).

Although the first act of eating resulted in death at once and YHWH prevented man eating a second time (from a different tree), the story does not end there. The very YHWH who prevented man from the possibility to "eat and live forever" in Gen 3:22 is going to offer man another chance to "eat and live forever" in John 6:27–58—both actions show an act of kindness on the part of YHWH.

The LXX translates וְאָכַל וָחַי לְעֹלָם as καὶ φάγῃ καὶ ζήσεται εἰς τὸν αἰῶνα. The phrase φάγῃ καὶ ζήσεται εἰς τὸν αἰῶνα "eat and live forever" appears only twice more in the entire canonical Scripture. It is found in John 6:51—φάγῃ ἐκ τούτου τοῦ ἄρτου ζήσει εἰς τὸν αἰῶνα and in John 6:58—ὁ τρώγων τοῦτον τὸν ἄρτον ζήσει εἰς τὸν αἰῶνα. Special focus needs to be given to "eating" that results in "living forever."

Could the eating of the fruit of the tree of life have led to life forever? Rabbinical interpretation takes the view that by not allowing man to eat from the tree of life after he had disobeyed, God was giving him an opportunity to repent. Otherwise, he could have lived forever in his state of rebellion.²³ The fact that man was not allowed to eat from the tree of life, after having disobeyed God's commandment and that he was expelled from the garden of Eden, it is appropriate to ask, as does Gerhard von Rad, "Could man at all, after his sentencing, break through the ban of death?"²⁴ The answer to this question is found in Jesus' emphatic statement that it is possible for man to break through the ban of death, albeit not on his own, for he says "I am the living bread which came down from heaven. If anyone eats from this bread, he will live forever" (John 6:51 cf. 58).

In John 6:27–58 Jesus presents himself as the bread that came down from heaven and eating his flesh grants eternal life (live forever).²⁵ Rudolf

---

21. Kessler and Deurloo, *Commentary on Genesis*, 57–58.

22. Mathews, *Genesis*, 256.

23. R. Abba b. Kahana writes, "This teaches that the Holy One, blessed be He, provided him with an opportunity of repentance. . . . Then the Holy One, blessed be He, said: SHALL HE PUT FORTH HIS HAND, AND EAT ALSO OF THE TREE OF LIFE? while if he does eat, HE WILL LIVE FOR EVER. Therefore THE LORD SENT HIM FORTH FROM THE GARDEN OF EDEN." Freedman, *Midrash Rabbah: Genesis*, 175–76.

24. Rad, *Genesis*, 97.

25. Haenchen, *John*, 291. See also his commentary on 50a (293–94). ὁ ἄρτος in 6:33 is masculine gender. It could refer to either the bread or to Jesus Christ, reasons

Bultmann suggests that vv. 51b–58 are a reference to the Lord's Supper.[26] Until v. 51, we see Jesus' reference to eating his flesh, but in v. 53 we see the addition of "drinking my blood," suggesting a shift in Johannine language from believing in Jesus for eternal life to partaking in the Lord's Supper for eternal life. This act of eating and drinking grants eternal life and they are guaranteed of their resurrection (v. 54).[27] Ignatius writes to the Ephesians that the breaking of bread in the Eucharist is the "medicine of immortality, the antidote that we should not die."[28] John Calvin in his commentary on Gen 3:22 writes that the "life forever" that Adam was denied was regained through Christ.[29]

Knowing the intention of those who were seeking him for bread, Jesus, in John 6:27, told them that they must not work for the food that perishes, but for the food that supplies eternal life. The language here is very similar to Jesus' conversation with the Samaritan woman in 4:14.[30] Not to confuse about what he meant by "work," Jesus immediately clarifies that the work that he has in mind is their "belief" in the one whom God has sent—their faith in Jesus Christ (29).

Haenchen. He states that the interchange between bread and flesh in this pericope of John is noteworthy as they are used synonymously for the body of Christ. Jesus asserts in 6:53 that "unless you eat the flesh of the Son of Man and drink His blood, you have no life in yourselves" (NASB). Earlier in 6:35 Jesus compared eating and drinking akin to believing in him. The question of whether or not this passage is a reference to the Eucharist has been debated. Haenchen, *On Gospel of John*, 1:295. For a detailed discussion on the different discourses in John 6, see Mackay, *John's Relationship with Mark*.

26. Rudolf Bultmann asserts that vv. 51b–58 is an interpolation of the editor and this passage is a reference to the Eucharist. Bultmann, *Gospel of John*, 234–37. Craig Keener is not certain that this refers to the Eucharistic. He understands Jesus' language in terms of midrashic exegesis and compares "bread of life" with the Torah as in Rabbinical Judaism. The mention of bread and wine does not automatically make it eucharistic since most of the Jewish meals would have those components present. He concludes that John's eucharistic language applies to Jesus' death itself and not merely to the symbols that point to his death. Keener, *Gospel of John*, 679–91. See also Schnackenburg, *Gospel according to St. John*, 30–69. Andreas Köstenberger suggests that this section is not eucharistic because σάρξ is used for the "flesh" and not σῶμα (1 Cor 11:24), which is commonly used in relation to the Lord's Supper. Köstenberger, *John*, 215.

27. Bultmann, *Gospel of John*, 235–36.

28. Ignatius, "Epistle to the Ephesians," 68. Schnackenburg highlights the fact that most of the church fathers viewed 6:52–59 as Eucharistic. Schnackenburg, *Gospel according to St. John*, 2:65–69. For a summary of patristic commentary on 6:53–58, see Elowsky, *John 1–10*, 238–43.

29. Calvin, *First Book of Moses*, 184.

30. Carson, *John*, 284.

An important point to be noted in Jesus' reference to himself as the "bread of life" in vv. 35–49 is that he does not talk about eating this bread nor does he talk about his flesh being the bread. Instead, we see the phrase "the one who believes" immediately after his statement of "I am the bread of life" (35, 40, 44–48 NASB).[31] The first time we read about eating the bread is in v. 50. From here on, the language changes from believing in Jesus being the bread of life for eternal life to eating this bread (specifically his flesh) for eternal life. Whether or not 6:51b–58 is reference to Eucharist is beside the point. One needs to understand vv. 51b–58 in light of vv. 27–48. Together, they reveal two complementary elements. First, belief in Jesus, and second, eating his flesh and drinking his blood allow the reversal of what happened long ago in the garden of Eden, that is, man is now given the opportunity to "eat and live forever."

Man was not allowed to attain eternal life on his own by eating from the tree of life in Gen 3:22; he is now granted access to eternal life through his dependence on God's provision in Jesus Christ—through the very act of "eating." YHWH once denied man the opportunity to "eat and live forever." The same YHWH is now giving him the opportunity to "eat and live forever"—a mysterious yet an incredible relationship with YHWH. If the consequences of sin and disobedience resulted in punishment and denial of access to eating that results in living forever, its remedy also comes through eating, which results in living forever. This connection between Gen 3:22 and John 6:51, 58 appears relevant and clear once "eating" and "living forever" are understood from the perspective of Trinitarian interpretation. This transition between Gen 3:22 and John 6:51, 58 is possible because the identity of YHWH is understood to be Trinitarian and therefore, justifiable.

"And the Rock *Was* Christ"—1 Cor 10:4

It is necessary to place 1 Cor 10:1–13 in its immediate context to better understand what Paul meant when he wrote "and the rock was Christ."[32] In chapters 8–11 Paul instructs the Corinthians about how they should exercise their Christian liberty, especially given the possibility that the very exercising of their liberty could be detrimental to a weak brother's Christian life. In chapter 8, Paul discusses the issue of eating "food offered

---

31. Carson, *John*, 288–94.
32. Davidson, *Typology in Scripture*, 203–7; Thiselton, *Corinthians*, 723.

to idols." In 8:4–8, Paul states that idols are nothing; it is permissible for someone to eat from the food offered to the idols if that person's conscience permits. However, Paul reminds the Corinthians that they need to be careful in the way they exercise this freedom because such an exercise could be a hindrance to the one who is weak on such matters (v. 9). Paul exhorts the Corinthians to be responsible and caring in the exercise of their rights as Christians. Paul himself mentions in 9:11–12, 24–27, and 10:22–31 that he voluntarily makes no use of his own freedom for the sake of his fellow believers. The Golden Rule of "love one another" is perfected in such acts; 1 Cor 10:1–13 should be understood within this larger context.

In 1 Cor 10:1–13 Paul directs the attention of the Corinthians to an important matter.[33] The paraenetic section (vv. 6–11) seems to be a continuation of 9:24–27 where Paul expresses his awareness of the danger of being disqualified in ministry and the prize for which he runs.[34] He expresses similar concerns for the Corinthian believers. They too face the danger of being unapproved by God just as those with whom God was displeased during the wilderness journey.[35] What happened to Israelites serves as an example (10:6, 11) and a warning for the Corinthian believers (10:12). It is in this context that we read Paul's reference to Christ as the rock that followed the Israelites during the wilderness journey from which they drank.

Paul makes two explicit references to Christ in the first thirteen verses (vv. 4, 9). Some call vv. 1–13 Paul's midrash on Num 21:16–20.[36] Peter Enns calls Paul's reference to a moveable rock in v. 4 as "one witness

---

33. Han, *Swimming in the Sea*, 79, 85–86, 110. There are similarities between 1 Cor 10:1–13 and 2 Cor 6:14—7:1 in that Paul sees the OT Scriptures speaking about the believers in general and the Corinthian believers in particular. This is not an isolated instance of Paul seeing Christ and the church in the OT Scriptures.

34. Lockwood, *1 Corinthians*, 322. γὰρ in 10:1 seems to suggest that 10:1–13 is a justification or further evidence for his statement in 9:24–27.

35. Ciampa and Rosner, *Corinthians*, 443.

36. Enns, "The 'Moveable Well,'" 23–38. Enns is in agreement with many scholars with his focus on the apparent extrabiblical tradition behind this text. For example, see Collins, *First Corinthians*, 364. See also, Strack and Billerbeck, *Kommentar zum Neuen Testament*, 408; Lietzmann, *An die Korinther 1-2*; Pickup, "New Testament Interpretation," 353–81. Pickup argues that the midrashic exegesis was acceptable and takes biblical inspiration seriously. In his view, midrashic exegesis should not be perceived as allegorical; instead, its atomistic use of the OT texts must be seen as a legitimate way of finding additional significance for an earlier word or phrase at a later time within the framework of the entire canon. Pickup, "New Testament Interpretation," 357–63.

to an established exegetical tradition."³⁷ His conclusion is based on the rabbinic interpretation of a "moveable well." Enns focuses on the aspect of "mobility."³⁸ After analyzing the extrabiblical sources, Enns concludes that Paul must have been aware of this tradition because outside this tradition one cannot find any reference to a "mobile" source of water. His argument is built on the premise that the midrashic tradition is necessary to understand 1 Cor 10:4.³⁹

Contrary to Enns' conclusion, Richard Davidson argues that Pauline interpretation of the OT events does not have to be dependent on rabbinic Midrashim.⁴⁰ Davidson points out the fact that the legend of the "moveable well" is solely based on Num 21:17–18 and not on the passages in which water from the rock is mentioned. Paul does not follow any of the details of the rabbinic legends.⁴¹ Instead of finding a midrashic origin for Pauline reference to the "rock that followed," Davidson finds

---

37. Enns, "'Moveable Well,'" 25. See also Hanson, *Jesus Christ*, 11–23; Ellis, *Prophecy and Hermeneutic*, 209–12. Ellis addresses the loose equation between the rabbinic legends of Num 21:17–18 and 1 Cor 10:4. He concludes that, although there are several dissimilarities between the two, it is not impossible to see such a connection between the two; 1 Cor 10:4 can be considered an allusion to rabbinic midrash. For rabbinic references to a "moveable well," see Charlesworth, "Pseudo-Philo (First Century A.D.)," 297–378; Grossfeld, *Targum Onqelos*. Contra Enns, Garland contends that Paul could have wondered, as did ancient exegetes, what were the water sources for the Israelites between Exod 17:1–7 and Num 20:1–11? The first time the "rock" appears is in Exod 17:1–7 and the last time it appears is in Num 20:1–11. It could be that it was the same rock in both places; if so, the rock must have followed them. For Paul to make such a conclusion is a small step because he has already mentioned Christ as the source of all spiritual gift (1:4–7) and source of creation (8:6). Garland, *1 Corinthians*, 456–57. For similar arguments to that of Garland, see Kaiser, *Uses of the Old Testament*; Godet, *Commentary on First Corinthians*; Bruce, *1 and 2 Corinthians*. Bruce concludes that Paul did not follow the midrashic tradition; instead, he might have alluded to YHWH as "rock" (Deut 32:4, 15, 18, 30, 31; Ps 18:2, 31; 19:14; 28:1; 62:2; 78:35; 89:26; 144:1; Isa 26:4) and the angel of YHWH (Exod 14:19; 23:20–23; 32:34; 33:2 cf. Acts 7:30, 38), seeing the preexistent Christ. Bruce, *1 and 2 Corinthians*, 91.

38. Enns, "'Moveable Well,'" 23.

39. Enns, "'Moveable Well,'" 27–28.

40. Davidson, *Typology in Scripture*, 223–48.

41. Details such as the well were created on the evening of the sixth day. It was given to Israel on account of Miriam. It had the shape of a beehive; it functioned like sieve. Its water flowed from a flask's many openings. Occasionally it delivered water to individual doors and caused the growth of many plants and trees. Its verdure provided wine for the drink offering and perfume for women. It was an effective deodorant. Long ago it flooded the valley and killed the armies of Israel's enemies, and it is still visible in the Sea of Tiberias. Davidson, *Typology in Scripture*, 235–37.

OT evidences that better explain Pauline rationale, especially in light of the immediate context of 1 Cor 10:4.

At first, Paul mentions that all Israelites ate the same spiritual food and drank the same spiritual drink (10:3–4) before remarking on the identity of that rock. Another place where food and water appear in such a close proximity is in Exod 16–17 (cf. Deut 8:15, 16; Neh 9:15; Ps 78:16; 105:41; 114:8; Isa 48:21).[42] The water from the rock is preceded by food—the bread that came down from heaven (Exod 16:4). Moses' song in Deuteronomy 32 repeatedly mentions YHWH as "the Rock" (32:4, 15, 18, 30–31).[43] It is possible that Paul makes some connection between the "rock" in Deut 32 and Christ. This possibility is even stronger when we consider the fact that Paul quotes from Deut 32:17 in 1 Cor 10:20 only few verses after he referred to the rock as Christ, argues Davidson.[44]

Davidson concludes, "It appears that for Paul, Jesus is the Rock because he is Yahweh of the OT, and not because Philo has allegorically equated the rock with wisdom and Paul sees Jesus as the true Wisdom."[45] Though it is beyond the scope of this book to deal any further with the question of whether Paul did or did not appropriate an already existing form of exegesis, it can be concluded that one does not have to resort to attributing a midrashic origin for Pauline thought, especially in light of Paul's own conviction as outlined in chapter 3 of this book. Paul had no qualms attributing to Jesus what was once said exclusively of YHWH (cf. Isa 45:21–23; Phil 2:9–11 or Joel 2:32; Rom 10:13).[46] It was because Paul saw Jesus in the person of YHWH. The question is not whether Paul could have used any materials from an already existing midrashic tradition or alluded to it. Paul made references to pagan materials elsewhere to make his point (for example, Acts 17:23; Titus 1:12).

---

42. Davidson, *Typology in Scripture*, 239.

43. Davidson, *Typology in Scripture*, 244–45. See also Bauckham, *Jesus and the God*, 100.

44. This argument of Davidson goes both ways because in Num 21:4–9 we read about the Israelites being bitten by snakes because of their rebellion against the Lord, which is mentioned in 1 Cor 10:9. The well legend has its origin in Num 21:17–18.

45. Davidson, *Typology in Scripture*, 243. James Dunn argues for divine wisdom as Paul's preferred way of referring to preexistent Christ. Dunn, *Theology of Paul the Apostle*, 266–77.

46. Such a connection between YHWH and Christ is not an aberration in Pauline thought, but Paul's way of explicating faith in one true YHWH who is the Father, Son, and Spirit.

The important question seems to be whether there is something within this passage (or within Pauline corpus) that reveals Paul's own understanding of Christ's relationship to the Israelites. If such evidence exists, that might help explain Paul's reference to Christ as the "rock" in v. 4. In fact, such evidence exists and can be found within this section itself. Going beyond Paul, we also find other references within the NT that would have influenced Paul's conclusion. They can be found in Jesus' own statements concerning the "bread of life" and "living water."

In v. 9, Paul makes explicit the presence of Christ during the wilderness journey.[47] Here Paul mentions that it was Christ whom the Israelites tested in the wilderness (Num 21:5–9) when they tested the LORD (v. 7) and were bitten by the snakes.[48] Whether or not Χριστόν was the original reading in v. 9 is debated.[49] Bruce M. Metzger makes an important observation in his critical examination of the textual variants: "The reading that best explains the origin of the others is Χριστόν, attested by the oldest Greek manuscript ($\mathfrak{P}^{46}$) as well as by a wide diversity of early patristic and versional witnesses.... The difficulty of explaining how the ancient Israelites in the wilderness could have tempted Christ prompted some copyists to substitute either the ambiguous or the unobjectionable. *Paul's reference to Christ here is analogous to that in ver. 4*" (italics mine).[50] Metzger suggests that vv. 4 and 9 have similar referent.

"And the rock was Christ" was an original Pauline thought; it did not have to come from a midrashic tradition.[51] What does it mean? It means that, for Paul, the God who provided the manna and the water

---

47. Bates, *Apostolic Proclamation*, 88. Paul clearly believed in the preexistence of Christ (Rom 8:3; 10:6; 1 Cor 8:6; Gal 4:4; Phil 2:6–11; Col 1:15–20). Therefore, it was not difficult for him to see the presence of the preexistent Christ during the wilderness journey.

48. As discussed in chapter 3, Jesus was already recognized within the identity of YHWH (not added to the identity of YHWH); Paul nuances that understanding when he identifies Christ as the one whom the Israelites tested in the wilderness. For Paul, there was no doubt to the identity of Jesus and YHWH. Paul's conviction becomes evident in his interchangeable use of YHWH and Christ for the identity of the God of Israel during the wilderness journey. Cf. Jude 5.

49. See chapter 3 for a detailed text-critical analysis of this verse.

50. Metzger, *Textual Commentary*, 494.

51. Enns ignores the words of 1 Cor 10:9 that the Israelites tested Christ in the wilderness. According to his acceptance of 10:4 as a midrashic reading, one would expect to find a similar tradition for v. 9. In its absence, one could certainly argue that if Paul did not need a midrashic tradition to substantiate that the Israelites tested Christ in the wilderness, perhaps he did not have to depend on a similar tradition to determine that "the rock was Christ."

in the wilderness is the same God whom the Israelites tested and whom the Corinthians are in danger of displeasing just as the Israelites did (cf. 1 Cor 8:6).[52]

Hans Hübner explains the NT interpretation of the OT events this way:

> The New Testament authors did not consider themselves as writers who provided the holy Scripture of Israel with a new conclusion that supposedly included an ultimate validity because they were proclaiming an ultimately valid message. They were firmly convinced, however, that their writings had final authority. After all, their intention was to mediate in a literal form the final word of God, which is the Kerygma of God's final act of salvation in Jesus Christ; consequently, they intended to present the only correct interpretation of Israel's Scripture. It was their conviction that the Christological understanding of the holy Scripture would supply it with the indisputable and indispensable eschatological-messianic meaning, which, in pointing toward the Christ event, already was the original meaning.[53]

Statements such as this can be overcome if, as asserted in chapter 3, the identity of YHWH can be understood as Trinitarian. A Trinitarian reading does not see Paul's reference to Christ as the "rock" problematic because Christ is the same God who provided food and water to the Israelites. In fact, the Trinitarian identity of YHWH helps explain how Paul sees God's work in the past and his work in the present. There is continuity because he is the same God.

Paul calls the exodus generation "fathers" of the Corinthians (v. 1) and proceeds to argue that what happened in the history of Israel is very relevant to them. Paul focuses on the aspect of the "journey."[54] He compares the journey of the exodus generation with the Christian life (journey) of the Corinthian believers. Certain aspects of their wilderness journey are pertinent and instructive to the Christian journey. The Corinthian believers cannot be complicit or unwitting participants in similar tragedy (here the reference is to those with whom God was not pleased).

---

52. Bauckham, *Jesus and the God*, 97–104. Bauckham argues that Paul clearly saw Jesus within the identity of YHWH. This is especially evident in 1 Cor 10:4, 9.

53. Hübner, "New Testament Interpretation," 334.

54. In 9:24–27 he used the analogy of race. He moves between "race" and "journey" to make the same point—disqualification is a possibility.

Bridging the Gap

The exodus generation ate the same spiritual[55] food and drank the same spiritual drink from the spiritual rock that followed them and the rock was Christ (vv. 3-4; Exod 16:4—17:7; Num 11:6-9; 20:1-13; Ps 78:15-16).[56] What did Paul mean by ἡ πέτρα δὲ ἦν ὁ Χριστός (and the rock *was* Christ)? Paul does not have a particular "rock" in mind as indicated by the anarthrous πέτρας (γὰρ ἐκ πνευματικῆς ἀκολουθούσης πέτρας).[57] As a result Paul may have had in mind not just one act of drinking, but an ongoing action in the past, as indicated by the imperfect ἔπινον (v. 4).[58] The Israelites needed water throughout their journey and we do not read about them lacking water except in couple of places where God instructed Moses to strike or speak to the rock for water. It means that God provided them with water as if the water or the source of water followed them. Just as God provided them food so also he provided them water.[59]

Davidson suggests that Paul's use of "spiritual" food and "spiritual" drink somehow points to the Lord's Supper:

> By describing the sustenance of Israel with Eucharistic terminology, Paul indicates that the OT events/elements (eating the manna and drinking water from the Rock) point forward as advance-presentations of the Lord's Supper. In parallel to the Corinthians' participation in the Eucharist, the apostle seems to intimate that ancient Israel also partook of sacramental gifts which conveyed the Spirit.... If ancient Israel received sacramental gifts of the Spirit and yet experienced divine retribution when they persisted in sin, so it 'must-needs-be' with the new Israel, the Christian Church.[60]

---

55. Πνευματικῆς (spiritual) in Paul's writings means more than figurative (cf. Rom 1:11; Gal 6:1; Eph 1:3; Col 3:16). Collins notes that Paul's use of spiritual "describes reality that is thoroughly influenced by the Spirit, the creative and salvific power of God." Collins, *First Corinthians*, 369.

56. Regarding Exod 17:6 Rabbi H. Lehrman comments that God granted Moses permission to strike any rock to produce water: "They can have their choices of rocks; from whichever they want water, give it to them." Freedman and Simon, *Midrash Rabbah*, 318. See also rabbinical commentary on Num 20:6-11. Freedman and Simon, *Midrash Rabbah*, 759-60.

57. Compare that with τὸ βρῶμα and τὸ πόμα (vv. 3-4). See also BDF, 141. Lockwood suggests that the imperfect here covers not just the two incidents where water from the rock quenched the thirst of the Israelites, but the forty years of the journey. Lockwood, *1 Corinthians*, 322.

58. BDF, 169.

59. Davidson, *Typology in Scripture*, 244-45.

60. Davidson, *Typology in Scripture*, 246.

The material elements in both the wilderness nourishment of Israel and the Lord's Supper point beyond themselves to something deeper.[61] Both are supernatural experiences and both speak of a spiritual reality.

In fact, Paul does not have to look anywhere else, such as rabbinic traditions, for making this leap from manna in the wilderness to the bread in the Lord's Supper or water from the rock to Christ as the rock.[62] Jesus himself provides him with such connections. For example, see passages such as John 4:13–14; 6:31–33; 7:37–39. After equating "manna" with "bread from heaven" (6:31), Jesus says that he was the bread that comes down from heaven (6:33). It is he who gives life. Similarly, Paul could find Jesus' own reference to a spiritual source of water in John 7:37–39—"rivers of living water." Or, one can hear Paul echoing Jesus' statement to the Samaritan woman in John 4:13–14—"the water that I will give." So it is not abstruse for Paul to see Christ as the source of the bread and the water during the wilderness journey. This makes even more sense given the warning Paul gives concerning the Lord's Supper in 1 Cor 10:14–22.

Although the elements in the Eucharist are not the literal body and blood of Christ, it is as such in the spiritual sense because consuming the elements is as good as consuming the flesh and blood of Christ (cf. John 6:51–58; Matt 26:26–28; Luke 22:19–20; 1 Cor 11:23–26). An important point to note is that the "all" Israelites in 10:1–4 is compared with the "all" those who take part in the Lord's Supper in 16–22.[63] Just as they "all" ate from the same bread, we all too share the same bread, the bread in the Lord's Supper (v. 17). God was not pleased with most of the Israelites.[64] Similarly, some of those who take part in the Lord's Supper

---

61. Davidson, *Typology in Scripture*, 247.

62. "Just as Christ the Lord is for Paul the mediator of creation (1 Cor. 8:6), so also for Paul the pre-existent Christ was present with the Israelites. He was as much the source of the spiritual food and drink of the Israelites as he is the one present in the Lord's Supper at Corinth (1 Cor. 10:16–21; 11:17–34)" (Bandstra, "Interpretation in I Corinthians 10:1–11," 14). Cf. Hays, *Echoes of Scripture*, 87–102. Richard Hays reasons that even if one were to accept the premise of midrashic exegesis as the backdrop for Paul's conclusion in 1 Cor 10:4, it still does not explain his rationale for his particular theological conclusion concerning the gentiles being part of Israel, for Paul sees the gentile Christians as those who have already become part of Israel (Rom 4; 11:17–24; 1 Cor 12:1–31; Gal 3:6–16; Eph 2:11–22).

63. Davidson, *Typology in Scripture*, 224.

64. Lockwood, *1 Corinthians*, 325. Lockwood suggests that it is an understatement to say that God was not pleased with most of them (v. 5) because, except for Joshua and Caleb who were under the cloud with Moses, everyone of the exodus generation died in the wilderness (cf. Num 14:20–35). So the Corinthians faced a grave danger in their Christian lives and needed to take heed from Israel's history.

unworthily would also be subject to God's displeasure and punishment (1 Cor 11:28–32). The Israelites were punished for their rebellion and sin (10:5–10). Paul does not want similar fate to befall the Corinthians. That is why Paul concludes with a strong warning against the mishandling of the Lord's Supper (vv. 21–33). The Corinthian believers need to be careful to not belittle the Eucharist. Paul's paraenesis against such practice among the Corinthians is derived from the fact that God's punishment in the past should serve as an example for Christians and that they should avoid continuing in sin because they could incur similar punishment as those in the wilderness journey who did not obey Christ and rebelled against him even while enjoying his blessings of food and water.[65]

Paul's reference to Christ is more than a figural or typological reading of the OT or silent witness to an already established rabbinic tradition of a "moveable well."[66] For Paul, the rock was Christ.[67] Whenever and wherever the Israelites drank from the "rock" (or for that matter the continued supply of water) it was Christ who supplied that water.[68] Thus, they drank from Christ the rock. Paul sees YHWH's intervention in the lives of Israel as the intervention of the triune God. Jesus' claims allow him to make that connection. Paul read the OT that way based on seeing the work of YHWH and the work of the Father, Son, and Spirit as one and the same. For him such a reading was natural extension of that understanding and not an allegorical or midrashic leap. Paul reveals a new way of understanding the OT just as it happened to the disciples when Jesus opened their minds to a new way of understanding the OT Scriptures in Luke 24:45.

---

65. Lockwood, *1 Corinthians*, 331–36.

66. Hurtado, *Lord Jesus Christ*, 576–77.

67. The use of the imperfect ἦν as opposed to the present indicative ἐστίν suggests that Paul sees Christ literally (preexistence) and not allegorically (cf. Matt 13:19–30; Gal 4:22–31—these passages use present tense to convey the fact that the comparisons are more symbolical than literal). Conzelmann, *1 Corinthians*, 167n26; Robertson and Plummer, *First Epistle of St. Paul*, 201.

68. "'Was' indicates that the divine Christ was really a part of Israel's history, providing them life-giving water. What happened then is relevant for the instruction of the Corinthians now because their situation is analogous and because the benefits from Christ are comparable. The argument cuts both ways" (Witherington, *Conflict and Community in Corinth*, 218–19).

Conclusion

These two case studies have demonstrated how the proper identification of YHWH as the triune God can enable a Trinitarian interpretation that is robust and faithful to the identity of God in Scripture. This type of a reading is possible because YHWH is understood to be the Father, Son, and Spirit. As a result, what was once said of YHWH can later be attributed to any one person of the Godhead without having to question the legitimacy of such a move. This view of the identity of YHWH also answers the question regarding how to make better sense of the NT quotations of the OT and how they reveal the NT's own understanding of the identity of YHWH and by extension, the identity of the one true God as the Father, Son, and Spirit.

As demonstrated, the misconstrual of the identity of YHWH as the first person (P1) of the Trinity is the reason for the isolationist tendency to be present in the current models of Trinitarian interpretation. Part of the reason for identifying YHWH as P1 is the failure to differentiate between the appellation "Father" for God in the OT and Jesus' use of "Father" in the Trinitarian sense—addressing the first person of the Trinity. As I have established in chapter 3, there is a difference between calling God "Father" and Jesus' use of that appellation. Most, if not all, of the proposals I evaluated in chapter 2 could have claimed the mantle of Trinitarian interpretation legitimately if they had ascertained the identity of YHWH as the triune God. Until that happens, those proposals are of limited use for a comprehensive view of Trinitarian interpretation.

5

Conclusion

THE MODERN GENESIS OF theological interpretation of Scripture needs to be understood against the particular background of its origin. Historical-critical thinking made a case for the removal of confessional elements from biblical interpretation because dogmas were considered a corrupting influence.[1] Benjamin Jowett captures that sentiment of historical-critical thinking:

> The office of the interpreter is not to add another, but to recover the original one; the meaning, that is, of the words as they struck on the ears or flashed before the eyes of those who first heard and read them. He has to transfer himself to another age; to imagine that he is a disciple of Christ or Paul; to disengage himself from all that follows. The history of Christendom is nothing to him; but only the scene at Galilee or Jerusalem, the handful of believers who gathered themselves together at Ephesus, or Corinth, or Rome. . . . He has no theory of interpretation; a few rules guarding against common errors are enough for him. His object is to read Scripture like any other book, with a real interest and not merely a conventional one. He wants to be able to open his eyes and see or imagine things as they truly are.
>
> Nothing would be more likely to restore a natural feeling on this subject than a history of the interpretation of Scripture. It would take us back to the beginning; it would present in one

---

1. Gabler, "Oration on the Proper Distinction," 494–95.

view the causes which have darkened the meaning of words in the course of ages; it would clear away the remains of dogmas, systems, controversies, which are encrusted upon them. It would show us the "erring fancy" of interpreters assuming sometimes to have the Spirit of God Himself, yet unable to pass beyond the limits of their own age, and with a judgment often biased by party.... Such a work would enable us to separate the elements of doctrine and tradition with which the meaning of Scripture is encumbered in our own day.[2]

Consequently, biblical interpretation since the eighteenth century distanced itself from the influences of dogmatic elements for the sake of objective interpretation. This has been the dominant method of biblical interpretation in the academy until Karl Barth challenged such norms and urged the incorporation of theological elements in biblical interpretation.

Summary of the History of TIS

Theological interpretation is not something new in the history of biblical interpretation. In fact, Christians have practiced theological interpretation of Scripture at all times although their number has reduced drastically in the last few centuries. R. R. Reno summarizes the continuity of theological interpretation: "With countless variations of a doctrinally ruled reading of scripture characterizes the broad sweep of the Christian tradition from Gregory the Great through Bernard and Bonaventure, continuing across Reformation differences in both John Calvin and Cornelius Lapide, Patrick Henry and Bishop Bossuet, and on to more recent figures such as Karl Barth and Hans Urs von Balthasar."[3] However, the academy argued against the practice of theological interpretation for a long time because it was not considered a serious method of biblical interpretation. The modern genesis of TIS needs to be understood against this particular background to make sense of its claim to be a relatively new enterprise in biblical interpretation.

Historical-critical thinking already heavily influenced the discipline of biblical studies by the time of Barth and Hans Urs von Balthasar.

---

2. Jowett, "On the Interpretation of Scripture," 338–39. Even though systematic theology was affected by such changes in biblical interpretation, it was the discipline of biblical studies that was most affected.

3. Reno, *Genesis*, 11.

Historical-critical interpretation divorced history, especially biblical history, from revelation, and conceived history apart from any recourse or relationship to revelation. As a result, biblical interpretation became a matter of attending to the literary, philological, polemical, and cultural features of the text.

Barth, having realized historical-critical interpretation was of little use to the church and that it did not go beyond the first step in exegesis, argued for the reintegration of history and revelation in biblical interpretation. Because the Bible and history are part of God's revelation, he believed that the same God who inspired the biblical writers is still present in its contemporary reading. Therefore, the reading of these texts must attend to God's revelation in Jesus Christ because it is through him that we receive the complete revelation. This particular argument of Barth challenged both Protestant and Catholic interpreters who believed in human ability to ascertain truth apart from any outside help—divine grace available only through Christ.

Barth's arguments influenced Balthasar who wanted to renew Catholic biblical interpretation, which was heavily influenced by historical-critical thinking. Barth and Balthasar influenced Protestant and Catholic interpretations respectively and the enduring effects of their works can be seen in interpretive practices of many scholars from both groups. Today, TIS has become an ecumenical movement where scholars from Catholic and Protestant traditions collaborate for the purpose of theological interpretation to benefit the church.

As noted in the introduction, theological interpretation of Scripture is an ecumenical movement in another sense—it involves the participation of scholars from different disciplines and diverse philosophical backgrounds. Today, there are disagreements among the participants on a whole range of issues due to ecclesial, disciplinary, and philosophical differences, but these disagreements are minor compared to the havoc historical-criticism caused for theological interpretation.

Isolationist Tendency in Trinitarian interpretation

Theological interpretation tends to read Scripture through certain theological lenses. Trinitarian interpretation has become a constant; however, there is considerable ambiguity as to what exactly Trinitarian interpretation means. This ambiguity is exacerbated by competing proposals for the same. A survey of the works that promote Trinitarian interpretation reveals that often times "Trinitarian interpretation" is a placeholder for christological, pneumatological, ecclesial, figural, and the presumed theories of Trinitarian interpretation.

As discussed in chapters 1 and 2, there is an isolationist tendency prevalent in these proposals. Assigning the OT mainly to God the Father and the NT to the Son and the Spirit is what I call an isolationist tendency. This tendency emerges from the misidentification of YHWH as P1. The NT tends to assign several of the OT passages to the Son and the Spirit where the OT simply had YHWH as the original referent. Misconstruing the identity of YHWH as P1 leads to questions such as these: What is the manner in which the NT quotes and alludes to the OT? Does the change in the referent make any difference in the understanding of those passages that are being quoted? How can they be attributed to another person of the Godhead if he was not the original referent? How could Jesus claim that the OT Scriptures speak concerning him if they were not originally about him? All proposals—christological, pneumatological, ecclesial, figural, and the so-called Trinitarian proposals—that claim the mantle of Trinitarian interpretation exhibit the isolationist tendency. All of them identify YHWH as the first person of the Trinity.

The arguments of Francis Watson and Kevin Vanhoozer for a christological interpretation depend on speech-act theory just as Nicholas Wolterstorff, John Webster, and Mark Bowald's argument for the so-called theories of Trinitarian interpretation. God the Father in these proposals is the locution, the Son is the illocution, and the Spirit is the perlocution. Since the Father, Son, and the Spirit are identified as different parts of the same speech, an interpretation that stems from this view and attends to these various speech-acts is considered Trinitarian. What we witness in both of these kinds of proposals is the heavy influence of philosophical hermeneutics (speech-act theory in particular) in theological interpretation, but these proposals themselves either do not often attend to the identity of YHWH or when they do, they identify YHWH as P1.

Similarly, Christopher Holmes and Todd Billings argue for a type of Trinitarian interpretation starting either from the perspective of the present ministry of Jesus Christ (Holmes) or from the perspective of the present ministry of the Holy Spirit (Billings). The ecclesial proposal is no different since Stephen Fowl argues that a Spirit-led interpretation will be Trinitarian just because the Spirit is God. If so, anyone can claim his or her interpretation to be Spirit-led and, therefore, Trinitarian. They do not show how their proposals would necessarily result in Trinitarian interpretation. And when they identify YHWH in the OT, they view him as P1. The common tendency in theological interpretation to start from the NT and go back to the OT is reversed in figural interpretation. Brevard Childs and Christopher Seitz maintain that biblical interpretation must address the discrete voice of the OT. Since God of the OT is known as the one who raised Jesus from the dead, we must begin our theological interpretation with the revelation of that God in the OT. The movement in interpretation should be from OT to NT and not vice versa. Their proposal too identifies YHWH as P1. As a result, figural interpretation does not help advance a robust view of Trinitarian interpretation.

John Goldingay demonstrated that these works overwhelmingly identify YHWH in the OT as P1. When there is an attempt to read the OT through a Trinitarian lens, they do so by arguing that they can find references to the Father, Son, and Spirit in the OT as in the case of Richard Schultz. One of the major reasons of identifying YHWH in the OT as God the Father is because of the failure to differentiate between the OT use of the appellation "Father" for God and Jesus' own use. For the solution to overcome the isolationist tendency in Trinitarian interpretation and to embrace a robust view, we need to first reconsider the identity of YHWH in the OT the Father, Son, and Spirit—the triune God.

YHWH as the Triune God

YHWH reveals his name to Moses in Exod 3:14–15 and 6:2–3. As presented in chapter 3, the identity of YHWH cannot be understood purely based on an etymological study. In order to understand his identity, we have to look at how he revealed himself throughout the OT. What emerges from that study is that YHWH's revelation of his name to Moses was the beginning of a new epoch in the history of Israel. Until this time, God spoke to the patriarchs directly, but from now on he spoke to his people through the representatives he chose. This change in Moses' own understanding can be noted in his invocation of God's name as YHWH in Exod 32:11–13, where Moses addresses his God as YHWH and reminds YHWH of his covenant with the patriarchs. Moses was convinced of the name of the God of the patriarchs once he revealed himself in Exod 3:14–15 and 6:2–3. Included in that revelation is YHWH's unique claim that he alone is God and none beside him. The Shema reminds the people to give him their complete devotion because he alone is God (Deut 6:4b).

The modern concept of monotheism complicated the way the identity of YHWH was viewed. In light of Deut 4 and 32, and other passages, it was argued that a better way to translate the Shema is "YHWH is our God, YHWH alone." The emphasis was not on number (one), but on his uniqueness. However, an inquiry into the identity of YHWH is complicated by the reference to YHWH as Father and Jesus' reference to the first person of the Trinity as his Father. As was shown, there is a difference between calling God Father in the OT and Jesus' own reference to the first person of the Trinity as Father—the former is a title of endearment and the latter reveals an ontological relation (between Jesus and the first person of the Trinity). The Jews who wanted to kill Jesus understood that Jesus called God "Father" in the ontological sense (John 5:18; cf. 8:41–42; 17:5).

In addition, Jesus called God "Father" contrary to the claims of Joachim Jeremias and others. Jesus also told us that we have this knowledge only through him because he alone reveals the Father (John 14:3–23). Our knowledge of the Father is a new kind of knowledge that was not available before (John 14:7—"from now on you know him, and have seen him"), and this knowledge is possible only through Jesus. Jesus has revealed that his reference to the Father is different from our own. Because the Father and the Son are one (John 10:30), our prayer and thanksgiving addressed to Jesus is also addressed to the Father and vice versa (John 14:10, 13–14). That there is a difference between calling God Father in the OT and Jesus' address to God as his Father can be established from Scripture.

The church fathers used the appellation "Father" for God in a number of ways. They were not always consistent in their use. The apologists often used the name in the Platonic sense ("father of the Universe") because of their disputations with the non-Christians. However, from the time of Irenaeus we see a more nuanced use of the name to refer to the first person of the Trinity, especially in Athanasius. Again, his focus was not on establishing whether YHWH was P1, but rather proving the eternality of the Son—if God has always been Father, then he could not have been Father without the Son; there was no time when the Son was not. Augustine, referring to the Shema, writes that "Hear, O, Israel: The Lord our God is one Lord" does not exclude the Son and the Spirit (*Trin.* 5.11.12). However, Gregory of Nazianzus mentions that the OT reveals the Father openly and the Son obscurely, but the NT proclaims the Son openly and indicates the Deity of the Spirit).[4] The church fathers' use of the appellation "Father" for God needs to be evaluated in light of the relevant biblical passages. It becomes obvious, as presented in chapter 3, that there is a difference between calling God "Father" in the OT and Jesus' reference to God as his "Father."

How do we understand the identity of YHWH? As asserted in chapter 3, a careful study of several OT passages reveals that multiple persons or entities are identified by the name YHWH. For example, יהוה and מלאך יהוה sometimes appear together (Judg 6:11–24), other times first the מלאך יהוה appears and then without any warning or hint מלאך יהוה becomes יהוה (Exod 3:2, 4). The Spirit of YHWH is sometimes equated with YHWH (Judg 13:25, 14:6, 19; 15:14; cf. 16:20). The OT also associates the exodus with יהוה (Exod 13:3, 9, 14, 16; 14:25; 16:6), מלאך יהוה (Judg 2:1–5), and רוח יהוה (Isa 63:14). Similarly, the Israelite sin during the wilderness journey was against יהוה (Exo 16:8; Num 11:1; Deut 1:26; 9:23; Jer 3:25), מלאך יהוה (Judg 2:2), and רוח יהוה (Isa 63:10). These OT passages reveal an important point—multiple persons are identified by the name YHWH and still it is not against YHWH's claim that he alone is God.

The NT ascribes to Jesus what was once said of YHWH: his name (John 1:18; Rev 1:17; 22:13; cf. Exod 3:14 [LXX]; Rev 1:4, 8), receiving glory and honor (Phil 2:9–11; cf. Isa 45:21–23), and confessing his name for salvation (Rom 10:9–13; cf. Isa 28:16; Joel 2:32; and Acts 2:21; 4:12; cf. Joel 2:32). Similarly, the NT attributes the exodus to Jesus (Jude 5) and the Israelites sinning against him (1 Cor 10:9). The Spirit is also identified with YHWH in the NT (Heb 3:7–11; cf. Ps 95:7–11). Ultimately, Paul identifies the Shema with the Father, Son, and Spirit (1 Cor 8:6). In light of the many biblical evidence, we can deduce that multiple persons are identified by the name YHWH in the OT and the NT identifies the Shema with the Father, Son, and the Spirit and ascribes to him what was once exclusively ascribed to YHWH; therefore, YHWH is the Father, Son, and Spirit.

The creeds claim that the Father is God, the Son is God, and the Spirit is God, but there is one God. Similarly, it can be argued that the Father is YHWH, the Son is YHWH, and the Spirit is YHWH, but only one YHWH. Just as the Father receives his being from no one, but the Son and the Spirit eternally receive their being from the Father, so also

---

4. NPNF[2], vol. 7, 326.

the Father is YHWH by his own being, but the Son and the Spirit receive the name YHWH from the Father. The identification of YHWH as the triune God is biblically sustainable and creedally orthodox.

This identification of YHWH as the triune God is necessary for a robust view of Trinitarian interpretation. This may also offer a way to understand the NT quotations of the OT and open a window into the NT's and the early church's understanding of the Godhead. Taking YHWH as the triune God also helps overcome the isolationist tendency prevalent in the current models of Trinitarian interpretation.

The Impact of the Trinitarian Identity of YHWH

If YHWH is the triune God, then a Trinitarian interpretation of Scripture can be undertaken with virtue and verve. The Trinitarian identity of YHWH will help make better sense of Jesus' own claim that things concerning him were written in the Scriptures such as the OT Scriptures (Luke 24:25–27, 44; John 5:39–47). The identity of YHWH as the Father, Son, and Spirit facilitates a holistic reading of Scripture—it allows the whole Scripture (Genesis to Revelation) to be taken as witnessing to the triune God. It will also allow one to traverse the so-called Lessing's ditch (the gap between history and faith) in biblical interpretation by bringing history and revelation together to understand the whole Scripture as a single witness to the one true God—an end to which Barth labored so vigorously. What often prevents one from traversing the testamental and historical divide in Trinitarian interpretation is one's failure to recognize the triune identity of YHWH.

When Gen 3:22 is read in light of the identity of YHWH as the triune God, it will help make some connections that would otherwise be lacking. A link between YHWH who prevents man from eating from the tree of life so that he may not "eat and live forever" in his state of rebellion and Jesus who offers man the opportunity to "eat and live forever" in John 6:27–58 can be established if the identity of YHWH is taken as triune. It was God's gracious act that prevented Adam and Eve from taking from the tree of life and eat from it. It is also God's gracious act in inviting humans into this intimate and mysterious relationship with him in which they are allowed to eat once again so that they may live forever as a result of that eating.

Of course, in John 6 the eating is more than just mere eating of Jesus' flesh. It is symbolic of one's faith in Jesus and also symbolic of the mystery of the Eucharist in which the bread and wine mysteriously appropriated as the flesh and blood of Christ without it actually becoming one literally. YHWH always wanted humans to "eat and live forever," not on human terms but on YHWH's terms. YHWH did not allow Adam and Eve to eat from the tree of life. He expelled them from the garden to teach them obedience (Gen 3:24). But the children of Adam are given the opportunity to eat as an act of obedience. YHWH has proven himself to be a good and compassionate God. That act of compassion can be seen in Jesus, in his life, death, and resurrection. He is YHWH's compassion personified.

The impact of the Trinitarian identity of YHWH in interpretation is also evident in the reading of 1 Cor 10:4. Paul uses the phrase "and the rock was Christ" just before the paraenetic section of 10:6–11. When this passage is read within the larger section of chapters 8–11, it can be seen that Paul is concerned about the proper use of Christian liberty by the Corinthians and their need to be careful about their spiritual journey because it is possible for them to displease the Lord just like the Israelites did during their wilderness journey. The Corinthians are in a position to offend the same Lord who provided the Israelites with their supply of water during the wilderness journey. The Lord provided them food and drink (10:3–4) and then Paul says that the rock Israelites drank from was Christ.

Naturally, one may wonder how Paul could make such a statement. Did Paul believe that Jesus was present during the wilderness journey? What to make of Paul's statement in 10:4? These are good questions and quite natural for someone to ask. The answer to these questions can be found in Paul's own statement in 10:9—the Israelites tested Christ in the wilderness. Moreover, Jesus himself claimed in John's Gospel that he is the bread of life and the living water (John 4:13–14; 6:31–33; 7:37–39). So Paul could have easily connected Jesus' statement and his own conviction that the Shema includes Christ (1 Cor 8:6).

For Paul, the identity of Jesus is included in the identity of YHWH. That is why he could make such statements. Unless they heed the warning, the disobedient Corinthians could share a similar fate to the disobedient Israelites. It is the same God who judges. Paul connects this section to his particular advice regarding the Lord's Supper (10:16–22) where he again references OT materials to make his point. He sees no division within the Godhead in terms of their work. The Father, Son, and Spirit have always been active and at work since the beginning of creation. The

YHWH who called Israel is the same YHWH who calls other to be his people. He both provides and punishes. It is up to Christians to decide whether they want to enjoy his provision or receive his punishment (cf. Jude 4–5). The same warning Paul presented to the Corinthians is before the present community of God as well because it is the same Lord who is at work in both communities. A connection can be seen here—the same Lord who provided for the Israelites and punished them during their wilderness journey was presented to the Corinthians as able and ready to both provide and punish. The same YHWH is presented in the Scriptures to the contemporary Christians as the one who is ready to provide for them and punish them if necessary. The question that remains is whether Christians take Paul's warning about hardening their hearts against YHWH seriously (Heb 3:7–11—the Spirit is called YHWH here).

Further Research

This book was confined to exploring the identity of YHWH in Scripture in order to offer a solution to overcome the isolationist tendency that exists in current models of Trinitarian interpretation. A study of the history of Trinitarian interpretation was deemed outside the bounds of this research although such a study could certainly have enlightened the thought process and strengthened some of the arguments. Similarly, this research did not pursue the fluidity model proposed by Benjamin Sommer and Mark Smith because the focus here was to elucidate the supports for my claim from scriptural data, as much as possible.[5] Also, I chose to work mainly within the contours of Christian thought. Their research could throw more light on the question of how monotheism was understood within the Bible and whether the various ideas concerning the identity of YHWH can be representative of biblical ideas themselves or the result of comparative-religion studies.

Another fruitful area of research would be to explore the recent contribution from Kendall Soulen, especially his idea of supersessionism influencing the replacement of the Tetragrammaton with the name of the Father, Son, and Spirit and the oblique references to YHWH that are found in the NT and in the creedal language that have been unexplored.[6]

---

5. Sommer, *Bodies of God*; Smith, *Origins of Biblical Monotheism*.
6. Soulen, *Divine Name(s)*; Soulen, *God of Israel*; Soulen, "YHWH the Triune God," 25–54.

Conclusion

Soulen mentions that by AD first century, Jewish theology had dropped using the Tetragrammaton and replaced it with הַשֵּׁם, meaning "the NAME." Soulen gives several NT examples where "the NAME" appears and suggest that these uses of "the NAME" are the NT's own way of retaining the Tetragrammaton (Matt 6:9—"hallowed be your NAME"; Matt 23:39; Mark 11:9; Luke 19:38; John 12:13—"Blessed is the one who comes in the NAME of the LORD"; cf. Lev 24:11).[7]

Both claims of Soulen have the potential to offer more clarity on the identity of YHWH and why Christians have not always acknowledged these facts. If the oblique reference of the NAME is indeed the accepted replacement for Tetragrammaton in the AD first century, that adds more support for what I have already presented here. Thus, both of his ideas are worth pursuing.

---

7. Soulen, *Divine Name(s)*, 163–73.

Bibliography

Aageson, James W. *Written Also for Our Sake: Paul and the Art of Biblical Interpretation*. 1st ed. Louisville: Westminster John Knox, 1993.
Aitken, James K. "Divine Will and Providence." In *Ben Sira's God: Proceedings of the International Ben Sira Conference, Durham, Upshaw College 2001*, edited by Renate Egger-Wenzel, 282–302. Berlin: Walter de Gruyter, 2002.
Alston, William P. "Truth: Concept and Property." In *What Is Truth?*, edited by Richard Schantz. Berlin: Walter de Gruyter, 2002.
Anatolios, Khaled. *Athanasius: The Coherence of His Thought*. London: Routledge, 1998.
Athanasius. *De decretis Nicaenae synodi*. Athanasius Werke 2. Edited by Hans-Georg Opitz. Berlin: Walter de Gruyter, 1935.
———. *De synodis 13,3—Apologia ad Constantium 3,4*. Athanasius Werke 2. Edited by Hans-Georg Opitz. Berlin: Walter de Gruyter, 1935.
———. *Orationes contra Arianos*. Athanasius Werke 1. Edited by Martin Tetz et al. 2nd ed. Berlin: Walter de Gruyter, 1998.
———. "Orationes contra Arianos." In *Select Writings and Letters of Athanasius, Bishop of Alexandria*, edited by Philip Schaff and Henry Wace, translated by Archibald Robertson, 303–47. A Select Library of the Nicene and Post-Nicene Fathers Second Series 4. Grand Rapids: Eerdmans, 1971.
Athenagoras. *Legatio and De Resurrectione*. Edited and translated by William R. Schoedel. Oxford: Clarendon, 1972.
———. *Supplique au sujet des chrétiens et Sur la Résurrection des morts*. Sources chrétiennes 379. Translated by Bernard Pouderon. Paris: Editions du Cerf, 1992.
Augustine. *De Trinitate*. Corpus Christianorum Latinorum 50A. Edited by William J. Mountain. Turnhout, Belgium: Brepols, 1954.
———. *The Trinity*. Edited by John E. Rotelle. Translated by Edmund Hill. New York: New City, 1991.
Ausloos, Hans. "The 'Angel of YHWH' in Exod. 23:20–33 and Judg. 2:1–5: A Clue to the 'Deuteronom(ist)ic' Puzzle?" *Vetus Testamentum* 58 (2008) 1–12.
Austin, John Langshaw. *How to Do Things with Words*. 2nd ed. William James Lectures. Edited by J. O. Urmson and Marina Sbisà. Cambridge, MA: Harvard University Press, 1975.
Ayres, Lewis. *Augustine and the Trinity*. Cambridge: Cambridge University Press, 2010.

———. "'There's Fire in That Rain': On Reading the Letter and Reading Allegorically." In *Heaven on Earth? Theological Interpretation in Ecumenical Dialogue*, edited by Hans Boersma and Matthew Levering, 33–51. Directions in Modern Theology. Chichester: Wiley-Blackwell, 2013.

Balthasar, Hans Urs von. *Glory of the Lord: A Theological Aesthetics, Vol 1; Seeing the Form*. Edited by John Riches. Translated by Erasmo Levia-Merikakis. Edinburgh: T&T Clark, 1982.

———. *The Theology of Karl Barth: Exposition and Interpretation*. Translated by Edward T. Oakes. San Francisco: Ignatius, 1992.

Bandstra, Andrew J. "Interpretation in I Corinthians 10:1–11." *Calvin Theological Journal* 6.1 (1971) 5–21.

Barrett, C. K. *The Gospel According to St. John: An Introduction with Commentary and Notes on the Greek Text*. 2nd ed. Philadelphia: Westminster, 1978.

Barr, James. "Abbā Isn't 'Daddy.'" *Journal of Theological Studies* 39.1 (1988) 28–47.

———. *History and Ideology in the Old Testament*. The Herbert Hensley Henson Lectures in the University of Oxford. Oxford: Oxford University Press, 2000.

———. *The Semantics of Biblical Language*. Oxford: Oxford University Press, 1961.

Barth, Karl. *Church Dogmatics: 1.1, the Doctrine of the Word of God*. Edited by G. W. Bromiley and T. F. Torrance. Translated by G. W. Bromiley. Peabody, MA: Hendrickson, 2010.

———. *Church Dogmatics: 2.1, the Doctrine of God; Part 1—The Knowledge of God*. Edited by G. W. Bromiley and T. F. Torrance. Translated by T. H. L. Parker et al. Edinburgh: T&T Clark, 2000.

———. *Church Dogmatics: 2.2, the Doctrine of God*. Edited by G. W. Bromiley and T. F. Torrance. Edinburgh: T&T Clark, 1957.

———. *Church Dogmatics: 3.2, the Doctrine of Creation*. Edited by G. W. Bromiley and Thomas F. Torrance. Translated by G. W. Bromiley. Peabody, MA: Hendrickson, 2010.

———. *Church Dogmatics: 4.2, the Doctrine of Reconciliation: Jesus Christ, the Servant as Lord*. Edited by T. F. Torrance and G. W. Bromiley. Translated by G. W. Bromiley. Edinburgh: T&T Clark, 1958.

———. *The Epistle to the Romans*. Translated by Edwyn C. Hoskyns. Oxford: Oxford University Press, 1968.

———. *How I Changed My Mind*. Richmond: John Knox, 1966.

———. *Der Römerbrief*. Zweite Fassung. Zürich: Theologischer Verlag Zürich, 1922.

———. *Das Wort Gottes und die Theologie: Gesammelte Vorträge I*. Munich: Chr. Kaiser, 1924.

———. *The Word of God and Theology*. Translated by Amy Marga. New York: T&T Clark, 2011.

Barth, Karl, and Eduard Thurneysen. *Briefwechsel, Band I, 1913–1921*. Edited by Eduard Thurneysen. Karl Barth Gesamtausgabe V Briefe. Zürich: Theologischer Verlag Zürich, 1973.

Bartholomew, Craig G. *Introducing Biblical Hermeneutics: A Comprehensive Framework for Hearing God in Scripture*. Grand Rapids: Baker, 2015.

———. "Listening for God's Address: A Mere Trinitarian Hermeneutic for the Old Testament." In *Hearing the Old Testament: Listening for God's Address*, edited by Craig G. Bartholomew and David J. H. Beldman, 3–22. Grand Rapids: Eerdmans, 2012.

———. "Uncharted Waters: Philosophy, Theology and the Crisis in Biblical Interpretation." In *Renewing Biblical Interpretation*, edited by Craig G. Bartholomew et al., 1:1–35. Scripture and Hermeneutics Series. Grand Rapids: Zondervan, 2000.

Bartholomew, Craig G., and Heath A. Thomas, eds. *A Manifesto for Theological Interpretation*. Grand Rapids: Baker, 2016.

Bates, Matthew W. *The Birth of the Trinity: Jesus, God, and Spirit in New Testament and Early Christian Interpretations of the Old Testament*. Oxford: Oxford University Press, 2015.

———. *The Hermeneutics of the Apostolic Proclamation: The Center of Paul's Method of Scriptural Interpretation*. Waco, TX: Baylor University Press, 2012.

Bauckham, Richard. *God Crucified: Monotheism and Christology in the New Testament*. Didsbury Lectures. Grand Rapids: Eerdmans, 1999.

———. *Jesus and the God of Israel: God Crucified and Other Studies on the New Testament's Christology of Divine Identity*. Grand Rapids: Eerdmans, 2008.

Bauer, Walter, et al. *A Greek-English Lexicon of the New Testament and Other Early Christian Literature*. 3rd ed. Chicago: University of Chicago Press, 2000.

Baumgarten, Siegmund Jakob. *Evangelische Glaubenslehre: Mit Einigen Anmerkungen, Vorrede und Historischen Einleitung*. Edited by Johann Salomo Semler. Halle: Johann Justinus Gebauer, 1760. https://www.google.com/books/edition/D_Siegmund_Jacob_Baumgartens_Evangelisch/oqi51UHZrTYC?hl=en&gbpv=1.

Beale, G. K. *Handbook on the New Testament Use of the Old Testament: Exegesis and Interpretation*. Grand Rapids: Baker, 2012.

Bechard, Dean Philip. *The Scripture Documents: An Anthology of Official Catholic Teachings*. Edited and translated by Dean P. Béchard. Collegeville, MN: Liturgical, 2002.

Behr, John. *The Nicene Faith, Part One: True God of True God*. The Formation of Christian Theology 2. Crestwood, NY: St. Vladimir's Seminary Press, 2004.

Beitzel, B. J. "Exodus 3:14 and the Divine Name: A Case of Biblical Paronomasia." *Trinity Journal* 1 (1980) 5–20.

Bekkum, Wout Jacues van. "What's in the Divine Name? Exodus 3 in Biblical and Rabbinic Tradition." In *The Revelation of the Name YHWH to Moses Perspectives from Judaism, the Pagan Graeco-Roman World, and Early Christianity*, edited by Geurt Hendrik van Kooten, 9:3–15. Themes in Biblical Narrative. Leiden: Brill, 2006.

Betz, John R. "Beyond the Sublime: The Aesthetics of the Analogy of Being (Part One)." *Modern Theology* 21.3 (2005) 367–411.

———. "Beyond the Sublime: The Aesthetics of the Analogy of Being (Part Two)." *Modern Theology* 22.1 (2006) 1–50.

Billings, J. Todd. *The Word of God for the People of God: An Entryway to the Theological Interpretation of Scripture*. Grand Rapids: Eerdmans, 2010.

Blass, Friedrich, et al. *A Greek Grammar of the New Testament and Other Early Christian Literature*. Translated by Robert W. Funk. Chicago: University of Chicago Press, 1961.

Blenkinsopp, Joseph. *Isaiah 56–66: A New Translation with Introduction and Commentary*. 1st ed. Vol. 3. Anchor Bible. New York: Doubleday, 2003.

Block, Daniel Isaac. *Judges, Ruth*. New American Commentary 6. Nashville: Broadman & Holman, 1999.

Bockmuehl, Markus. "God's Life as a Jew: Remembering the Son of God as Son of David." In *Seeking the Identity of Jesus: A Pilgrimage*, edited by Beverly R. Gaventa and Richard B. Hays, 60–78. Grand Rapids: Eerdmans, 2008.

———. *Jewish Law in Gentile Churches: Halakhah and the Beginning of Christian Public Ethics*. Edinburgh: T&T Clark, 2000.

Boersma, Hans. *Nouvelle Théologie and Sacramental Ontology: A Return to Mystery*. New York: Oxford University Press, 2009.

Boersma, Hans, and Matthew Levering, eds. *Heaven on Earth? Theological Interpretation in Ecumenical Dialogue*. Directions in Modern Theology. Chichester: Wiley-Blackwell, 2013.

Bokedal, Tomas. "The Rule of Faith: Tracing Its Origins." *Journal of Theological Interpretation* 7.2 (2013) 233–55.

Bowald, Mark Alan. *Rendering the Word in Theological Hermeneutics: Mapping Divine and Human Agency*. Burlington, VT: Ashgate, 2007.

Brett, Mark. "Four or Five Things to Do with Texts: A Taxonomy of Interpretive Interests." In *The Bible in Three Dimensions: Essays in Celebration of Forty Years of Biblical Studies in the University of Sheffield*, edited by David J. A. Clines et al., 357–78. Sheffield: Sheffield Academic Press, 1990.

Brezik, Victor B., ed. *One Hundred Years of Thomism: Aeterni Patris and Afterwards, a Symposium*, 7–22. Houston: Center for Thomistic Studies, 1981.

Briggs, Richard S. "The Book of Genesis." In *A Theological Introduction to the Pentateuch: Interpreting the Torah As Christian Scripture*, edited by Richard S. Briggs and Joel N. Lohr, 19–50. Grand Rapids: Baker, 2012.

———. *The Virtuous Reader: Old Testament Narrative and Interpretive Virtue*. Studies in Theological Interpretation. Grand Rapids: Baker, 2010.

Brown, David. "Sacramentality." In *The Oxford Handbook of Theology and Modern European Thought*, edited by Nicholas Adams et al., 615–32. New York: Oxford University Press, 2013.

Brown, Raymond E. *The Critical Meaning of the Bible*. New York: Paulist, 1981.

Brown, William P. *Character and Scripture: Moral Formation, Community, and Biblical Interpretation*. Grand Rapids: Eerdmans, 2002.

Bruce, F. F. *1 and 2 Corinthians*. New Century Bible Commentary. Edited by Matthew Black. Grand Rapids: Eerdmans, 1980.

Brueggemann, Walter. *Genesis*. Interpretation: A Bible Commentary for Teaching and Preaching. Edited by James Luther Mays. Atlanta: John Knox, 1982.

———. *Theology of the Old Testament: Testimony, Dispute, Advocacy*. Philadelphia: Fortress, 1997.

Bultmann, Rudolf. *The Gospel of John: A Commentary*. Translated by G. R. Beasley-Murray. Philadelphia: Westminster, 1971.

Burnett, Richard E. "Historical Criticism." In *Dictionary for Theological Interpretation of the Bible*, edited by Kevin J. Vanhoozer et al., 290–93. Grand Rapids: Baker, 2005.

Busch, Eberhard. *Karl Barth: His Life from Letters and Autobiographical Texts*. Philadelphia: Fortress, 1976.

Butler, Trent C. *Judges*. Word Biblical Commentary 8. Nashville: Thomas Nelson, 2009.

Calvin, John. *Commentaries on the First Book of Moses Called Genesis*. Calvin's Commentaries 1. Translated by John King. Grand Rapids: Baker, 1999.

Carey, Patrick W. *Avery Cardinal Dulles, SJ: A Model Theologian, 1918–2008*. New York: Paulist, 2010.

Carson, D. A. *The Gospel According to John*. Pillar New Testament Commentary. Leicester: Inter-Varsity, 1991.
Cary, Phillip. *Jonah*. Brazos Theological Commentary on the Bible. Grand Rapids: Brazos, 2008.
Cassuto, Umberto. *A Commentary on the Book of Exodus*. Jerusalem: Magnes Press, Hebrew University, 1967.
———. *A Commentary on the Book of Genesis, Part I: From Adam to Noah, Genesis 1–6:8*. 1st English ed. Jerusalem: Magnes Press, Hebrew University, 1961.
Chafer, Lewis Sperry. *Systematic Theology: Prolegomena, Bibliology, Theology Proper*. Vol. 1. Dallas: Dallas Seminary Press, 1947.
Chapman, Stephen B. "Modernity's Canonical Crisis: Historiography and Theology in Collision." In *Hebrew Bible, Old Testament: The History of Its Interpretation, from the Renaissance to the Enlightenment*, edited by Magne Saebø, 2:651–87. Göttingen: Vandenhoeck & Ruprecht, 1996.
Charlesworth, James H., ed. "Pseudo-Philo (First Century A.D.)." In *The Old Testament Pseudepigrapha*, 297–378. Peabody, MA: Hendrickson, 2010.
Childs, Brevard S. *Biblical Theology in Crisis*. Philadelphia: Westminster, 1970.
———. *Biblical Theology of the Old and New Testaments: Theological Reflection on the Christian Bible*. Philadelphia: Fortress, 1993.
———. *The Book of Exodus: A Critical, Theological Commentary*. Old Testament Library. Philadelphia: Westminster, 1974.
———. *Old Testament Theology in a Canonical Context*. Philadelphia: Fortress, 1986.
———. *The Struggle to Understand Isaiah as Christian Scripture*. Grand Rapids: Eerdmans, 2004.
———. "Toward Recovering Theological Exegesis." *Pro Ecclesia* 6.1 (1997) 16–26.
Christensen, Duane L. *Deuteronomy 1:1—21:9*. 2nd ed. Word Biblical Commentary 6A. Nashville: Thomas Nelson, 2001.
Ciampa, Roy E., and Brian S. Rosner. *The First Letter to the Corinthians*. Pillar New Testament Commentary. Grand Rapids: Eerdmans, 2010.
Clarke, Kent D., and Stanley E. Porter. "What Is Exegesis? An Analysis of Various Definitions." In *Handbook to Exegesis of the New Testament*, edited by Stanley E. Porter, 3–21. Leiden: Brill, 1997.
Collins, John J. *The Bible after Babel: Historical Criticism in a Postmodern Age*. Grand Rapids: Eerdmans, 2005.
Collins, Raymond F. *First Corinthians*. Sacra Pagina 7. Edited by Daniel J. Harrington. Collegeville, MN: Liturgical, 1999.
Conzelmann, Hans. *1 Corinthians: A Commentary on the First Epistle to the Corinthians*. Edited by George W. MacRae. Translated by James W. Leitch. Hermeneia: A Critical and Historical Commentary on the Bible. Philadelphia: Fortress, 1975.
Critchley, Simon. *The Ethics of Deconstruction: Derrida and Levinas*. Oxford: Blackwell, 1992.
Cummins, Steven A. "The Theological Interpretation of Scripture: Recent Contributions by Stephen E. Fowl, Christopher R. Seitz and Francis Watson." *Currents in Biblical Research* 2.2 (2004) 179–96.
Dahl, N. A., and Alan F. Segal. "Philo and the Rabbis on the Names of God." *Journal for the Study of Judaism in the Persian, Hellenistic and Roman Period* 9.1 (1978) 1–28.
Dahlke, Benjamin. *Die Katholische Rezeption Karl Barths: Theologische Erneuerung im Vorfeld des Zweiten Vatikanischen Konzils*. Tübingen, Germany: Mohr Siebeck, 2010.

———. *Karl Barth, Catholic Renewal and Vatican II*. T&T Clark Studies in Systematic Theology. New York: T&T Clark, 2012.

Daley, Brian E. "'In Many and Various Ways': Towards A Theology of Theological Exegesis." In *Heaven on Earth?: Theological Interpretation in Ecumenical Dialogue*, edited by Hans Boersma and Matthew Levering, 13–31. Directions in Modern Theology. Chichester: Wiley-Blackwell, 2013.

Daniélou, Jean. *God and the Ways of Knowing*. Translated by Walter Roberts. San Francisco: Ignatius, 1957.

Davidson, Richard M. *Typology in Scripture: A Study of Hermeneutical Typos Structures*. Andrews University Seminary Doctoral Dissertation Series 2. Berrien Springs, MI: Andrews University Press, 1981.

DelCogliano, Mark. "The Influence of Athanasius and the Homoiousians on Basil of Caesarea's Decentralization of 'Unbegotten.'" *Journal of Early Christian Studies* 19.2 (2011) 197–223.

Deleuze, Gilles. "The Image of Thought." In *Postmodernism: Critical Concepts*, edited by Victor E. Taylor and Charles E. Winquist, translated by Paul Patton, 63–103. Foundational Essays. New York: Routledge, 1998.

Derrida, Jacques. *Writing and Difference*. Translated by Alan Bass. Chicago: University of Chicago Press, 1978.

Doering, Lutz. "God as Father in Texts from Qumran." In *The Divine Father: Religious and Philosophical Concepts of Divine Parenthood in Antiquity*, edited by Felix Albrecht and Reinhard Feldmeier, 18:107–35. Themes in Biblical Narrative: Jewish and Christian Traditions. Boston: Brill, 2014.

Dorrien, Gary J. *The Barthian Revolt in Modern Theology: Theology without Weapons*. Louisville: Westminster John Knox, 2000.

Drazin, Israel, and Stanley M. Wagner, trans. *Onkelos on the Torah: Understanding the Bible Text: Genesis*. Vol. 1. New York: Gefen, 2006.

Dulles, Avery. "Revelation, Scripture, and Tradition." In *Your Word Is Truth: A Project of Evangelicals and Catholics Together*, edited by Charles W. Colson and Richard John Neuhaus, 35–58. Grand Rapids: Eerdmans, 2002.

———. "Vatican II on the Interpretation of Scripture." *Letter and Spirit* 2 (2006) 17–26.

Dunn, James D. G. *Christology in the Making: A New Testament Inquiry into the Origins of the Doctrine of the Incarnation*. London: SCM, 1980.

———. "Ex Akoēs Pisteōs." *Ex Auditu* 16 (2000) 35–46.

———. *The Theology of Paul the Apostle*. Grand Rapids: Eerdmans, 1998.

Ellis, E. Earle. *Prophecy and Hermeneutic in Early Christianity: New Testament Essays*. Wissenschaftliche Untersuchungen zum Neuen Testament 18. Grand Rapids: Eerdmans, 1978.

Elowsky, Joel C., ed. *John 1–10*. Ancient Christian Commentary on Scripture 4A. Downers Grove, IL: InterVarsity, 2006.

Enns, Peter E. "The 'Moveable Well' in 1 Cor 10:4: An Extrabiblical Tradition in an Apostolic Text." *Bulletin for Biblical Research* 6 (1996) 23–38.

Ermarth, Elizabeth Deeds. "Postmodernism." In *Routledge Encyclopedia of Philosophy*, edited by Edward Craig, 587–90. London: Routledge, 1998.

Farkasfalvy, Denis M. *Inspiration and Interpretation: A Theological Introduction to Sacred Scripture*. Washington, DC: Catholic University of America Press, 2010.

Fehr, Jakob. *Das Offenbarungsproblem in Dialektischer und Thomistischer Theologie*. Leipzig: Verlag der Universitätsbuchhandlung Freiburg, 1939.

Fiorenza, Francis Schüssler. "Systematic Theology: Task and Methods." In *Systematic Theology: Roman Catholic Perspectives*, edited by Francis Schüssler Fiorenza and John P. Galvin, 1:1–89. Minneapolis: Fortress, 1991.

Fish, Stanley E. *Is There a Text in This Class? The Authority of Interpretive Communities*. Cambridge, MA: Harvard University Press, 1980.

Fitzmyer, Joseph A. *The Biblical Commission's Document "The Interpretation of the Bible in the Church": Text and Commentary*. Subsidia Biblica 18. Rome: Editrice Pontificio Istituto Biblico, 1995.

———. *The Interpretation of Scripture: In Defense of the Historical-Critical Method*. New York: Paulist, 2008.

Fossum, Jarl E. *The Name of God and the Angel of the Lord: Samaritan and Jewish Concepts of Intermediation and the Origin of Gnosticism*. Wissenschaftliche Untersuchungen zum Neuen Testament 36. Tübingen, Germany: Mohr, 1985.

Foucault, Michel. *Madness and Civilization: A History of Insanity in the Age of Reason*. Translated by Richard Howard. New York: Routledge, 1971.

Fowl, Stephen E. "Book Review: Is There a Meaning in This Text? By Kevin J. Vanhoozer." *Modern Theology* 16.2 (2000) 260–62.

———. *Engaging Scripture: A Model for Theological Interpretation*. Malden, MA: Blackwell, 1998.

———. "The Ethics of Interpretation or What's Left over after the Elimination of Meaning." In *The Bible in Three Dimensions: Essays in Celebration of Forty Years of Biblical Studies in the University of Sheffield*, edited by David J. A. Clines et al., 379–98. Sheffield: Sheffield Academic Press, 1990.

———. "Further Thoughts on Theological Interpretation." In *Reading Scripture with the Church: Toward a Hermeneutic for Theological Interpretation*, by A. K. M. Adam et al., 125–30. Grand Rapids: Baker, 2006.

———. "The Importance of a Multivoiced Literal Sense of Scripture: The Example of Thomas Aquinas." In *Reading Scripture with the Church: Toward a Hermeneutic for Theological Interpretation*, by A. K. M. Adam et al., 35–50. Grand Rapids: Baker, 2006.

———. "The Role of Authorial Intention in the Theological Interpretation of Scripture." In *Between Two Horizons: Spanning New Testament Studies and Systematic Theology*, edited by Joel B. Green and Max Turner, 71–87. Grand Rapids: Eerdmans, 2000.

———. *The Story of Christ in the Ethics of Paul: An Analysis of the Function of the Hymnic Material in the Pauline Corpus*. Journal for the Study of the New Testament Supplement 36. Sheffield: JSOT, 1990.

———. *The Theological Interpretation of Scripture: Classic and Contemporary Readings*. Cambridge, MA: Blackwell, 1997.

———. *Theological Interpretation of Scripture*. Eugene, OR: Cascade, 2009.

Fowl, Stephen E., and L. Gregory Jones. *Reading in Communion: Scripture and Ethics in Christian Life*. Eugene, OR: Wipf & Stock, 1998.

Freedman, David Noel. "Name of the God of Moses." *Journal of Biblical Literature* 79.2 (1960) 151–56.

Freedman, H., trans. *Midrash Rabbah: Genesis*. 3rd ed. Vol. 1. London: Soncino, 1983.

Freedman, H., and M. Simon, eds. *Midrash Rabbah: Numbers II*. 3rd ed. Vol. 6. Translated by Judah J. Slotki. London: Soncino, 1983.

Frei, Hans W. *The Doctrine of Revelation in the Thought of Karl Barth, 1909 to 1922: The Nature of Barth's Break with Liberalism.* New Haven, CT: Yale University Press, 1956.

———. *The Eclipse of Biblical Narrative: A Study in Eighteenth and Nineteenth Century Hermeneutics.* New Haven, CT: Yale University Press, 1974.

———. *The Identity of Jesus Christ: The Hermeneutical Bases of Dogmatic Theology.* Philadelphia: Fortress, 1967.

Fretheim, Terence E. "Yahweh." Edited by Willem A. VanGemeren. *New International Dictionary of Old Testament Theology and Exegesis.* Grand Rapids: Zondervan, 1997.

Gabler, Johann P. "An Oration on the Proper Distinction between Biblical and Dogmatic Theology and the Specific Objectives of Each." In *The Flowering of Old Testament Theology: A Reader in Twentieth-Century Old Testament Theology, 1930–990,* edited by Ben C. Ollenburger et al., translated by John Sandy-Wunsch and Laurence Eldredge, 489–502. Sources for Biblical and Theological Study 1. Winona Lake, IN: Eisenbrauns, 1992.

Gadamer, Hans-Georg. *Truth and Method.* Translated by Joel Weinsheimer and Donald G. Marshall. 2nd rev. ed. New York: Continuum, 2004.

Gadenz, Pablo. "Overcoming the Hiatus between Exegesis and Theology: Guidance and Examples from Pope Benedict XVI." In *Verbum Domini and the Complementarity of Exegesis and Theology,* edited by Scott Carl, 41–62. Catholic Theological Formation. Grand Rapids: Eerdmans, 2015.

Garland, David E. *1 Corinthians.* Baker Exegetical Commentary on the New Testament. Grand Rapids: Baker, 2003.

Garrett, Susan R. "'Lest the Light in You Be Darkness': Luke 11:33–36 and the Question of Commitment." *Journal of Biblical Literature* 110.1 (1991) 93–105.

Geddert, Timothy J. "The Implied YHWH Christology of Mark's Gospel: Mark's Challenge to the Reader to 'Connect the Dots.'" *Bulletin for Biblical Research* 25.3 (2015) 325–40.

Gignilliat, Mark S. *Karl Barth and the Fifth Gospel: Barth's Theological Exegesis of Isaiah.* Burlington, VT: Ashgate, 2013.

Godet, Frédéric Louis. *Commentary on First Corinthians.* Kregel Reprint Library. Grand Rapids: Kregel, 1977.

Goheen, Michael W., and Christopher J. H. Wright. "Mission and Theological Interpretation." In *A Manifesto for Theological Interpretation,* edited by Craig G. Bartholomew and Heath A. Thomas, 171–96. Grand Rapids: Baker, 2016.

Goldingay, John. *Do We Need the New Testament? Letting the Old Testament Speak for Itself.* Downers Grove, IL: InterVarsity, 2015.

Green, Joel B. *Practicing Theological Interpretation: Engaging Biblical Texts for Faith and Formation.* Grand Rapids: Baker, 2011.

———. "The (Re-)Turn to Theology." *Journal of Theological Interpretation* 1.1 (2007) 1–3.

Green, Joel B., and T. J. Meadowcroft, eds. *Ears That Hear: Explorations in Theological Interpretation of the Bible.* Sheffield: Sheffield Phoenix, 2013.

Greidanus, Sidney. *Preaching Christ from the Old Testament: A Contemporary Hermeneutical Method.* Grand Rapids: Eerdmans, 1999.

Grenz, Stanley J. *A Primer on Postmodernism.* Grand Rapids: Eerdmans, 1996.

———. *Theology for the Community of God.* Grand Rapids: Eerdmans, 2000.

Grenz, Stanley J., and John R. Franke. *Beyond Foundationalism: Shaping Theology in a Postmodern Context*. Louisville: Westminster John Knox, 2001.

Grindheim, Sigurd. *God's Equal: What Can We Know about Jesus' Self-Understanding in the Synoptic Gospels?* Library of New Testament Studies 446. Edited by Mark Goodacre. New York: T&T Clark, 2011.

Grossfeld, Bernard, ed. *The Targum Onqelos to Leviticus and the Targum Onqelos to Numbers*. Aramaic Bible 8. Translated by Bernard Grossfeld. Wilmington, DE: M. Glazier, 1988.

Gunton, Colin E. *A Brief Theology of Revelation: The 1993 Warfield Lectures*. New York: T&T Clark, 2005.

———. *Father, Son, and Holy Spirit: Essays Toward a Fully Trinitarian Theology*. New York: T&T Clark, 2003.

Haenchen, Ernst. *John: A Commentary on the Gospel of John*. Edited by Ulrich Busse and Robert W. Funk. Translated by Robert W. Funk. Hermeneia: A Critical and Historical Commentary on the Bible 2. Philadelphia: Fortress, 1984.

Hamerton-Kelly, Robert. *God the Father: Theology and Patriarchy in the Teaching of Jesus*. Overtures to Biblical Theology. Edited by Walter Brueggemann and John R. Donahue. Philadelphia: Fortress, 1979.

Hamilton, Victor P. *The Book of Genesis. Chapters 1–17*. New International Commentary on the Old Testament. Grand Rapids: Eerdmans, 1990.

Han, Paul. *Swimming in the Sea of Scripture: Paul's Use of the Old Testament in 2 Corinthians 4.7–13.13*. Library of New Testament Studies 519. London: T&T Clark, 2014.

Hanson, Anthony Tyrrell. *Jesus Christ in the Old Testament*. London: SPCK, 1965.

Hanson, R. P. C. *Allegory and Event: A Study of the Sources and Significance of Origen's Interpretation of Scripture*. Louisville: Westminster John Knox, 1959.

———. *The Search for the Christian Doctrine of God: The Arian Controversy 318–381*. Edinburgh: T&T Clark, 1988.

Harnack, Adolf von. *History of Dogma*. Translated by Neil Buchanan. Eugene, OR: Wipf & Stock, 1997.

———. *Marcion: The Gospel of the Alien God*. Translated by John E. Steely and Lyle D. Bierma. Eugene, OR: Wipf & Stock, 2007.

Harris, R. Laird, et al., eds. *Theological Wordbook of the Old Testament*. Chicago: Moody, 1980.

Hart, David Bentley. *The Beauty of the Infinite: The Aesthetics of Christian Truth*. Grand Rapids: Eerdmans, 2003.

Hartwell, Herbert. *The Theology of Karl Barth: An Introduction*. Studies in Theology 62. Philadelphia: Westminster, 1964.

Harvey, Van A. *The Historian and the Believer: The Morality of Historical Knowledge and Christian Belief*. Chicago: University of Illinois Press, 1966.

Hays, Richard B. *Echoes of Scripture in the Letters of Paul*. New Haven, CT: Yale University Press, 1989.

———. "'Here We Have No Lasting City': New Covenantalism in Hebrews." In *The Epistle to the Hebrews and Christian Theology*, edited by Richard Bauckham et al., 151–73. Grand Rapids: Eerdmans, 2009.

———. "Reading the Bible with Eyes of Faith: The Practice of Theological Exegesis." *Journal of Theological Interpretation* 1. 1 (2007) 5–21.

Helmer, Christine. "Trust and the Spirit: The Canon's Anticipated Unity." *Journal of Theological Interpretation* 1.1 (2007) 61–77.

Heringer, Seth. "The Problem of 'History' in Recent Theological Commentary." In *Ears That Hear: Explorations in Theological Interpretation of the Bible*, edited by Joel B. Green and Tim J. Meadowcroft, 26–42. Sheffield: Sheffield Phoenix, 2013.

Hesse, Mary. "How to Be a Postmodernist and Remain a Christian: A Response to Nicholas Wolterstorff." In *After Pentecost: Language and Biblical Interpretation*, edited by Craig G. Bartholomew et al., 2:91–96. The Scripture and Hermeneutics Series. Grand Rapids: Zondervan, 2001.

Holmes, Christopher R. J. "Revelation in the Present Tense: On Rethinking Theological Interpretation in the Light of the Prophetic Office of Jesus Christ." *Journal of Theological Interpretation* 6.1 (2012) 23–42.

Holt, Robby, and Aubrey Spears. "The Ecclesia as Primary Context for the Reception of the Bible." In *A Manifesto for Theological Interpretation*, edited by Craig G. Bartholomew and Heath A. Thomas, 72–93. Grand Rapids: Baker, 2016.

Howard, George. "The Tetragram and the New Testament." *Journal of Biblical Literature* 96.1 (1977) 63–83.

Hübner, Hans. "New Testament Interpretation of the Old Testament." In *Hebrew Bible, Old Testament: The History of Its Interpretation, From the Beginnings to the Middle Ages (until 1300)*, edited by Magne Saebø, 1:332–72. Göttingen: Vandenhoeck & Ruprecht, 1996.

Hunsinger, George. *How to Read Karl Barth: The Shape of His Theology*. Oxford: Oxford University Press, 1993.

Hurtado, Larry W. *Lord Jesus Christ: Devotion to Jesus in Earliest Christianity*. Grand Rapids: Eerdmans, 2003.

———. *One God, One Lord: Early Christian Devotion and Ancient Jewish Monotheism*. Philadelphia: Fortress, 1988.

Hütter, Reinhard. "Barth between McCormack and von Balthasar: A Dialectic." *Pro Ecclesia* 8 (1999) 105–9.

Ignatius. "The Epistle to the Ephesians." In *The Epistles of St. Clement of Rome and St. Ignatius of Antioch*, rev. ed., translated by James A. Kleist, 1:60–68. Ancient Christian Writers: The Works of the Fathers in Translation. New York: Paulist, 1946.

Irenaeus. *Contre Les Hérésies*. Edited by Adelin Rousseau and Louis Doutreleau. Sources chrétiennes 100.1–100.2, 152–53, 210–11, 263–64, 293–94. Paris: Éditions du Cerf, 2006.

Janzen, J. Gerald. "On the Most Important Word in the Shema (Deuteronomy 6:4–5)." *Vetus Testamentum* 37.3 (1987) 280–300.

Jeanrond, Werner G. *Text and Interpretation As Categories of Theological Thinking*. Translated by Thomas J. Wilson. New York: Crossroad, 1988.

Jenson, Robert W. *Ezekiel*. Brazos Theological Commentary on the Bible. Grand Rapids: Brazos, 2009.

———. *Systematic Theology: The Triune God*. Vol. 1. New York: Oxford University Press, 2001.

———. *The Triune Identity: God According to the Gospel*. Philadelphia: Fortress, 1982.

Jeremias, Joachim. *Jesus and the Message of the New Testament*. Minneapolis: Fortress, 2002.

———. *The Prayers of Jesus*. Studies in Biblical Theology 6. Naperville, IL: Alec R. Allenson, 1967.

John Paul II, Pope. *Fides et Ratio: On the Relationship Between Faith and Reason*. Washington, DC: United States Conference of Catholic Bishops, 1998.

Johnson, Keith L. "Karl Barth and the Analogia Entis." *International Journal of Systematic Theology* 15.2 (2013) 219–21.

———. "Reconsidering Barth's Rejection of Przywara's Analogia Entis." *Modern Theology* 26.4 (2010) 632–50.

Johnson, Luke Timothy, and William S. Kurz. *The Future of Catholic Biblical Scholarship: A Constructive Conversation*. Grand Rapids: Eerdmans, 2002.

Jowett, Benjamin. "On the Interpretation of Scripture." In *Essays and Reviews*, 7th ed., 330–433. London: Longman, Green, Longman, & Roberts, 1861. https://archive.org/details/essaysreviewsoolonduoft/page/330/mode/2up?q=interpretation.

Justin. *Apologie pour les chrétiens*. Translated by Charles Munier. Sources chrétiennes 507. Paris: Cerf, 2006.

———. *Dialogue avec le Tryphon: Edition critique*. Edited and translated by Philippe Bobichon. Paradosis 47. Fribourg: Academic Press Fribourg, 2003.

———. *Dialogue with Trypho*. Edited by Michael Slusser. Translated by Thomas B. Falls. Selections from the Fathers of the Church 3. Washington, DC: Catholic University of America Press, 2003.

———. *Justin, Philosopher and Martyr: Apologies*. Translated by Denis Minns and P. M. Parvis. Oxford Early Christian Texts. Oxford: Oxford University Press, 2009.

Kaiser, Walter C., Jr. "חלס." In *Theological Wordbook of the Old Testament*, edited by R. Laird Harris, Gleason L. Archer, and Bruce K. Waltke, 2:627. Chicago: Moody, 1980.

———. *The Uses of the Old Testament in the New*. Chicago: Moody, 1985.

Kaiser, Walter C., Jr., et al. *Three Views on the New Testament Use of the Old Testament*. Edited by Kenneth Berding and Jonathan Lunde. Grand Rapids: Zondervan, 2008.

Keener, Craig S. *The Gospel of John: A Commentary*. Vol. 1. Peabody, MA: Hendrickson, 2003.

Kelsey, David H. *The Uses of Scripture in Recent Theology*. Philadelphia: Fortress, 1975.

Kessler, Martin, and Karel Adriaan Deurloo. *A Commentary on Genesis: The Book of Beginnings*. New York: Paulist, 2004.

Kittel, Gerhard, et al., eds. *Theological Dictionary of the New Testament*. 10 vols. Grand Rapids: Eerdmans, 1964–76.

Klappert, Bertold. "Die Trinitätslehre als Auslegung des NAMENs des Gottes Israels: Die Bedeutung des Alten Testaments und des Judentums für die Trinitätslehre." *Evangelische Theologie* 62.1 (2002) 54–72.

Knauf, Ernst A. "Yahwe." *Vetus Testamentum* 34.4 (1984) 467–72.

Köhler, Ludwig, and Walter Baumgartner. *The Hebrew and Aramaic Lexicon of the Old Testament*. Study ed. Vol. 1. Translated by M. E. J. Richardson. Leiden: Brill, 2001.

Kooten, Geurt Hendrik van, ed. *The Revelation of the Name YHWH to Moses: Perspectives from Judaism, the Pagan Graeco-Roman World, and Early Christianity*. Themes in Biblical Narrative 9. Leiden: Brill, 2006.

Köstenberger, Andreas J. *John*. Baker Exegetical Commentary on the New Testament. Grand Rapids: Baker, 2004.

Kuruvilla, Abraham. *Genesis: A Theological Commentary for Preachers*. Eugene, OR: Resource Publications, 2014.

Lampe, G. W. H., ed. *A Patristic Greek Lexicon*. Oxford: Clarendon, 1961.

Lane, Anthony N. S. "Tradition." In *Dictionary for Theological Interpretation of the Bible*, edited by Kevin J Vanhoozer et al., 809–12. Grand Rapids: Baker, 2005.

Lanfer, Peter Thacher. *Remembering Eden: The Reception History of Genesis 3:22–24*. New York: Oxford University, 2012.

Larson, E. "460. 4QNarrative Work and Prayer." In *Qumran Cave 4, Volume 26: Cryptic Texts and Miscellanea, Part 1; Miscellaneous Texts from Qumran*, edited by Stephen Pfann and Philip Alexander, 369–86. Discoveries in the Judaean Desert 26. Oxford: Oxford University Press, 2000.

Lashier, Jackson. *Irenaeus on the Trinity*. Supplements to Vigiliae Christianae 127. Leiden: Brill, 2014.

Lash, Nicholas. "Interpretation and Imagination." In *Incarnation and Myth: The Debate Continued*, edited by Michael D. Goulder, 19–26. Grand Rapids: Eerdmans, 1979.

———. *Theology on the Way to Emmaus*. London: SCM, 1986.

Law, David R. *The Historical-Critical Method: A Guide for the Perplexed*. New York: Continuum, 2012.

Lee, Aquila H. I. *From Messiah to Preexistent Son: Jesus' Self-Consciousness and Early Christian Exegesis of Messianic Psalms*. Wissenschaftliche Untersuchungen zum Neuen Testament 2.192. Edited by Jörg Frey. Tübingen, Germany: Mohr Siebeck, 2005.

Legaspi, Michael C. *The Death of Scripture and the Rise of Biblical Studies*. Oxford Studies in Historical Theology. Oxford: Oxford University Press, 2010.

Leith, John H., ed. *Creeds of the Churches: A Reader in Christian Doctrine, from the Bible to the Present*. Louisville: Westminster John Knox, 1982.

Levering, Matthew. *Participatory Biblical Exegesis: A Theology of Biblical Interpretation*. Notre Dame, IN: University of Notre Dame Press, 2008.

Liddell, Henry George, et al. *A Greek-English Lexicon*. 9th rev. ed. Edited by Eric Arthur Barber. Oxford: Clarendon, 1968.

Lietzmann, Hans. *An die Korinther 1–2*. Handbuch zum Neuen Testament 9. Edited by Werner Georg Kümmel. Tübingen, Germany: Mohr Siebeck, 1949.

Lindbeck, George A. *The Nature of Doctrine: Religion and Theology in a Postliberal Age*. 25th anniversary ed. Louisville: Westminster John Knox, 2009.

Livingston, James C. *Modern Christian Thought: The Enlightenment and the Nineteenth Century*. 2nd ed. Vol. 1. Minneapolis: Fortress, 2006.

Lockwood, Gregory J. *1 Corinthians*. Concordia Commentary. Saint Louis: Concordia, 2000.

Lonergan, Bernard J. F. *Method in Theology*. Toronto: University of Toronto Press, 1990.

Lowery, David K. "God as Father: With Special Reference to Matthew's Gospel." PhD thesis, University of Aberdeen, 1987.

Lubac, Henri de. *Exégèse médiéval: Les quatres sens de l'écriture*. Paris: Aubier, 1959.

Lyotard, Jean-François. *The Postmodern Condition: A Report on Knowledge*. Theory and History of Literature 10. Translated by Geoff Bennington and Brian Massumi. Minneapolis: University of Minnesota Press, 1984.

MacDonald, Nathan. *Deuteronomy and the Meaning Of "Monotheism."* Forschungen zum Alten Testament 2.1. Tübingen, Germany: Mohr Siebeck, 2003.

MacDonald, Neil B. "Theological Interpretation, the Historical Formation of Scripture, and God's Action in Time." In *The Bible as Christian Scripture: The Work of Brevard S. Childs*, edited by Christopher R. Seitz and Kent Harold Richards, 85–101. Society of Biblical Literature 25. Atlanta: Society of Biblical Literature, 2013.

Mackay, Ian D. *John's Relationship with Mark: An Analysis of John 6 in the Light of Mark 6–8*. Wissenschaftliche Untersuchungen zum Neuen Testament 2.182. Tübingen, Germany: Mohr Siebeck, 2004.

Marshall, I. Howard. "Acts." In *Commentary on the New Testament Use of the Old Testament*, edited by G. K. Beale and D. A. Carson, 513–606. Grand Rapids: Baker, 2007.
Martin, Dale B. *Pedagogy of the Bible: An Analysis and Proposal*. Louisville: Westminster John Know, 2008.
Martin, Francis. *Sacred Scripture: The Disclosure of the Word*. Naples: Sapientia Press of Ave Maria University, 2006.
Mathews, K. A. *Genesis*. New American Commentary 1A. Nashville: Broadman & Holman, 1996.
Mayes, A. D. H. *Deuteronomy: Based on the Revised Standard Version*. New Century Bible Commentary. Grand Rapids: Eerdmans, 1981.
Methuen, Charlotte. "On the Threshold of a New Age: Expanding Horizons as the Broader Context of Scriptural Interpretation." In *Hebrew Bible, Old Testament: The History of Its Interpretation, from the Renaissance to the Enlightenment*, edited by Magne Saebø, 2:665–90. Göttingen, Germany: Vandenhoeck & Ruprecht, 1996.
McCormack, Bruce L. *Karl Barth's Critically Realistic Dialectical Theology: Its Genesis and Development, 1909–1936*. Oxford: Oxford University Press, 1997.
McDonough, Sean M. *YHWH at Patmos: Rev. 1:4 in Its Hellenistic and Early Jewish Setting*. Wissenschaftliche Untersuchungen Zum Neuen Testament 2.107. Tübingen, Germany: Mohr Siebeck, 1999.
McGowan, John. *Postmodernism and Its Critics*. Ithaca, NY: Cornell University Press, 1991.
McReynolds, Paul R. "John 1:18 in Textual Variation and Translation." In *New Testament Textual Criticism: Its Significance for Exegesis; Essays in Honour of Bruce M. Metzger*, edited by Eldon Jay. Epp and Gordon D. Fee, 105–18. Oxford: Clarendon, 1981.
Meek, Theophile James. *Hebrew Origins*. Rev. ed. New York: Harper, 1950.
Metzger, Bruce M. *A Textual Commentary on the Greek New Testament*. 2nd ed. Stuttgart: Deutsche Bibelgesellschaft, 1994.
Michaelis, Johann David. *Beurtheilung der Mittel, Welche man Anwendet, die Ausgestorbene Hebräische Sprache zu Verstehen*. Göttingen: A. van den Hoeks Witwe, 1757. https://books.google.com/books?id=Cgk4AQAAMAAJ&newbks=1&newbks_redir=0&dq=Michaelis,+Johann+David.+Beurtheilung+der+Mittel,+Welche+man+Anwendet,+die+Ausgestorbene+Hebr%C3%A4ische+Sprache+zu+Verstehen&source=gbs_navlinks_s.
Michelfelder, Diane P., and Richard E. Palmer, eds. *Dialogue and Deconstruction: The Gadamer-Derrida Encounter*. Albany: State University of New York Press, 1989.
Milgrom, Jacob. *Leviticus 1–16: A New Translation with Introduction and Commentary*. Anchor Bible 3. New York: Doubleday, 1991.
Moberly, R. W. L. *The Old Testament of the Old Testament: Patriarchal Narratives and Mosiac Yahwism*. Overtures to Biblical Theology. Minneapolis: Fortress, 1992.
———. "What Is Theological Interpretation of Scripture?" *Journal of Theological Interpretation* 3.2 (2009) 161–78.
Moltmann, Jürgen. *God in Creation: An Ecological Doctrine of Creation*. The Gifford Lectures 1984–1985. London: SCM, 1985.
Morales, Xavier. *La théologie trinitaire d'Athanase d'Alexandrie*. Collection des études augustiniennes: Série Antiquité 180. Paris: Institut d'études augustiniennes, 2006.

Morris, Leon. *The Gospel according to John*. Rev. ed. New International Commentary on the New Testament. Grand Rapids: Eerdmans, 1995.
Motyer, J. A. *The Revelation of the Divine Name*. London: Tyndale, 1959.
Moyise, Steve. *The Old Testament in the New: An Introduction*. New York: T&T Clark, 2001.
Murphy, Francesca A. "Profiling Christ: The Psalms of Abandonment." In *Heaven on Earth?: Theological Interpretation in Ecumenical Dialogue*, edited by Hans Boersma and Matthew Levering, 173–87. Directions in Modern Theology. Chichester: Wiley-Blackwell, 2013.
Murray, Rae, et al. "Christ in/and the Old Testament." *Journal of Theological Interpretation* 2.1 (2008) 1–22.
Murtonen, A. *A Philological and Literary Treatise on the Old Testament Divine Names 'El, AElôah, AElohîm, and Yhwh*. Studia Orientalia 18.1. Helsinki: Societas Orientalis Fennica, 1952.
Nestle, Eberhard, et al., eds. *Novum Testamentum Graece*. 27th rev. ed. Stuttgart: Deutsche Bibelgesellschaft, 1993.
Nestle, Eberhard, et al., eds. *Novum Testamentum Graece*. 28th rev. ed. Stuttgart: Deutsche Bibelgesellschaft, 2012.
Neusner, Jacob, and Richard S. Sarason, eds. *The Tosefta*. Vol. 2. New York: Ktav, 1981.
Obbink, H. "The Tree of Life in Eden." In *The Expository Times*, edited by A. W. Hastings and E. Hastings, 44:475. Edinburgh: T&T Clark, 1932.
Oesterley, W. O. E., and Theodore H. Robinson. *Hebrew Religion: Its Origin and Development*. New York: Macmillan, 1930.
O'Keefe, John J., and Russell R. Reno. *Sanctified Vision: An Introduction to Early Christian Interpretation of the Bible*. Baltimore: Johns Hopkins University Press, 2005.
Olivier, J. P. J. "חלם." In *New International Dictionary of Old Testament Theology and Exegesis*, edited by Willem A. VanGemeren, 3:259–64. Grand Rapids: Zondervan, 1997.
Osborn, Eric. *Irenaeus of Lyons*. New York: Cambridge University Press, 2001.
Osburn, Carroll D. "The Text of 1 Corinthians 10:9." In *New Testament Textual Criticism: Its Significance for Exegesis; Essays in Honour of Bruce M. Metzger*, edited by Eldon Jay. Epp and Gordon D. Fee, 201–11. Oxford: Clarendon, 1981.
Palakeel, Joseph. *The Use of Analogy in Theological Discourse: An Investigation in Ecumenical Perspective*. Serie Teologia. Rome: Pontificia Universita Gregoriana, 1995.
Parke-Taylor, Geoffrey H. *Yahweh: The Divine Name in the Bible*. Waterloo, ON: Wilfrid Laurier University Press, 1975.
Payne, J. Barton. "Yahweh." *Theological Wordbook of the Old Testament*, edited by R. Laird Harris et al, 210–12. Chicago: Moody, 1980.
Pelikan, Jaroslav. *The Emergence of the Catholic Tradition (100–600)*. The Christian Tradition: A History of the Development of Doctrine 1. Chicago: University of Chicago Press, 1974.
Philo. *On Abraham. On Joseph. On Moses*. Vol. 6. Translated by F. H. Colson. Cambridge, MA: Harvard University Press, 1935. https://www.loebclassics.com/view/LCL289/1935/volume.xml.
Pickup, Martin. "New Testament Interpretation of the Old Testament: The Theological Rationale of Midrashic Exegesis." *Journal of the Evangelical Theological Society* 51.2 (2008) 353–81.

Pietersma, Albert. "Kyrios or Tetragram: A Renewed Quest for the Original LXX." In *De Septuaginta: Studies in Honour of John William Wevers on His Sixty-Fifth Birthday*, edited by Albert Pietersma and Claude E. Cox, 85–101. Mississuga: Benben Publications, 1984.

Plantinga, Cornelius, Jr. "Trinity." In *The International Standard Bible Encyclopedia*, edited by Geoffrey W. Bromiley, 4:913–21. Grand Rapids: Eerdmans, 1995.

Plato. *Timaeus, Critias, Cleitophon, Menexenus, Epistles*. Plato in Twelve Volumes 9. Translated by R. G. Bury. Cambridge, MA: Harvard University Press, 2005. https://www.loebclassics.com/view/LCL234/1929/volume.xml.

Pontifical Biblical Commission. *The Interpretation of the Bible in the Church*. Rome: Libreria Editrice Vaticana, 1993.

Popovic, Mladen. "God the Father in Flavius Josephus." In *The Divine Father: Religious and Philosophical Concepts of Divine Parenthood in Antiquity*, edited by Felix Albrecht and Reinhard Feldmeier, 18:181–97. Themes in Biblical Narrative: Jewish and Christian Traditions. Boston: Brill, 2014.

Porter, Stanley E., ed. *Hearing the Old Testament in the New Testament*. McMaster New Testament Studies. Grand Rapids: Eerdmans, 2006.

———. "What Exactly Is Theological Interpretation of Scripture, and Is It Hermeneutically Robust Enough for the Task to Which It Has Been Appointed?" In *Horizons in Hermeneutics: A Festschrift in Honor of Anthony C. Thiselton*, edited by Stanley E. Porter and Matthew Malcolm, 234–67. Grand Rapids: Eerdmans, 2013.

Porter, Stanley E., and Beth M. Stovell, eds. *Biblical Hermeneutics: Five Views*. Downers Grove, IL: InterVarsity, 2012.

Potterie, Ignace de la. "Biblical Exegesis: A Science of Faith." In *Opening Up the Scriptures: Joseph Ratzinger and the Foundations of Biblical Interpretation*, edited by Jos Granados et al., translated by Michelle Borras, 30–64. Grand Rapids: Eerdmans, 2008.

Prestige, G. L. "ΑΓΕΝ[Ν]ΗΤΟΣ and Cognate Words in Athanasius." *Journal of Theological Studies* 34 (1933) 258–65.

Pryzwara, Erich. *Analogia Entis: Metaphysics; Original Structure and Universal Rhythm*. Translated by John R. Betz and David Bentley Hart. Grand Rapids: Eerdmans, 2014.

———. *Analogia Entis: Metaphysik*. Vol. 1. Munich: Hösel and Pustet, 1932.

Quell, Gottfried. "El and Elohim in the OT." In *Theological Dictionary of the New Testament*, edited by Gerhard Kittel et al., translated by Geoffrey W. Bromiley, 3:78–89. Grand Rapids: Eerdmans, 1964.

———. "The Old Testament Name for God." In *Theological Dictionary of the New Testament*, edited by Gerhard Kittel et al., translated by Geoffrey W. Bromiley, 3:1058–81. Grand Rapids: Eerdmans, 1964.

Quine, W. V. O. *Word and Object*. Cambridge, MA: Massachusetts Institute of Technology Press, 1970.

Radde-Gallwitz, Andrew. *Basil of Caesarea, Gregory of Nyssa, and the Transformation of Divine Simplicity*. Oxford Early Christian Studies. Oxford: Oxford University Press, 2009.

Rad, Gerhard von. *Genesis: A Commentary*. Rev. ed. Translated by John H. Marks. The Old Testament Library. Philadelphia: Westminster John Knox, 1973.

———. *Old Testament Theology: The Theology of Israel's Historical Traditions*. Vol. 1. Translated by D. M. G. Stalker. Louisville: Westminster John Knox, 2001.

———. *Old Testament Theology*. Vol. 2. Translated by D. M. G. Stalker. New York: Harper & Row, 1965.

Rae, Murray. *History and Hermeneutics*. New York: T&T Clark, 2005.

———. "Theological Interpretation and Historical Criticism." In *A Manifesto for Theological Interpretation*, edited by Craig G. Bartholomew and Heath A. Thomas, 94–109. Grand Rapids: Baker, 2016.

Rahner, Karl. *Spirit in the World*. Translated by William Dych. New York: Herder & Herder, 1968.

Räisänen, Heikki. *Beyond New Testament Theology: A Story and A Programme*. 2nd ed. London: SCM, 2000.

Ramm, Bernard L. *The Pattern of Religious Authority*. Grand Rapids: Eerdmans, 1959.

Ratzinger, Joseph Cardinal. "Biblical Interpretation in Conflict: On the Foundations and the Itinerary of Exegesis Today." In *Opening up the Scriptures: Joseph Ratzinger and the Foundations of Biblical Interpretation*, edited by Jos Granados et al., translated by Adrian Walker, 1–29. Grand Rapids: Eerdmans, 2008.

———. *Jesus of Nazareth: From the Baptism in the Jordan to the Transfiguration*. Translated by Adrian J. Walker. New York: Doubleday, 2007.

Reno, R. R. *Genesis*. Brazos Theological Commentary on the Bible. Grand Rapids: Brazos, 2010.

Roberts, Alexander, and James Donaldson, eds. *The Apostolic Fathers with Justin Martyr and Irenaeus*. Ante-Nicene Fathers 1. Grand Rapids: Eerdmans, 1993.

Robertson, Archibald, and Alfred Plummer. *A Critical and Exegetical Commentary on the First Epistle of St. Paul to the Corinthians*. 2nd ed. The International Critical Commentary 33. Edinburgh: T&T Clark, 1986.

Rowe, C. Kevin. "The Doctrine of God Is a Hermeneutic: The Biblical Theology of Brevard S. Childs." In *The Bible as Christian Scripture: The Work of Brevard S. Childs*, edited by Christopher R. Seitz and Kent Harold Richards, 155–69. Society of Biblical Literature 25. Atlanta: Society of Biblical Literature, 2013.

Rusch, William G., ed. *The Trinitarian Controversy*. Translated by William G. Rusch. Sources of Early Christian Thought. Philadelphia: Fortress, 1980.

Sandy-Wunsch, John. "Early Old Testament Critics on the Continent." In *Hebrew Bible, Old Testament: The History of Its Interpretation, from the Renaissance to the Enlightenment*, edited by Magne Saebø, 2:971–84. Göttingen: Vandenhoeck & Ruprecht, 1996.

Saner, Andrea D. *"Too Much to Grasp": Exodus 3:13–15 and the Reality of God*. Journal of Theological Interpretation Supplements 11. Winona Lake, IN: Eisenbrauns, 2015.

Sasson, Jack M. *Judges 1–12: A New Translation with Introduction and Commentary*. Anchor Yale Bible 6. New Haven, CT: Yale University Press, 2014.

Scalise, Charles J. "Canonical Hermeneutics: Childs and Barth." *Scottish Journal of Theology* 47.1 (1994) 61–88.

Schaff, Philip, and Henry Wace, eds. *Cyril of Jerusalem, Gregory Nazianzen*. A Select Library of the Nicene and Post-Nicene Fathers Second Series 7. Peabody, MA: Hendrickson, 1994.

Schnackenburg, Rudolf. *The Gospel according to St. John*. Vol. 2. Translated by Cecily Hastings et al. New York: Crossroad, 1982.

Schuller, Eileen M. "4Q372 1: A Text about Joseph." *Revue de Qumran* 14 (1990) 349–76.

———. "The Psalm of 4Q372 1 within the Context of Second Temple Prayer." *Catholic Biblical Quarterly* 54.1 (1992) 67–79.
Schuller, E., and M. Bernstein. "372. 4QNarrative and Poetic Composition." In *Qumran Cave 4: Miscellanea*, edited by Douglas M. Gropp et al., 2:165–97. Discoveries in the Judaean Desert 28. Oxford: Clarendon, 2001.
Schultz, Richard. "Hearing the Major Prophets: 'Your Ears Are Open, but You Hear Nothing' (Isa. 42:20)." In *Hearing the Old Testament: Listening for God's Address*, edited by Craig G. Bartholomew and David J. H. Beldman, 332–55. Grand Rapids: Eerdmans, 2012.
Seitz, Christopher R. "The Call of Moses and the 'Revelation' of the Divine Name: Source-Critical Logic and Its Legacy." In *Theological Exegesis: Essays in Honor of Brevard S. Childs*, edited by Christopher R. Seitz and Kathryn Greene-McCreight, 145–61. Grand Rapids: Eerdmans, 1999.
———. *The Character of Christian Scripture: The Significance of a Two-Testament Bible*. Grand Rapids: Baker, 2011.
———. "Christological Interpretation of Texts and Trinitarian Claims to Truth: An Engagement with Francis Watson's Text and Truth." *Scottish Journal of Theology* 52.2 (1999) 209–26.
———. "The Divine Name in Christian Scripture." In *This Is My Name Forever: The Trinity and Gender Language for God*, edited by Alvin F. Kimel Jr., 23–34. Downers Grove, IL: InterVarsity, 2001.
———. *Figured Out: Typology and Providence in Christian Scripture*. Louisville: Westminster John Knox, 2001.
———. *Word without End: The Old Testament as Abiding Theological Witness*. Grand Rapids: Eerdmans, 1998.
Semler, Johann Salomo. *Abhandlung von Freier Untersuchung des Canon*. 4 vols. Halle, Germany: C. H. Hemmerde, 1771. https://www.google.com/books/edition/D_Joh_Salomo_Semlers_Abhandlung_Von_Frei/BvJUoAEACAAJ?hl=en.
———. *Historische Einleitung in die Dogmatische Gottesgelersamkeit*. Edited by Sigmund Jakob Baumgarten. Evangelische Glaubenslehre 2. Halle, Germany: Johann Justinus Gebauer, 1760. https://www.google.com/books/edition/D_Siegmund_Jacob_Baumgartens_Evangelisch/ktIOAAAAQAAJ?hl=en&gbpv=1.
Smith, Mark S. *The Origins of Biblical Monotheism: Israel's Polytheistic Background and the Ugaritic Texts*. New York: Oxford University Press, 2001.
Sommer, Benjamin D. *The Bodies of God and the World of Ancient Israel*. Cambridge: Cambridge University Press, 2009.
Soulen, R. Kendall. *The Divine Name(s) and the Holy Trinity: Distinguishing the Voices*. Vol. 1. Louisville: Westminster John Knox, 2011.
———. *The God of Israel and Christian Theology*. Minneapolis: Fortress, 1996.
———. "Supersessionism." In *A Dictionary of Jewish-Christian Relations*, edited by Edward Kessler and Neil Wenborn, 413–14. Cambridge: Cambridge University Press, 2005.
———. "YHWH the Triune God." *Modern Theology* 15.1 (1999) 25–54.
Spawn, Kevin L., and Archie T. Wright, eds. *Spirit and Scripture: Exploring a Pneumatic Hermeneutic*. New York: T&T Clark, 2012.
Spinks, D. Christopher. *The Bible and the Crisis of Meaning: Debates on the Theological Interpretation of Scripture*. New York: T&T Clark, 2007.

Stampe, Dennis. "Toward a Grammar of Meaning." In *On Noam Chomsky: Critical Essays*, edited by Gilbert Harman, 267–302. Garden City, NJ: Anchor, 1974.
Steinmetz, David C. "The Superiority of Pre-Critical Exegesis." *Theology Today* 37.1 (1980) 27–38.
Stendahl, Krister. *Meanings: The Bible As Document and As Guide*. Philadelphia: Fortress, 1984.
Storer, Kevin. *Reading Scripture to Hear God: Kevin Vanhoozer and Henri De Lubac on God's Use of Scripture in the Economy of Redemption*. Eugene, OR: Pickwick, 2014.
Stout, Jeffrey. "What Is the Meaning of a Text?" *New Literary History* 14.1 (1982) 1–12.
Strack, Hermann L., and Paul Billerbeck. *Kommentar zum Neuen Testament aus Talmud und Midrasch: Die Briefe des Neuen Testaments und die Offenbarung Johannis*. Munich, Germany: C. H. Beck, 1985.
Taylor, Victor E., and Charles E. Winquist, eds. *Postmodernism: Critical Concepts*. Foundational Essays 1. New York: Routledge, 1998.
Theophilus. *Théophile d'Antioche: Trois livres à Autolycus*. Edited by Gustave Bardy. Translated by Jean Sender. Sources chrétiennes 20. Paris: Éditions du Cerf, 1948.
———. *Theophilus of Antioch: Ad Autolycus*. Edited and translated by Robert M. Grant. Oxford Early Christian Texts. Oxford: Clarendon, 1970.
Thiselton, Anthony C. *The First Epistle to the Corinthians: A Commentary on the Greek Text*. New International Greek Testament Commentary. Grand Rapids: Eerdmans, 2000.
Thomas, Heath A. "The Telos (Goal) of Theological Interpretation." In *A Manifesto for Theological Interpretation*, edited by Craig G. Bartholomew and Heath A. Thomas, 197–217. Grand Rapids: Baker, 2016.
Thompson, Marianne Meye. *John: A Commentary*. 1st ed. The New Testament Library. Louisville: Westminster John Knox, 2015.
———. *The Promise of the Father: Jesus and God in the New Testament*. Louisville: Westminster John Knox, 2000.
Toorn, Karel van der. "Yahweh." In *Dictionary of Deities and Demons in the Bible*, edited by Karel van der Toorn et al., 910–19. Leiden: Brill, 1999.
Torrance, Thomas F. *Karl Barth: Introduction to Early Theology*. New York: T&T Clark, 2004.
Tracy, David. *Blessed Rage for Order: The New Pluralism in Theology*. Chicago: University of Chicago Press, 1996.
Treier, Daniel J. *Introducing Theological Interpretation of Scripture: Recovering a Christian Practice*. Grand Rapids: Baker, 2008.
———. "Typology." In *Dictionary for Theological Interpretation of the Bible*, edited by Kevin J. Vanhoozer et al., 823–27. Grand Rapids: Baker, 2005.
———. *Virtue and the Voice of God: Toward Theology as Wisdom*. Grand Rapids: Eerdmans, 2006.
———. "What Is Theological Interpretation? An Ecclesiological Reduction." *International Journal of Systematic Theology* 12.2 (2010) 144–61.
Treier, Daniel J., and Kevin J. Vanhoozer. *Theology and the Mirror of Scripture: A Mere Evangelical Account*. Studies in Christian Doctrine and Scripture. Downers Grove, IL: InterVarsity, 2015.
Troeltsch, Ernst. "Ueber Historische und Dogmatische Methode in der Theologie." In *Theologie als Wissenschaft*, 105–27. Munich: C. Kaiser, 1971.
Vanhoozer, Kevin J., ed. *The Cambridge Companion to Postmodern Theology*. New York: Cambridge University Press, 2003.

---. *The Drama of Doctrine: A Canonical-Linguistic Approach to Christian Theology*. Louisville: Westminster John Knox, 2005.

---. *First Theology: God, Scripture and Hermeneutics*. Downers Grove, IL: InterVarsity, 2002.

---. "Imprisoned or Free? Text, Status, and Theological Interpretation in the Master/Slave Discourse of Philemon." In *Reading Scripture with the Church: Toward a Hermeneutic for Theological Interpretation*, by A. K. M. Adam et al., 51–93. Grand Rapids: Baker, 2006.

---. *Is There a Meaning in This Text?: The Bible, the Reader, and the Morality of Literary Knowledge*. 10th anniversary ed. Grand Rapids: Zondervan, 2009.

---. *Remythologizing Theology: Divine Action, Passion, and Authorship*. Cambridge Studies in Christian Doctrine. New York: Cambridge University Press, 2010.

---. "What Is Theological Interpretation?" *Dictionary for Theological Interpretation of the Bible*, edited by Kevin J. Vanhoozer et al., 19–22. Grand Rapids: Baker, 2005.

Vaux, Roland de. "The Revelation of the Divine Name YHWH." In *Proclamation and Presence: Old Testament Essays in Honour of Gwynne Henton Davies*, edited by John I. Durham and J. R. Porter, 48–75. Richmond: John Knox, 1970.

Vermès, Géza. *Jesus and the World of Judaism*. Philadelphia: Fortress, 1984.

Vervenne, M. "The Phraseology of 'Knowing YHWH' in the Hebrew Bible: A Preliminary Study of Its Syntax and Function." In *Studies in the Book of Isaiah: Festschrift Willem A. M. Beuken*, edited by J. van Ruiten and M. Vervenne, 467–92. Bibliotheca Ephemeridum Theologicarum Lovaniensium 132. Louvain: Leuven University Press, 1997.

Wallace, Daniel B. *Greek Grammar beyond the Basics: An Exegetical Syntax of the New Testament with Scripture, Subject, and Greek Word Indexes*. Grand Rapids: Zondervan, 1996.

---. "The Semantics and Exegetical Significance of the Object-Complement Construction in the New Testament." *Grace Theological Journal* 61.1 (1985) 91–112.

Waltke, Bruce K. *The Book of Proverbs*. 2 vols. New International Commentary on the Old Testament. Grand Rapids: Eerdmans, 2004.

---. *An Old Testament Theology: An Exegetical, Canonical, and Thematic Approach*. Grand Rapids: Zondervan, 2007.

Warfield, Benjamin Breckinridge. *The Right of Systematic Theology*. London: FB&C, 2015.

Washburn, Christian D. "The Catholic Use of the Scriptures in Ecumenical Dialogue." In *Verbum Domini and the Complementarity of Exegesis and Theology*, edited by Scott Carl, 63–84. Catholic Theological Formation. Grand Rapids: Eerdmans, 2015.

Watson, Francis. "The Old Testament as Christian Scripture: A Response to Professor Seitz." *Scottish Journal of Theology* 52.2 (1999) 227–32.

---. *Text and Truth: Redefining Biblical Theology*. Grand Rapids: Eerdmans, 1997.

---. *Text, Church and World: Biblical Interpretation in Theological Perspective*. Grand Rapids: Eerdmans, 1994.

---. "The Triune Divine Identity: Reflections on Pauline God-Language, in Disagreement with J. D. G. Dunn." *Journal for the Study of the New Testament* 80 (2000) 99–124.

Watts, John D. W. *Isaiah 34–66*. Rev. ed. Edited by Bruce M. Metzger et al. Word Biblical Commentary 25. Nashville: Thomas Nelson, 2005.

Webb, Barry G. *The Book of Judges*. New International Commentary on the Old Testament. Grand Rapids: Eerdmans, 2012.
Webster, John. *The Domain of the Word: Scripture and Theological Reason*. T&T Clark Theology. New York: T&T Clark, 2012.
———. *Holy Scripture: A Dogmatic Sketch*. New York: Cambridge University Press, 2003.
———. *Karl Barth*. New York: Continuum, 2000.
———. *Word and Church: Essays in Church Dogmatics*. New York: Continuum, 2006.
Weinandy, Thomas G. *Athanasius: A Theological Introduction*. Great Theologians Series. Aldershot, UK: Ashgate, 2007.
Wenham, Gordon J. *Genesis 1–15*. Word Biblical Commentary 1. Waco, TX: Word, 1987.
Westermann, Claus. *Genesis: A Commentary*. Translated by John Scullion. Minneapolis: Augsburg, 1984.
Wevers, John William, ed. *Exodus*. Septuaginta: Vetus Testamentum Graecum 2.1. Göttingen: Vandenhoeck & Ruprecht, 1991.
Whitman, Jon, ed. *Interpretation and Allegory: Antiquity to the Modern Period*. Boston: Brill, 2003.
Whybray, R. N. "Genesis." In *The Oxford Bible Commentary*, edited by John Barton and John Muddiman, 38–66. Oxford: Oxford University Press, 2001.
Widdicombe, Peter. *The Fatherhood of God from Origen to Athanasius*. Oxford Theological Monographs. New York: Oxford University Press, 1994.
Wigley, Stephen D. *Karl Barth and Hans Urs von Balthasar: A Critical Engagement*. New York: T&T Clark, 2007.
———. "The von Balthasar Thesis: A Re-examination of von Balthasar's Study of Barth in the Light of Bruce McCormack." *Scottish Journal of Theology* 56 (2003) 345–59.
Wilkinson, Robert J. *Tetragrammaton: Western Christians and the Hebrew Name of God; From the Beginnings to the Seventeenth Century*. Boston: Brill, 2015.
Williamson, Peter S. "Catholic Biblical Interpretation." In *Dictionary for Theological Interpretation of the Bible,* edited by Kevin J. Vanhoozer et al., Grand Rapids: Baker, 2005.
Wisse, Maarten. "From Cover to Cover? A Critique of Wolterstorff's Theory of the Bible as Divine Discourse." *International Journal for Philosophy of Religion* 52.3 (2002) 159–73.
Witherington, Ben, III. *Conflict and Community in Corinth: A Socio-Rhetorical Commentary on 1 and 2 Corinthians*. Grand Rapids: Eerdmans, 1995.
———. *Revelation*. New Cambridge Bible Commentary. New York: Cambridge University Press, 2003.
Witherington, Ben, III, and Laura Michaels Ice. *The Shadow of the Almighty: Father, Son, and Spirit in Biblical Perspective*. Grand Rapids: Eerdmans, 2002.
Wolterstorff, Nicholas. *Divine Discourse: Philosophical Reflections on the Claim That God Speaks*. New York: Cambridge University Press, 1995.
———. "The Promise of Speech-Act Theory for Biblical Interpretation." In *After Pentecost: Language and Biblical Interpretation*, edited by Craig G. Bartholomew et al., 73–90. Grand Rapids: Zondervan, 2001.
Wrede, William. "The Task and Methods of 'New Testament Theology.'" In *The Nature of New Testament Theology: The Contribution of William Wrede and Adolf Schlatter*, translated by Robert Morgan, Studies in Biblical Theology 2.25. Naperville, IL: A. R. Allenson, 1973.

Wright, N. T. *Climax of the Covenant: Christ and the Law in Pauline Theology.* New York: T&T Clark, 1991.

Xun, Chen. *Theological Exegesis in the Canonical Context: Brevard Springs Childs's Methodology of Biblical Theology.* Studies in Biblical Literature 137. New York: Peter Lang, 2010.

Yeago, David S. "The Catholic Luther." In *The Catholicity of the Reformation*, edited by Carl E. Braaten and Robert W. Jenson, 13–34. Grand Rapids: Eerdmans, 1996.

———. "The New Testament and the Nicene Dogma: A Contribution to the Recovery of Theological Exegesis." *Pro Ecclesia* 3.2 (1994) 152–64.

Young, Frances. *Exegesis and Theology in Early Christianity.* Burlington, VT: Ashgate, 2012.

Zuntz, Günther. *The Text of the Epistles: A Disquisition upon the Corpus Paulinum.* The Schweich Lectures of the British Academy. London: Oxford University Press, 1953.

www.ingramcontent.com/pod-product-compliance
Lightning Source LLC
Chambersburg PA
CBHW062040220426
43662CB00010B/1584